MYSTERY SCIENCE THEATER 3000

THE CULTURAL HISTORY OF TELEVISION

MYSTERY SCIENCE THEATER 3000

A Cultural History

MATT FOY AND CHRISTOPHER J. OLSON

ROWMAN & LITTLEFIELD
Lanham • Boulder • New York • London

Published by Rowman & Littlefield
An imprint of The Rowman & Littlefield Publishing Group, Inc.
4501 Forbes Boulevard, Suite 200, Lanham, Maryland 20706
www.rowman.com

86-90 Paul Street, London EC2A 4NE, United Kingdom

British Library Cataloguing in Publication Information Available

Library of Congress Cataloging-in-Publication Data

Names: Foy, Matt, author. | Olson, Christopher J., author.
Title: Mystery science theater 3000 : a cultural history / Matt Foy and
    Christopher J. Olson.
Other titles: Mystery science theater three-thousand
Description: Lanham : Rowman & Littlefield, 2024. | Series: The cultural history of
    television | Includes bibliographical references and index.
Identifiers: LCCN 2024005862 (print) | LCCN 2024005863 (ebook) | ISBN
    9781538173480 (cloth) | ISBN 9781538173497 (ebook)
Subjects: LCSH: Mystery science theater 3000. | Cult television programs—
    Social aspects.
Classification: LCC PN1992.77.M97 F69 2024 (print) | LCC PN1992.77.M97 (ebook) |
    DDC 791.45/72—dc23/eng/20240327
LC record available at https://lccn.loc.gov/2024005862
LC ebook record available at https://lccn.loc.gov/2024005863

CONTENTS

ACKNOWLEDGMENTS

The authors would like to thank their loved ones for all their devotion and support during the process of writing this book. Matt is thankful for all the love and support from Bobbie, Gavin, Aydyn, Willow, Mom, Dad, and Grandma. Thank you, Drs. Ronald J. Pelias, Craig Gingrich-Philbrook, Jonathan Gray, Nathan Stucky, and Satoshi Toysaki for nurturing my embryonic attempts at making riffing a thing one can study. Finally, big thanks to Bryan Clark and Robert Fedeler for hyping up *Eegah* to the point I couldn't believe it could be as funny as you said because everything changed when we watched it, and you were right.

Chris wishes to extend deep gratitude to his longtime partner and very own Creepy Girl, Dr. CarrieLynn Reinhard of Dominican University, for her willingness to read each in-progress chapter and offer feedback on the prose and ideas. Thank you so much for all your love, patience, and help throughout the years. Additionally, Chris would like to recognize fellow MSTies Frank Beno, Jr., Megan Stemm-Wade, Joe Belfeuil, Chris Loseke, Clelia Sweeney, Dave Stanley, Sarah Stanley, Zach Anderson, and Amanda Bartelt for spending some of their valuable time on this planet watching MST3K and its various offshoots with me. Y'all make watching the show an even more enjoyable act than it already is. Finally, Chris thanks his three cats Bragi, Sif, and Tyr for keeping him company during the long, lonely hours of writing. I adore you all, you little ragamuffins.

The authors would also like to thank the editors of the Cultural History of Television series as well as all the fine folks at our publisher, Rowman & Littlefield, and their parent company Rowman & Littlefield for helping bring this project to fruition and carry it over the finish line. Without their assistance, this book would not exist, so we are eternally grateful to them for their willingness to take a chance and publish our ramblings about our favorite little cow-town puppet show.

Finally, Matt and Chris wish to thank the casts and crews of every iteration of MST3K as well as the makers of all the movies riffed throughout the years for providing hours upon hours of laughter and joy. Together, these creators have shaped our humor and our tastes in a variety of ways while also providing comfort in the form of background noise when performing household chores or enduring marathon sessions of grading student papers. To paraphrase a riff from episode 312, MST3K provides us with interest, and for that, we thank you!

INTRODUCTION

"Turn down your lights (where applicable)"

"We've got movie sign!"

With these words, Joel (or Mike, or Jonah, or Emily) descends, along with robot pals Tom Servo and Crow T. Robot, into the Mystery Science Theater, a secret cinema located deep within the bowels of the Earth-orbiting Satellite of Love (named after the Lou Reed song). Once there, the trio suffers through some of the cheesiest B- and Z-grade movies ever made, cracking jokes the entire time to preserve their sanity. This torture is all part of a devious experiment overseen by a rotating cast of evil mad scientists, starting with Dr. Clayton Forrester and his assistant Larry Erhardt, who was later replaced by TV's Frank. This evil duo eventually gave way to Clayton's wicked mother Pearl Forrester and her dim-witted henchmen Professor Bobo and Brain Guy (aka Observer), who in turn passed the reins to Clayton's daughter Kinga Forrester, her lovesick lackey Max (aka TV's Son of TV's Frank), and Pearl's defective clone Synthia.[1]

In 1988, quirky standup comic Joel Hodgson settled in Minneapolis, Minnesota, where he teamed with producer Jim Mallon to create *Mystery Science Theater 3000* (or MST3K for short), a little "cow-town puppet show"[2] that initially aired on Minnesota UHF station KTMA.[3] When developing their idea, the duo drew inspiration from a diverse group of influences that included the 1960s radio comedy troupe the Firesign Theater, Canadian sketch comedy show *SCTV*, long-running British sci-fi series *Doctor Who*, children's program *Matty's Funnies with Beany and Cecil*, and the films *What's Up, Tiger Lily?*, *Silent Running*, and *The Omega Man*. The duo then enlisted the help of fellow comics Kevin Murphy, Trace Beaulieu, and Josh Weinstein, who all worked diligently to make MST3K a reality. Debuting on KTMA on November 24, 1988, the new series immediately resonated with viewers throughout the Land of 10,000 Lakes.

Despite its smalltown origins, MST3K has since emerged as a venerable pop cultural institution that remains beloved to this day, and it has numerous spinoffs and imitators across a variety of media platforms. The series, which proudly boasts a do-it-yourself attitude that aligns with the punk culture prevalent at the time, would go on to influence internet culture, particularly in terms of the rise of comment sections and social media sites such as Twitter and Instagram, which allow everyday people to (often anonymously) speak back to media producers and celebrities in numerous ways. In addition, MST3K introduced the concept of riffing (i.e., making snarky and sometimes observational quips) to the wider populace, encouraging the rise of a diverse array of dedicated riffers, both amateur and professional, who keep the tradition of heckling movies and other media alive and well in the twenty-first century. The series shaped the sensibilities of several professional and amateur comedians, many of whom launched podcasts devoted to reviewing and mocking bad movies, including *The Flop House*, *We Hate Movies*, and *How Did This Get Made?*

These days, the spirit of MST3K lives on in the style of humor employed by YouTubers like Markiplier and the Game Grumps, comedy troupes such as Master Pancake Theater and Incognito Cinema Warriors XP, and even professional wrestlers like Colt Cabana and the Good Brothers, aka Karl Anderson and Luke Gallows. Cabana, along with a rotating cast of comedians that includes Brendan Burns, Marty DeRosa, and John Hastings, often hosts a live comedy show called "Colt Cabana and [guest host] Do Comedy and Commentary to Bad Wrestling Matches," in which they riff on disastrous wrestling matches. The Good Brothers, meanwhile, hosted the short-lived WWE-produced YouTube series Botch Club, cracking wise while watching the sports entertainment giant's "most hilarious bloopers and blunders."

Even the members of the horrorcore rap group Insane Clown Posse—alongside special guests like actor/musician Corey Feldman and professional wrestler Scott Hall aka Razor Ramon—got in on the act, riffing on music videos under the banner of *Insane Clown Posse Theater*.[4] Additionally, the popularity of Ugandan commentator/narrator V.J. Emmie, who gained cult fame thanks to his riffing on the Wakaliwood productions *Who Killed Captain Alex?* and *Bad Black*, as well as the appearance of international knockoffs such as the Russian "Project 'Popcorn,'" reveal that the show's outrageous attitude and infectious humor transcends both national and cultural boundaries.

This book traces MST3K's history from its humble beginnings as a beloved local UHF series to its rise as a cult sensation airing first on the Comedy Channel (later Comedy Central) and then the Sci-Fi Channel (later Syfy), up to its recent high-profile resurgence as a popular Netflix original series and a touring live show. We wrap things up with a discussion of the Gizmoplex, MST3K's dedicated streaming service that launched in 2022. Along the way, we consider the show's place within different historical, social, and cultural contexts to uncover how its unique brand of Midwestern-inflected humor came to influence the tone and techniques of subsequent generations of comics and media creators during the first three decades of the twenty-first century. The methods that the show's creators used to parody a wide variety of targets—including self-important celebrities, "bad" movies, newspaper comic strips, flash-in-the-pan trends, overzealous fans, and more—remain evident across the contemporary media landscape.

Indeed, MST3K aligned with or directly paved the way for numerous aspects of modern life, from the highly referential filmmaking of directors like Quentin Tarantino and Steven Spielberg, to humorous commentaries by YouTubers and Twitch streamers such as the Nostalgia Critic and the Angry Video Game Nerd, to real-time online discussion and liveblogging of everything from appointment television to professional wrestling matches to political debates. The riffing techniques pioneered by MST3K helped provide media practitioners and consumers with the tools needed to engage in the sort of active, critical media consumption and production that is essential in the present moment, as they assist media consumers around the world in developing both media literacy and communal vocabularies for practicing everyday media criticism. Such skills not only assist audiences in navigating the increasingly intertextual and metatextual media landscape of contemporary society, but also provide opportunities for people to gain the sort of cultural capital needed to develop and maintain personal brands, a core skill in the age of participatory media and fan cultures.[5]

We also take a deep dive into the post-MST3K projects produced by the show's creators and cast members in the years after the show initially went off the air. These official spinoffs include the early 2000s humor webzine Timmy Big Hands, as well as the movie riffing projects the Film Crew, RiffTrax, Cinematic Titanic, and the Mads. These ancillary projects kept the show's comedic sensibilities alive after executives at the Sci-Fi Channel canceled the series, an act that, at the time, seemingly ended MST3K once and for all. Yet the success of these offshoots, combined with the show's well-received relaunch—first on streaming giant Netflix and later its own proprietary streaming service the Gizmoplex—demonstrate that MST3K's humor and outlook have become thoroughly embedded within the culture at large. Furthermore, these projects all helped to establish the type of referential, metatextual humor that has become popular during the current post-postmodern age.[6] As such, they all helped facilitate, either directly or indirectly, the rise of the numerous disciples and imitators of MST3K that currently exist and enjoy massive popularity among niche audiences the world over.

Ultimately, this little cow-town puppet show is not directly responsible for the contemporary culture of speaking back to media texts. However, few shows can boast the enduring cult popularity and lasting influence of MST3K, and the series' legacy has only grown in the two decades since its initial run ended. The show's cultural significance extends far beyond its enduring critical acclaim and devotion from its passionate fanbase. Instead, MST3K's profound cultural impact lies in its visionary modeling of an accessible, artistic, and active way of consuming popular culture that would come to characterize media production and participation in the forty-plus years that followed the show's inauspicious debut on a tiny UHF station in wintry Minneapolis. Join us, won't you, as we explore how MST3K contributed to the development of the twenty-first-century media landscape.

To paraphrase the show's creators: "We've got book sign!"

CHAPTER ONE

"THERE WAS A GUY NAMED JOEL"

The KTMA Years

Though born in Stevens Point, Wisconsin, on February 20, 1960, Joel Hodgson spent most of his formative years roughly one hundred miles away in Green Bay, Wisconsin, home of beer, bratwurst, and beloved football team the Packers.[1] Raised in an Evangelical Christian household, the precocious Hodgson quickly developed an interest in entertaining that was fueled in part by the plays and events staged by a local church.[2] By the time he reached seventh grade, Hodgson had embarked on a career as a magician and ventriloquist, devoting much of his time to building his own puppets and performing at local events.[3] Upon graduating from Ashwaubenon High School in 1978, Hodgson packed up and moved to St. Paul, Minnesota, to study media at Bethel College.[4] There, Hodgson took a class on the theater of the absurd, which inspired him to incorporate comedy into his magic act,[5] and in 1981 he won the Bethel College Campus Comedy Contest. The following year, Hodgson won the first annual Twin Cities Comedy Invitational, cementing his decision to move to Los Angeles and try his hand at becoming a professional standup comedian.[6]

Hodgson quickly made a name for himself thanks to high-profile appearances on *Late Night with David Letterman*, *Saturday Night Live*, and an HBO Young Comedians special.[7] His act revolved mainly around the wacky "inventions" he claimed to have created in his Mystery Science Lab.[8] These included the cordless tin can telephone (two empty Campbell's soup cans adorned with antennae), the pocket mohawk (a bald cap with a strip cut down the middle through which Hodgson could stick his own hair), and a tuna and cheese casserole that hides an automatic rifle (perfect for the secret agent who also attends church potlucks). Additionally, Hodgson made amusing observations about popular culture, with gags informed by old sitcoms like *The Patty Duke Show*, largely forgotten toys such as the Whammo Air Blaster, and sporadically silly cultural imports like the *Godzilla* films.

Of course, with the benefit of hindsight, some of Hodgson's jokes from this period could now be considered questionable or problematic. For instance, during a bit that pokes fun at both the Showa-era *Godzilla* films produced between 1954 and 1974 and the 1950s TV show *Lassie*, Hodgson dons a pair of glasses that give him the appearance of a stereotypically racist caricature of a Japanese person and proceeds to mimic the poor English dubbing commonly found in the US releases of the Toho productions. Nevertheless, even racially insensitive gags such as these demonstrate the breadth and depth of Hodgson's pop culture acumen.

By 1985, a creatively exhausted Hodgson had grown tired of Los Angeles and, rather than wind up as the wacky neighbor on a formulaic sitcom, he decided to move back to Minnesota, this time settling in Minneapolis. During this time, Hodgson lived with his parents and spent his days building and selling sculptures, working at a t-shirt factory, designing toys, and constructing props for fellow comics. He also continued to dabble in comedy himself, co-writing an hour-long Showtime comedy special with a young Jerry Seinfeld in 1986.[9] Around the same time, Hodgson entertained offers to play dimwitted bartender Woody Boyd in the popular sitcom *Cheers* (a role that eventually went to a then-unknown Woody Harrelson) and the eccentric engineer Philo in the "Weird Al" Yankovic vehicle *UHF* (Anthony Geary of *General Hospital* fame ultimately won that role). Yet fate intervened when, in 1987, Hodgson met Jim Mallon, at that time a production manager at Minneapolis' recently launched independent UHF television station, KTMA. The acronym UHF, which stands for ultra-high frequency, refers to the band of electromagnetic radiation with a radio frequency range between three hundred megahertz and three gigahertz (three thousand megahertz). Due to its short wavelength and high frequency, which renders it less susceptible to environmental factors, UHF is commonly used for data transmission, including TV and radio transmission and channel broadcasting.[10]

Hodgson and Mallon became fast friends, and together they hatched an idea for a new cable-access show called *Mystery Science Theater 3000*, known to fans as MST3K. When developing the show, the duo looked to weekly television programs in which a host introduces an old movie in each episode. However, Hodgson came up with the novel idea of having the host provide a running commentary throughout the film, suggesting, "How about instead of having the host at the commercial breaks, we have the host be in the movie?"[11] Hodgson also drew inspiration from Elton John's 1973 album *Goodbye Yellow Brick Road*, the liner notes of which featured illustrations of silhouetted figures watching a movie to accompany the song "I've Seen That Movie Too." Using these elements as their foundation, Hodgson and Mallon then set about launching their new venture.

Mystery Science Theater 3000 (Comedy Central), 1988 to 1999. Shown: Crow, Joel Hodgson, Tom Servo.
COMEDY CENTRAL / PHOTOFEST © COMEDY CENTRAL

"THIS IS THE SATELLITE OF LOVE, IT'S A SPACE STATION OF MY OWN DESIGN": CREATING MST3K

With a title cribbed from Hodgson's standup routine and a premise inspired by both the post-apocalyptic thriller *The Omega Man*[12] and the environmentalist sci-fi film *Silent Running*,[13] the original incarnation of MST3K followed a hapless janitor who finds himself trapped in space and forced to watch cheesy movies, which he gleefully mocks alongside a trio of homemade robots. To produce the show, Hodgson and Mallon enlisted the help of some other local comics, starting with KTMA employee Kevin Murphy. Prior to his stint on MST3K, Murphy created and hosted the satirical news show *15 Minutes*—a parody of the CBS news series *60 Minutes*—that likewise aired on KTMA in the late 1980s. The show, which was used to fill time after airings of films culled from the station's tape library, featured Murphy as journalist Bob Bagadonuts, who offered a comedic look at issues affecting the Twin Cities area. These included a wave of alien abductions related to a local bowling organization and the construction of a wall between Minneapolis and St. Paul. The series also featured the "Team 23 News" spoof, a send up of news shows that predated *The Daily Show* by a decade.[14]

In addition to Murphy, Hodgson and Mallon recruited Minnesota-based comics Trace Beaulieu and Josh Weinstein, who later adopted the stage name J. Elvis Weinstein in honor of singer/songwriter Elvis Costello. The newly assembled group of five then set about making a fourteen-minute-long pilot episode of MST3K, pillaging the station's library of movies to find the "cannon fodder" for their jokes.[15] In the unaired pilot, laid-back astronaut Joel Hodgson (played, naturally, by Hodgson) orbits the earth aboard the Satellite of Love, where he watches and ridicules segments from the campy Japanese sci-fi flick *The Green Slime*. Periodically throughout the episode, Hodgson ventures out of the theater to engage in shenanigans alongside his robot companions Crow T. Robot, Beeper, and Gypsy, all played by Beaulieu and Weinstein, who later doubled as the mad scientists overseeing the entire operation. Originally, Hodgson modeled the robots (or bots, as they are affectionately known to fans) after the characters of C-3PO and R2-D2 from the *Star Wars* films, with Beeper speaking in beeps and whistles understood only by Crow. Yet Beeper was left out of the show's first episode and retooled into a new character named Servo who debuted in the second episode and quickly morphed into Tom Servo as Weinstein developed and refined the character's personality via a deep voice and an overinflated ego.

Upon seeing the pilot, KTMA station manager Donald O'Connor[16] somewhat reluctantly authorized production on thirteen episodes of MST3K with the first one debuting at 6:00 pm on Thanksgiving Day, November 24, 1988.[17] Almost immediately, MST3K gained a cult following among Minnesotans, many of whom sent letters of appreciation[18] and inundated the station's answering machine with messages praising the quirky new series.[19] These messages likely helped save MST3K from an early cancellation and convinced O'Connor—who apparently failed to understand the show and was poised to axe it from the station's schedule—to expand the first season order to twenty-one episodes.

From the start, MST3K exhibited a delightfully lo-fi, do-it-yourself (DIY) aesthetic and attitude, with Hodgson and pals handling nearly all duties both behind and in front of the camera. Mallon and Hodgson founded a production company called Best Brains to produce the show. Hodgson, meanwhile, built the original robot puppets the night before shooting the pilot, making them out of found objects including a bowling pin, plastic soap dishes, an Eveready "All American Lantern" flashlight, and rubber tubing. He later redesigned and rebuilt the puppets when it came time to shoot the actual episodes, introducing a fourth robot named Cambot, who handles camera duties, and replacing Beeper with Servo, named after the "Servotron" vending machine located inside Minneapolis' Southdale shopping center.[20] In addition, the entire group set out to scrounge up the materials needed to build the modest but imaginative set, which included "Goodwill toy rejects, Masonite, insulating foam, hot glue, and spray paint."[21]

During these early years, the quintet worked tirelessly to produce MST3K's inaugural season, writing and shooting each episode at a breakneck pace due to sharing production equipment with *Saturday Night at Ringside*, a program devoted to reviewing local professional wrestling shows. As stated in the introduction to *The Mystery Science Theater 3000 Amazing Colossal Episode Guide*, "These five intrepid pioneers would sit and write the famous 'host segments' in the morning,"[22] after which Mallon typed up the scripts on his Xerox 8088 four-megahertz PC half an hour before production commenced. The crew would then grab a quick lunch "at the mediocre deli, and return to shoot the famous 'host segments.'"[23] Afterward, Hodgson, Beaulieu, and Weinstein "would sit uncomfortably close to a blue wall and, with puppets in hand, see a movie, quite often for the first time in their lives, and make jokes about it."[24] All this before 5:00 pm. Thus, much like the plucky teens in *The Giant Gila Monster* and other cheesy B-movies heckled by Hodgson and his cohorts, the group approached production of MST3K with a bold "Let's turn this old barn into a theater!" mindset common to youth.

This fiercely independent ethos aligns the show with the punk and zine cultures of the era, a time when the lines between producer and consumer had begun to blur. In the mid- to late 1980s, punk rock enjoyed a resurgence, thanks in part to the underground popularity of hardcore bands like Suicidal Tendencies and Bad Religion, and the genre's unconstrained, outsider attitude soon seeped into the broader mainstream culture (see the rise of mall staple Hot Topic for evidence of this phenomenon). In many ways, this period was defined by the idea that anyone could pick up a guitar, learn three chords, and become a musician. Likewise, anybody with access to a photocopier could produce and distribute their own zine devoted to a variety of topics, from local music scenes (*Maximum RocknRoll*, *Profane Existence*) to cult movies (*Gorezone, Shock Cinema*) to feminist ideology (*Shocking Pink, Bikini Kill*).

Both punk culture and zines aim to disrupt established gatekeepers by disregarding traditional modes of production as well as promoting alternative forms of creation and consumption, an idea that became increasingly important in the 1980s as Reagan-era deregulation and media consolidation left mainstream popular culture more homogenized than ever before. MST3K demonstrated similar disruptive tendencies during its early years thanks to the creators' efforts to remain in Minneapolis, far outside the established media production centers based in Hollywood and New York. Conventional wisdom states that media producers should try to appeal to the widest possible audience and thus generate maximum profits, but the creators of MST3K instead opted to produce something aimed at a small but devoted fanbase. As Hodgson notes in the behind-the-scenes special *This is MST3K*, "We never say 'Who's gonna get this?' We always say, 'the right people will get this.'"[25] This declaration could easily serve as the show's unofficial slogan, as it emphasizes the idea that MST3K has always courted a small, subcultural audience comprised of people who share the creators' unconventional sense of humor.

In the book *Subculture: The Meaning of Style*, author Dick Hebdige writes that media tend to privilege certain groups over others, reinforcing dominant social and cultural ideologies, but subcultures help to turn these power structures completely on their head.[26] For instance, subcultures frequently confront established social mores by wearing shabby clothing or performing eccentric actions intended to shine a light on culturally forbidden content such as class structures or racial injustices. Ultimately, according to Hebdige, subcultures respond to specific historical conditions and reveal the tensions that exist between those in power and those who occupy more marginalized positions within society. Punk and zine cultures are prime examples of Hebdige's ideas, as they each challenge conventional, mainstream attitudes and express a desire for a different way of life. For instance, punk espouses a revolutionary rhetoric that stems from a desire to disrupt the status quo.[27] Punk performances frequently involve nudity, profanity, and other "rude" behaviors, all with the aim of upending the established social order.[28] Likewise, zines tend to ignore the conventions of professional design while encouraging people to indulge their creativity, share their specific skills or knowledge, and develop a sense of identity.[29] In other words, punk and zines both defy conventional attitudes by aspiring to create something new and, hopefully, change the world.

Since its inception, MST3K has performed a similar function. As mentioned, Hodgson drew a great deal of inspiration from the theater of the absurd. Theatre critic Martin Esslin coined the term to refer to a form of drama developed in the 1950s by primarily European playwrights such as Samuel Beckett, Arthur Adamov, and Eugène Ionesco. Here, absurd refers to "that which has no purpose, or goal, or objective."[30] Absurdist plays tend to explore questions regarding the meaning (or lack thereof) of human existence using illogical dialogue, aimless situations, and nonsensical plots, all elements that can be found in MST3K. In addition, when making the pilot episode, Hodgson and his associates also looked to the Firesign Theater, a surrealist comedy troupe of the 1960s and 1970s known for a highly referential brand of humor that relied on allusions to obscure songs and their own previous routines. MST3K regularly employs a similarly intertextual type of comedy, featuring jokes that require at least a cursory knowledge of everything from the Pia Zadora Golden Globe scandal[31] to the writings of author Kurt Vonnegut[32] to local Minnesota rock band Trip Shakespeare.[33]

Throughout the series, the MST3K crew mined humor from the popular culture of the past and present, but they also (perhaps unwittingly) inspired viewers to reconsider existing power structures, challenge established taste hierarchies, and poke some good-natured fun at prevailing institutions. On the surface, MST3K is little more than a goofy, ultra-low-budget comedy show about a guy and a couple of snarky robots mocking corny old movies.[34] Dig a little deeper, though, and you will find a wealth of incisive comedy that pokes fun at nearly every aspect of contemporary society while subverting dominant sociocultural ideologies.

Hodgson and his crew routinely reference widely accepted bastions of quality such as Akira Kurosawa, Ingmar Bergman, and Jack Kerouac right alongside models of supposedly disposable mass entertainment like *Beanie and Cecil*, *Terry and the Pirates*, and *Tutor Turtle*. By cracking wise about how *The Green Slime* was produced "the same year as *2001: A Space Odyssey*" or joking that an obviously papier-mâché "asteroid" is instead a "battle station" (an obvious nod to *Star Wars: Episode IV—A New Hope*), Hodgson obliterates the distinctions between high art and low trash, thereby upending traditional notions of good and bad taste. Through their numerous intertextual references, the makers of MST3K reveal themselves as fans of all popular culture rather than elitists who only devoured "important" art (such as foreign films) while dismissing "tacky" mass media texts (such as children's television shows) as rubbish.

"OOH, VERY SCARY, I'M TREMBLING": THE INFLUENCE OF HORROR HOSTS ON MST3K

MST3K continues a tradition of simultaneously mocking and celebrating cheesy B-movies as established by late-night horror hosts such as Vampira, Zacherley, and others. Vampira, often credited as the first horror host,[35] initially rose to prominence in 1954 thanks to *The Vampira Show* (originally titled *Dig Me Later, Vampira*), which aired fifty episodes on Los Angeles' KABC-TV Channel 7 from April 30, 1954, until April 2, 1955. In each installment, the slim-waisted Vampira (portrayed by former pin-up model Maila Nurmi) slinked around a fog-enshrouded soundstage and introduced such campy horror flicks as *White Zombie*, *Return of the Ape Man*, and *The Flying Serpent*. At different points throughout each episode, Vampira would stop the film to comment on the events unfolding onscreen, which usually involved her making corny, pun-filled jokes. Following the show's cancellation, Vampira gained cult immortality by co-starring alongside former prince of darkness Bela Lugosi and hulking Swedish professional wrestler Tor Johnson in the camp classic *Plan 9 from Outer Space*. She also, depending on who you ask, inspired actress/comedian Cassandra Peterson to create the equally alluring Elvira, Mistress of the Dark, who likewise ridiculed tawdry B-movies on her own late-night show, *Elvira's Movie Macabre*, which ran on KHJ-TV (also out of Los Angeles) from September 26, 1981, to November 2, 1986. In fact, the character was so similar to Vampira that Nurmi sued Peterson for intellectual property theft in the late 1980s, but the case was ultimately dismissed.[36]

Following Vampira's brief tenure lounging on the velvet Victorian sofa, Zacherley the Cool Ghoul, alter ego of radio and TV personality John Zacherle, emerged to haunt late-night viewers throughout the late 1950s and early 1960s. The cadaverous character, initially named Roland, debuted as the host of *The Shock Theater* (later shortened to simply *Shock Theater*), which first aired on WCAU-TV Channel 10 in Philadelphia, Pennsylvania, from October 7, 1957, to September 13, 1958. Like Vampira before him, Roland lurked around a dank dungeon and introduced somewhat goofy horror movies like *Return of the Vampire* and *Zombies on Broadway* to a sleep-deprived audience. The show proved quite popular with teenaged viewers, so much so that a local record producer convinced Zacherle to record a rock-and-roll single titled "Dinner with Drac," which landed in the Top 10 in March 1958. The following year, after CBS purchased WCAU, Zacherle opted to relocate to New York, taking Roland and *Shock Theater* with him. There, the show aired on WABC-TV from September 2, 1958, until March 27, 1959, with a producer adding a "Y" to the end of Zacherle's name in the credits to help with pronunciation. At that point, Zacherle officially changed the character's name to Zacherley, and he continued to host various horror movie shows throughout the 1950s and 1960s, including *Zacherley at Large* (1959), *The Zacherley Show* (1959–1960), and, perhaps most famously, *Chiller Theater* (1964–1965).

To this day, fans still regard Vampira and Zacherle as the queen and king of late-night horror hosts. However, they are hardly the only performers to slather on some white grease paint and portray ghoulish characters who quipped their way through some of the silliest Z-grade horror films ever made. The duo spawned a legion of disciples who similarly shambled across local independent TV stations in the four decades following their reign. In addition to Elvira, their ranks include Ghoulardi,[37] Svengoolie,[38] Joe Bob Briggs,[39] Commander USA,[40] and Ned the Dead,[41] the latter of whom hailed from Hodgson's old stomping grounds of Green Bay. With the help of inexpensive syndication packages, these morbidly funny emcees introduced generations of viewers to obscure, cheaply made horror and science fiction flicks produced throughout the 1950s, 1960s, 1970s, and 1980s. In the process, they helped create the "bad movie" culture that later fueled MST3K's success. Folks tuning in to shows like *Creature Feature* (starring the vampiric Count Gore Devol) or *Nightmare Theater* (hosted by the hirsute Dr. Cadaverino) were treated to such trashy gems as *It Conquered the World* and *Zontar: The Thing from Venus*. Many of the offerings presented by these horror hosts went on to become regarded as cult classics with fans engaging in an ironic appreciation of their supposed badness, as in the cases of *Glen or Glenda* and *Santa Claus Conquers the Martians*. Thus, as Kristen Hunt notes,[42] late-night horror hosts helped foster the emergence of trash cinema culture, which encompasses MST3K.

Film scholar Guy Barefoot observes that trash cinema has existed in one form or another since the 1930s and that, like cult cinema, it tends to involve specific ways of watching and appreciating films that frequently fail to conform to conventional notions of quality. He compares trash cinema to punk, arguing that both labels push back against dominant mainstream values.[43] Barefoot considers the term trash cinema a label rather than a judgment of taste, because it encourages viewers to explore the world of so-called bad movies without dismissing them due to their shortcomings, technical or otherwise. Horror hosts helped promote such viewing via their sardonic observations about the films and their quality (or lack thereof). The simple act of showing half-forgotten oddities like *Devil Bat's Daughter* and *The Incredible Melting Man* kept those films alive in the public's imagination. As Hunt writes, "Anyone at home and bored on a weekend night could catch these movie shows, and despite the varied quality of the films, they made an impression on countless kids."[44] Hodgson counts himself among those kids, explaining in an interview with the *Green Bay Press Gazette* that he looked to such shows for inspiration. He states, "When I started 'Mystery Science Theater,' I kind of went back to that and said how could I do a show locally that's inexpensive and would be novel. I kind of started with that, like what do I remember from Green Bay? What do I remember growing up? And it was kind of those shows."[45]

MST3K follows a similar structure and performs a similar function as the shows hosted by Vampira, Zacherley, and their numerous offspring, most notably in terms of how the creators excavate trash cinema to uncover comedy gold. Each episode of MST3K features a complete (though sometimes lightly edited) film that is periodically interrupted by comedic host segments. Yet MST3K differs from shows like *Chiller Theater* and *Commander USA* in that the performers remain inside the Mystery Science Theater as the film unspools and speak back to it in real time. Hodgson and his comedic conspirators refer to this activity as "riffing," which consists mainly of making humorous comments on the content of each film while it plays. In the show's early days, Hodgson, Beaulieu, and Weinstein frequently came up with jokes on the fly as they suffered through such cinematic atrocities as *Gamera vs. Zigra*, *City on Fire*, and *The Last Chase*. This explains why they use the word riffing—a term borrowed from the world of jazz that refers to the act of performing a solo in a personal and/or improvisational manner—to describe their specific brand of wisecracking. In terms of comedy, riffing suggests an energetic and often improvisational verbal outpouring, as exemplified by Robin Williams' early standup performances in which he unleashed a rapid-fire torrent of jokes targeting a variety of subjects. In MST3K, Hodgson and his collaborators engage in a similar activity, poking fun at a film's numerous shortcomings while dropping hundreds of intertextual references culled from all corners of popular culture.

"FORCED TO WATCH THEIR OWN MOVIE . . . HOW HORRIBLE": DEFINING MOVIE RIFFING

The concept of riffing can easily be applied to the act of ridiculing movies, TV shows, public speeches, poems, music videos, and more. In each case, a performer uses humor to appropriate texts from their original context and repurpose them in ways not intended by the original creators, thereby changing their meaning. Media scholar Henry Jenkins refers to such activity as "poaching," a term he borrows from French philosopher Michel De Certeau. For Jenkins, poaching describes how fans actively appropriate parts of their favorite TV shows, films, books, etc., and use them to create new cultural materials such as fan fiction and fan art.[46] MST3K performs a similar function, with Hodgson and his fellow mischief-makers critically talking back to what could charitably be described as flawed films and poking fun, both good-natured and otherwise, at their perceived inadequacies. Here, the performers utilize riffing mainly as a vehicle for comedy and entertainment, marking and responding to specific content within each film through sarcastic comments, humorous gestures, or informative observations, all of which serve to place the movies and their narratives into a new context.

At the same time, though, riffing demonstrates a fascinating blend of theoretical and political implications that suggest there is more going on than simply denigrating lousy movies for cheap laughs. The act of riffing, which in the case of MST3K involves speaking back to movies and other media texts, challenges assumptions about how audience members should behave when consuming a cultural text and disrupts ideas regarding how consumers are expected to interpret not only the text on the screen but also the texts evoked via intertextual references. Riffing thus harbors political potential because it allows both media producers and consumers alike to confront the ideological content of films and other pop culture texts. Ultimately, riffing creates an entirely new experience for media consumers, one that opens avenues for new dialogues on the nature of film, culture, and reality itself.

The animated series *Beavis and Butt-Head*, which originally aired on MTV from March 8, 1993, to November 28, 1997, serves as another example of this phenomenon. Each episode features the foul-mouthed duo heckling music videos by such then-popular musical acts as White Zombie, Primus, Tori Amos, and more. Throughout each video, the title characters make comedic (not to mention lewd and crude) observations about what they see happening onscreen. For instance, while watching the video for "I Love it Loud" by KISS, Beavis jokes, "These guys are pretty cool for a bunch of mimes." In another episode, during the video for AC/DC's "Highway to Hell," Butt-Head observes that lead singer Brian Johnson "looks like he's taking a dump." While puerile, such jokes nevertheless call attention to the symbols, tropes, and iconography routinely found in music videos of the period, imbuing them with new meaning via comedic juxtaposition (likening the members of KISS to mimes) or humorous observations about the performers (noting that Johnson's grimace resembles someone straining to empty their bowels). Thus, Beavis, Butt-Head, and those who watch them all become active consumers as they reinterpret and recontextualize the videos and challenge the meanings encoded within the lyrics, images, and performances.

Yet, as scholars Jef Burnham and Joshua Paul Ewalt observe, *Beavis and Butt-Head* differs from MST3K in that the former series "alternately positions the audience toward Beavis and Butt-Head's television set on which the music videos they criticize play and toward the characters themselves mocking the videos." Thus, the eponymous duo "become just as much an object of mockery as the videos they watch." The in-theater segments on MST3K, meanwhile, do not allow the show's audience to "directly confront the riffers," thereby creating a "unique form of dialogue between the secondary audience and the text" in which viewers are forced to "adapt and find new ways to dialogically address the inherent meanings of the series."[47]

Created by animator Mike Judge, *Beavis and Butt-Head* debuted soon after MST3K gained a national audience via its move to Comedy Central. Both series tapped into the same sort of postmodernist humor that appealed to the pop culture savvy members of Generation X (often simplified as Gen-X), the demographic cohort born sometime between the mid- to late 1960s and the early to mid-1980s. This generation came of age during the time of punk rock, hip hop, *Star Wars*, John Hughes, Bret Easton Ellis, and other highly postmodern genres, texts, and creators. Postmodernism often involves a suspicion of reason and an acute sensitivity to things like political and economic power. It is a philosophy that suggests "everything and nothing becomes relevant in its transformation into consumption."[48] Gen-Xers, as they came to be known within the popular press, overwhelmingly demonstrated such traits as many members rejected the values of their parents' generation (i.e., Baby Boomers) and denounced such entrenched social institutions as corporations, government organizations, and the nuclear family. At the same time, Gen-Xers consumed a lot of media as most were latchkey kids raised on television due to growing up in households in which both parents worked full-time jobs to maintain their middle-class lifestyle.

This idea is perhaps best encapsulated by the single-season cult TV series *Freaks and Geeks*, created by Paul Feig and featuring both Hodgson and Beaulieu (who also served as a writer on the show) in small recurring roles. In the episode titled "Dead Dogs and Gym Teachers," perennial outsider Bill Haverchuck (Martin Starr) endures another day of high school bullying only to return to an empty house, where he makes a dinner consisting of a grilled cheese sandwich, a glass of milk, and a large homemade brownie. He then sits down to watch comedian Garry Shandling perform a standup routine which leaves Bill laughing so hard that milk squirts out of his nose. Executive producer Judd Apatow, himself a member of Generation X born in 1967, states that he did the same thing every afternoon during his own high school years,[49] as did many other members of this specific age group. This cultural moment is possibly best summed up by Tyler Durden, the character played by Brad Pitt in the cult film *Fight Club*:

> We're the middle children of history, man. No purpose or place. We have no Great War. No Great Depression. Our Great War's a spiritual war. Our Great Depression is our lives. We've all been raised on television to believe that one day we'd all be millionaires, and movie gods, and rock stars . . . but we won't, and we're slowly learning that fact. And we're very, very pissed off.

Perhaps no other quote so accurately describes Generation X's cynical outlook and sarcastic sense of humor.

Of the original MST3K crew, only Josh Weinstein, born in 1971, can claim membership in Generation X. Yet this did not prevent the show's creators, most of whom were born between the late 1950s and the early 1960s, from utilizing the same sort of postmodern, referential humor that appealed to members of that community, thereby creating a show that truly captured the cultural zeitgeist of the time. This period, which also saw the rise of hip hop music and culture, was in many ways characterized by the often-intertwined concepts of intertextuality and appropriation. Intertextuality refers to the idea that artists, readers, viewers, etc., can appropriate a text and place its elements in different contexts that potentially alter the meaning of the original text and change its intended purpose.

For instance, the tracks featured on the 1989 album *Paul's Boutique* by hip hop legends the Beastie Boys (with an assist from Michael Simpson and John King, aka the Dust Brothers, who helped produce the record) are comprised primarily of samples appropriated from 105 different songs, including "Funky Snakefoot" by Alphonze Mouzon, "Loose Booty" by Sly & the Family Stone, and "Party Time" by Kurtis Blow. Similarly, the quintessential Gen-X film *Pulp Fiction* contains numerous references, homages, and allusions to other films such as *The Warriors*, *Dressed to Kill*, and, most prominently, *Band à part*, which also inspired the name of Tarantino's production company, A Band Apart. Ultimately, as evidenced by these examples, intertextuality suggests that a text's meaning does not reside solely with the original text and its author but rather emerges from the interplay that occurs between text, consumer, and other texts that are assembled by consumers.

While intertextuality and appropriation served as the primary tools of postmodern Gen-X artists, from musicians to filmmakers to comedians, both concepts have a long history. The two examples most pertinent to MST3K and its legacy are the TV show *Fractured Flickers* and the film *What's Up, Tiger Lily?* The former featured humorous dialogue dubbed over silent film footage and is perhaps the first popular example (in the United States, at least) of the explicit appropriation and subsequent riffing of mediated texts. The basic formula for each *Fractured Flickers* segment combines a melodramatic short clip from a silent film dubbed over with hilariously incongruent narration and dialogue, with host Hans Conried humorously setting up the premise of each "flicker." In the pilot episode, 1918's *Tarzan of the Apes* is repurposed as *Tarfoot of the Apes*, with Conried poking fun at star Elmo Lincoln's doughy physique and comedic superimposed dialogue joking about Jane's "cheap perfume" and renaming a British scientist Reginald Snively Wappington-Jones. While the jokes featured on *Fractured Flickers* rarely venture beyond relatively shallow commentary on the action or quality of the film itself, several of its segments predict future riffing tactics such as breaking the fourth wall, drawing attention to the medium (e.g., the narrator suggests that the devious "Wappington-Jones" has been waiting to get Jane alone "for three reels, which is a very long time for a cad to wait").

Meanwhile, for his directorial debut, controversial filmmaker Woody Allen appropriated the comedic Japanese spy movie *Kokusai himitsu keisatsu: Kagi no kagi* (also known by its English title *International Secret Police: Key of Keys*) and dubbed over its soundtrack with new ridiculous dialogue and music. In the original film, which was directed by Senkichi Taniguchi and premiered in Japan on October 23, 1965, special agent Jiro Kitami (Tatsuya Mihashi) is tasked with stealing a large amount of money from anti-government guerrillas but is soon swept up in a bigger mystery. Meanwhile, Allen's reworked version, renamed *What's Up, Tiger Lily?*, centers on secret agent Phil Moscowitz's quest to recover the world's best egg salad recipe, which has improbably been stolen. Early in the film, Allen appears onscreen to explain his process while simultaneously challenging his own authorship by exposing the film's origin. Later, near the middle of the film, he appears onscreen again and flatly refuses to clarify what is supposed to be happening in the intentionally incoherent plot.

In addition to the farcical superimposed narrative and humorous (though, at times, racist) dialogue, *What's Up, Tiger Lily?* is further convoluted thanks to self-aware dialogue that breaks the fourth wall (at one point, Moscowitz reports to intelligence that he "was nearly shot before the opening credits"), non-sequitur pop culture references (such as jokes about the Mormon Tabernacle Choir and Hugh Hefner), and a gunfight that pauses for a shadow puppet performance and a couple kissing in silhouette. By utilizing these different tactics, Allen not only exposes the medium (in this case, cinema) but reminds the audience of the space that exists between them and the screen. In the process, he assembles a breakthrough viewing experience by incongruently intermingling soundtrack and iconography.

Rhetorical tactics such as these were more fully realized on MST3K and its riffing offspring (explored in chapter 3). The show's rise coincides with the idea that consumers of popular culture are increasingly comfortable with treating texts as disposable and vulnerable to their personal whims. Critics and scholars continue to argue about whether activities such as movie riffing, text appropriation, and intertextual commentary—a move Steven Johnson refers to as a shift "from host organism to parasite"[50]—represent another step in the death of the author or the cynical manifestation of a collective creative bankruptcy. Either way, both *Fractured Flickers* and *What's Up, Tiger Lily?* represent important steps in the development of movie riffing generally and MST3K specifically because they each approach films as texts that can be both deconstructed and ridiculed. These examples resurrect forgotten—and, without modification, largely irrelevant to history—works and remove them from their original context, effectively creating Frankenstein films with all the seams on full display.

Of course, it must be noted that while some see riffing as a good thing, others consider it obnoxious, narcissistic, destructive, and entirely disrespectful to the films and those involved in making them. For instance, one KTMA viewer compared watching MST3K to "sitting in a theater with a bunch of rude junior high teenagers."[51] Likewise, actor Joe Don Baker, star of such riff-worthy stinkers as *Mitchell* and *Final Justice*, both of which appeared on later seasons of MST3K, reportedly hated how Hodgson and his merry band of riffers treated his films. Apparently, he was so upset that he threatened the show's creators with physical violence,[52] though Murphy believed that Baker was only kidding.

Similarly, Joe Dante, director of such classic genre films as *The Howling*, *Gremlins*, and *The 'Burbs*, also expressed disdain toward the show. On an episode of the podcast *The Movies That Made Me*, Dante informs guest Jonah Ray Rodriguez—who assumed hosting duties when the rebooted MST3K debuted on Netflix in 2017 (see chapter 5)—that he dislikes how the show's creators only riff on subpar, selectively edited prints of the films and periodically interrupt them with the "torturous" host segments.[53] Dante especially takes offense to the show's heckling of *This Island Earth*, the classic Cold War–era science fiction film riffed by Hodgson's replacement Michael J. Nelson and the crew of the Satellite of Love in *Mystery Science Theater 3000: The Movie* (see chapter 2). Dante considers *This Island Earth* one of his favorite films and did not appreciate it being edited into near-incomprehensibility and mocked. Nonetheless, even Dante concedes that the performers occasionally come up with funny jokes, and he appreciates the deep dives into the riffed films provided by the short documentaries included on the MST3K DVDs released first by Rhino and later by Shout Factory. Thus, it appears that even those who hate the show understand that MST3K and riffing both have a place in popular culture.

"PLEASE PUT YOUR BRAIN UNDER THE SEAT IN FRONT OF YOU": THIS IS MST3K

While MST3K's creators would later disavow the KTMA episodes due to what they perceived as technical and comedic inadequacies, these installments nevertheless set the tone for the rest of the series in two significant ways. First, they established the type of movies that would serve as targets for MST3K's brand of idiosyncratic, pop-culture-inflected humor: namely cheesy, campy, poorly made B-movies and telefilms that primarily spanned the genres of horror, science fiction, and fantasy. The first two episodes saw Joel and the bots riff *Invaders of the Deep* and *Revenge of the Mysterons from Mars*, two films that repackaged episodes of TV series produced by Gerry and Sylvia Anderson,[54] infamous for populating their shows with creepy, dead-eyed marionettes. Other films riffed during the KTMA years include *City on Fire, The Last Chase, The Million Eyes of Sumuru,*[55] *Phase IV,*[56] *SST Death Flight, Superdome, Hangar 18, Humanoid Woman* aka *To the Stars by Hard Ways,* and *Cosmic Princess.* This last one was another compilation film, this time comprised of two episodes of the short-lived science fiction TV series *Space: 1999* (1975–1977). Such films represent the castoffs of cinema due to their varying levels of competence and quality, thus serving as prime riffing fodder.

The season also featured several Japanese sci-fi flicks and giant monster movies, including *Mighty Jack, Fugitive Alien, Star Force: Fugitive Alien II, Time of the Apes, Gamera: The Giant Monster, Gamera vs. Barugon, Gamera vs. Gyaos, Gamera vs. Guiron, Gamera vs. Zigra,* and *The Legend of Dinosaurs.* Aside from *The Legend of Dinosaurs,* each of these films would reappear in episodes produced for Comedy Central (see chapter 2). Moreover, four of them—*Mighty Jack, Fugitive Alien, Starforce: Fugitive Alien II,* and *Time of the Apes*—were compiled from episodes of old TV shows à la *Invaders of the Deep* and *Revenge of the Mysterons from Mars.* American exploitation distributors such as American International Pictures and King Features Entertainment frequently purchased such films, editing them and dubbing them into English for release into US theaters, thereby removing them from their historical and cultural contexts. Nevertheless, even these often-incomprehensible dubbed versions still offer plenty of wacky fun, inspiring cult devotion from viewers who appreciate the low-budget charms of campy *Planet of the Apes* ripoffs and movies in which men stuffed into latex monster suits demolish model cities.

The second thing these episodes helped to solidify is the act of riffing itself. As mentioned, these early entries featured Hodgson, Beaulieu, and Weinstein engaging in extemporaneous riffing while watching the films, often for the first time ever. As such, the episodes often feature few jokes, as Hodgson and the other members of the crew frequently struggle to come up with zingers on the fly. Moreover, many of the jokes are simply not all that funny but rather just observational (e.g., mentioning how badly made the film is) or referential (e.g., joking that the word "dinosaur" kind of sounds like "Dinah Shore"). In this regard, these early installments truly recall the widespread communal activity that helped inspire the premise, that is, watching and making fun of "bad" movies.

The KTMA episodes genuinely feel like a few friends getting together on a Friday night to maybe get a little drunk while watching a hilariously awful movie about a giant flying turtle battling a creature that sort of resembles a dog mixed with a large kitchen knife. The movie proves so grueling, however, that it prompts the group to crack jokes to try and make each other laugh. However, not all the jokes land, and there are long, dull stretches when no one knows exactly what to say. That description pretty much sums up MST3K during the KTMA years. Even the creators admit that these episodes are not up to snuff, writing in the *Amazing Colossal Episode Guide*, "the shows were seminal and formative, which is to say *they weren't very good*."[57] Yet these episodes unquestionably helped establish the template for what riffing would become; throughout the show's run, the practice of riffing remained highly referential and intertextual, with the writers and performers drawing on the entirety of popular culture to generate laughs. They just needed time to learn that to generate the maximum amount of comedy, the jokes needed to be planned out in advance and placed strategically throughout any given film. The crew would develop and perfect this skill over the course of the Comedy Central episodes.

More importantly, though, the humor that defined MST3K was in place from the start, with Hodgson and his fellow performers making jokes inspired by a wide variety of influences, from Frank Zappa tunes to old *Variety* headlines to small-town water parks like the Wisconsin Dells. Given the depth and breadth of the witticisms fired off in each episode, it seemed as though the show's creators knew a little bit about everything under the sun, revealing them as rabid consumers of popular culture who somehow lucked into working in the entertainment industry. Yet they also remained firmly outside that industry thanks to producing the show in Minneapolis, far from the glitz and glamour of Hollywood. This distance provided Hodgson and his colleagues with an outsider's perspective on popular culture, and they regularly used that viewpoint to call out things they found silly or offensive. They were simultaneously part of and external to the culture industries.

Moreover, MST3K and the films riffed by the crew appeared cheap in comparison to the big-budget spectaculars churned out by major studios, but MST3K always felt quaint rather than shoddy. This charm stems largely from the creators' Midwestern sensibilities, which frequently involve a folksy, down-home attitude and a blunt honesty that tends to upset the executives who preside over the big studios situated in Los Angeles (for more on this idea, turn to chapter 3). As TV critic Tom Shales put it in a 1991 article for the *Washington Post*, "One of the many endearing things about the program is its Midwestern grass-roots ambiance. 'MST3K' is clearly homemade and not a store-bought cookie."[58] The homemade quality arose in part from the existence of UHF stations and cable access channels, which in the years before the development of the World Wide Web served as a medium for democratic local community expression.[59] This can-do, DIY spirit immediately helped endear MST3K to its legions of devoted fans.

MST3K struck a chord with viewers because it replicated something that almost everyone does but refined it in such a way that pretty much every joke generates laughter. The show's creators took an activity performed in living rooms, basements, bedrooms, and movie theaters around the world and turned it into a formula for a successful television show. As comedian Penn Jillette puts it in *This is MST3K*, "Don't you love talking back to something cheesy on the screen? And wouldn't you love it even better if everything you said were really clever and funny instead of the incoherent grunts you can usually squeeze out? That's the whole idea behind *Mystery Science Theater 3000*."[60] The show's simple hook appealed to viewers who likely participated in their own riffing sessions with friends, but they were probably nowhere near as funny as those written and performed by the professional comedians who developed MST3K and wrote every installment. Significantly, while the early episodes are considered inferior by both fans and the show's creators, they nevertheless resonated with viewers who stayed up way past their bedtime to watch a sleepy-eyed comic make fun of a cheesy B-movie about a square-jawed marionette battling to save the earth from some weird alien puppets. As one viewer put it in a message left on the station's answering machine, "Pretty hokey movie . . . great commentary."[61] The sacks of letters celebrating MST3K that bombarded KTMA simultaneously corroborated this assessment and saved the show from an early demise. A winning combination of familiarity and DIY attitude helped make MST3K a hit with fans of eccentric comedy.

By the time 1989 rolled around, a punishing production schedule had left the tiny crew feeling burnt out, but this did not stop them from sending a seven-minute MST3K demo reel to executives at HBO, who liked what they saw and picked up the series for their fledgling cable network, The Comedy Channel. With the help of their agent, Rick Leeds, the Satellite of Love crew took their little homemade cow-town puppet show to cable,[62] where they garnered a national audience while remaining true to their small-town, DIY roots. The next chapter explores the show's Comedy Central years, focusing on its trajectory from the verbally and visually clunky KTMA years to a more sophisticated style of movie commentary and presentation (though one that remains decidedly "lo-fi" in appearance). Chapter 2 also delves deeper into MST3K's premise to consider how it presents fans with a much-needed model for navigating and finding one's voice through pop culture literacy. Finally, the chapter explores how the show's repeated admonition to "keep circulating the tapes" encouraged fans to record episodes of the show and then share those recordings with one another, actively fostering a culture of engaged fan participation and dynamic media consumption.

CHAPTER TWO

"THEY HIRED A TEMP BY THE NAME OF MIKE"

The Comedy Central Years

With the move to the newly launched Comedy Channel (later rechristened Comedy Central) in 1988, the crew of the Satellite of Love (SoL) bid farewell to KTMA but not to their Midwestern roots or their do-it-yourself attitude. Opting against relocating production of *Mystery Science Theater 3000* to Los Angeles, Joel Hodgson and his band of merry pranksters, which at that point had grown beyond the original five members, remained in Minneapolis and continued to produce the show there. As such, MST3K's lo-fi aesthetic and smalltown sensibilities remained intact and would endure throughout the series' various incarnations. Crucially, the showrunners continued to write and perform regionally specific jokes even after MST3K gained (slightly) increased notoriety on a national stage. This meant that folks in Hodgson's hometown of Green Bay, Wisconsin, could continue enjoying gags about local landmarks like the Port Plaza Mall or familiar activities such as traveling up to Rhinelander to fish for crappies even as those japes likely flew over the heads of viewers based elsewhere.

Yet, rather than alienate non-Midwestern viewers and relegate the series to little more than a weird footnote in the history of television, MST3K's ethnographic dimensions helped the series build a devoted audience in every corner of the United States and beyond. The regionalism that defined MST3K's humor proved useful in hailing a wider though still niche audience comprised of people from all walks of life, many of whom resided outside the Midwest and therefore beyond the realm of hot fish shops or Sven-and-Ole jokes. As scholars (and Wisconsin natives) Claire Schmidt and Laurel Schmidt observe, MST3K's regionally specific humor allowed viewers in the flyover states to recognize them-selves in the show—and maybe laugh at themselves, as well—while also inviting outsiders to find humor in the broad Midwestern stereotypes frequently employed by the performers.[1] The show may have made the leap to a bigger platform, but its folksy, peculiarly accented, wisecracking personality persisted.

Of course, the transition from local UHF station to HBO-owned basic cable network was not without difficulties, and the denizens of the SoL soon found them-selves facing a whole new set of challenges that impacted MST3K throughout its Comedy Central years. While MST3K cost little to make and generated a great deal of positive press for the fledgling network, the series perpetually struggled to find a larger audience and thus lagged in the Nielsen ratings.[2] In addition, the showrunners occasionally experienced legal headaches when trying to acquire broadcast rights to the films they wanted to riff, an issue they had not faced during the KTMA years. Throughout those early days, Hodgson and his collaborators merely pulled their riffing fodder from the small station's existing film library. Upon moving to basic cable, however, the crew found clearing films to be much more difficult, due largely to increased red tape and prohibitively expensive li-censing fees. Meanwhile, a combination of creative burnout and growing tensions between Hodgson and his producing partner Jim Mallon inspired the former to step away from both the show and production company Best Brains after just a few years aboard the newly relaunched SoL. Hodgson would be replaced by head writer Michael J. Nelson starting with episode 513, in which the bots show their new crewmate the riffing ropes as they heckle the schlocky 1962 horror flick *The Brain That Wouldn't Die.*

Despite these various hardships, the Best Brains team still managed to produce 129 mirth-filled episodes across seven seasons during their partnership with HBO and Comedy Central. They even ventured beyond the confines of TV, piloting the SoL onto the silver screen in 1996 with *Mystery Science Theater 3000: The Movie,* which proved to be a bone of contention between Hodgson and Mallon. For their first (and thus far only) cinematic outing, the crew navigated a turbulent production and an abbreviated theatrical release to riff on a selectively edited ver-sion of the big-budget sci-fi spectacular *This Island Earth.* This period also gave rise to the first-ever official MST3K convention, the ConventioCon ExpoFest-A-Rama, which drew two thousand rabid MST3K fans, aka MSTies—including author Christopher J. Olson—to the Radisson South in downtown Bloomington, Minnesota, between September 16, 1994, and September 18, 1994.[3] The event proved so popular it spawned a sequel, ConventioCon ExpoFest-A-Rama 2: Electric Boogaloo, held from August 30, 1996, to September 2, 1996. Throughout it all, the crew of the SoL refined and perfected the art of movie riffing, provided viewers with a playful model for speaking back to media texts, and fostered a vibrant culture of active fan participation and dynamic media consumption.

Mystery Science Theater 3000 (Comedy Central), 1988 to 1999. Shown: Crow, Michael J. Nelson, Tom Servo.
COMEDY CENTRAL / PHOTOFEST © COMEDY CENTRAL

"YOU'RE WATCHING TURKEY DAY AT COMEDY CENTRAL!": MAKING MST3K

Along with finding a new home on a recently launched national basic cable network, MST3K also enjoyed a slight increase in its production budget. Nonetheless, the show's look and feel remained largely unchanged from the KTMA years as Hodgson and his team opted to maintain the delightfully handmade appearance of those early episodes. This consistency no doubt stems from the showrunners' conviction to continue producing the show in Minneapolis. Initially, executives at HBO wanted to move production of MST3K to New York, but the cast and crew rejected this idea, citing family and other obligations.[4] Thankfully, the network relented and allowed production to remain in Minneapolis, a decision that almost certainly helped the show avoid a quick cancellation and thereby build its rabid cult audience.

According to Ben Svetky, former staff writer for *Entertainment Weekly*, "I think being in the middle of nowhere kind of helps keep [the MST3K crew] focused on what they're doing."[5] Dan O'Shannon, an executive producer on the popular sitcom *Cheers*, corroborates Svetky's assertion, noting that the decision to remain in Minnesota ensures that MST3K is "amazingly different from anything that would be turned out [in Los Angeles]."[6] Kevin Murphy appears to agree with both of them, stating in *Wired*'s oral history of MST3K, "If we had done the show in New York, it would have been canceled within a season or two. There would have been people in there sticking their fingers in it. And the reason the show got to grow was because nobody wanted to come out to Minnesota."[7]

The decision to stay put may have also contributed to MST3K's emergence as one of the Comedy Channel's signature shows during the nascent network's first few years of existence. At the time, the Comedy Channel was still trying to establish an identity and executives were therefore throwing a lot of things at the wall to see what might stick. The new-and-improved basic cable version of MST3K, which looked and felt a lot like the old UHF version, established a reputation as a modest cult hit pretty much right from the start. As such, network execs decided to push the show and ride its success as a way of growing an audience for the recently launched cable channel.

Much like the show's aesthetic and down-home sensibilities, MST3K's basic format also stayed the same. In each episode, a pair of mad scientists (known as the Mads) force laidback janitor Joel Robinson (Hodgson) and his homemade robot pals to watch a bad movie as part of an ongoing search for a film awful enough to break Joel's will. The evil Dr. Clayton Forrester (Trace Beaulieu) would then use this film to conquer the world. Rather than enduring the experiment in silent agony, however, Joel and the bots unleash an almost nonstop torrent of jokes as a defense mechanism against the film's offensive badness. Though the stalwart pals occasionally encountered a film so putrid they would emerge from the theater in tears and sobs (as when they suffered through director Harold P. Warren's 1966 stinker *Manos: The Hands of Fate*), they never cracked as intended by their captors. In most cases Joel and the bots skewered the films with relative ease, returning from the theater in good spirits and as sharp-tongued as ever. Despite being subjected to some of the worst films ever made, the SoL crew always emerged victorious thanks to their quick wits and vast knowledge of popular culture.

While most aspects of MST3K remained constant, some differences did surface following the move to the new nationwide cable network. For instance, the character of Joel Hodgson was renamed Joel Robinson. Likewise, Servo became Tom Servo. More importantly, perhaps, the core group of Hodgson, Josh Weinstein, Trace Beaulieu, Kevin Murphy, and Jim Mallon expanded to include Michael J. Nelson (who served as head writer from seasons two through ten),

Bridget Jones,[8] Mary Jo Pehl, Frank Conniff, Paul Chaplin, and Beth "Beez" McKeever. Like the original crew, the new members performed a variety of roles both behind the scenes and in front of the camera. For instance, in addition to working as writers on the show, Pehl, Jones, and Nelson all made onscreen appearances during the Comedy Central years, playing such fan-favorite characters as Jan in the Pan,[9] Nuveena,[10] and Jack Perkins.[11] Pehl also became synonymous with the role of Magic Voice, the unseen computer intelligence that alerts the crew to an imminent Commercial Sign (signaling an ad break) or Movie Sign (the crew's cue to return to the theater and endure more torment), as she spent the most time inhabiting the role. Following performers Jann L. Johnson and Alexandra B. Carr, Pehl played Magic Voice from episode 415[12] to episode 706,[13] the final installment of MST3K's Comedy Central years. She would be succeeded first by Beth "Beez" McKeever, who played Magic Voice in a handful of episodes produced during the show's Sci-Fi Channel years, and later by producer/writer Sharyl Volpe, who inhabited the role during season thirteen, the first produced for MST3K's proprietary streaming service the Gizmoplex (see chapter 5).

Throughout this period, the show also employed a rotating team of contributing writers that included Rob Schrab,[14] Mike Gandolfi,[15] and Christopher Whiting.[16] This development was perhaps the most significant departure from the original KTMA incarnation of MST3K, which was written and performed entirely by the core group of Hodgson, Mallon, Beaulieu, Weinstein, and Murphy. Originally, these five weisenheimers wrote the host segments and improvised the riffs during theater segments, with each member adding their own quirky sensibility to the mix by drawing on a specific area of pop culture knowledge. For instance, Hodgson knew a great deal about sitcoms and kids shows from the 1950s and 1960s, while Murphy was well-versed in musical theater and sports trivia. With the expansion of the writers' room, however, came an expansion of perspectives and thus a wider selection of riffs. Newcomer Frank Conniff, who joined the show at the beginning of season two and played beloved second banana TV's Frank until episode 624, brought with him a deep well of obscure movie and literary references. Nelson, meanwhile, drew on his love of Shakespeare to inject numerous intertextual allusions to the Bard's most famous works. Introducing this new blood into the writing staff allowed the MST3K crew to direct their mockery at an even wider range of pop culture targets during the show's Comedy Central era.

Without access to the KTMA studios, the Best Brains crew needed a new space in which to produce MST3K. They found it in a warehouse located in what writer/performer Bill Corbett refers to as an "industrial park in a second-ring suburb" of Minneapolis.[17] The team had to convert the space into a feasible studio while also paying the show's ever-growing staff, but both tasks proved difficult as MST3K's budget remained limited. However, this did not stop the plucky crew from entering the age of personal computers as they purchased a Zeos 286 desktop computer that they used to transcribe the riffs generated during improvisational rehearsal sessions. The MST3K team would also construct a new set, establish an office for the Best Brains execs, and set up the show's production, all on next to no money. This meant that many members of the crew received a pittance on payday, but everyone stuck it out because they were getting the opportunity to live out their dream of working on a comedic TV series. According to Mallon, this lifestyle proved "intoxicating" and provided both cast and crew with an energy that "helped carry the day for the first season."[18]

In addition to a new studio space, the intrepid SoL crew also needed movies to riff, preferably bad ones. These could not be just any old run-of-the-mill bad movies, though; for a film to be riffed on MST3K, it needed to be bad in the right way. The showrunners set their sights on films that boasted ridiculous premises, preachy dialogue, and an intention of quality on the part of the filmmakers. Films riffed during the Comedy Central years include *The Robot vs. The Aztec Mummy*, *Catalina Caper*, *Pod People* aka *Extra Terrestrial Visitors*, *Monster a Go-Go*, *The Wild World of Batwoman*, and *The Violent Years*. Overall, the MST3K team tackled 129 feature-length films of dubious quality (though most are not without their charms) throughout the show's Comedy Central run. Each one fits the bill of being bad in the right way, meeting most or all the criteria sought by the show's creators.

The films riffed during this period all offered up an abundance of daft premises. See, for instance, *Eegah*, in which two teenage sweethearts run afoul of a seven-foot-tall caveman (played by the statuesque Richard Kiel) who falls for the girl à la King Kong. Many of the movies also featured delightfully preachy dialogue; in *Bride of the Monster*, police captain Tom Robbins (Harvey B. Dunn) observes that the villainous Dr. Eric Vornoff (Bela Lugosi) lost his life in a massive explosion during the film's climax because he "tampered in God's domain" due to trying to create a race of atomic supermen. Finally, some of the films aspired to greatness, such as *The Day the Earth Froze* aka *Sampo*, a lavish Soviet-Finnish retelling of the legend of Finnish folk hero Lemminkäinen. Such films proved perfect for riffing, as they provided MST3K's performers with plenty of material that seemed tailor-made for mockery.

At the same time, however, acquiring these movies often proved more difficult compared to the KTMA years, a time when Hodgson and his crew could simply pull a tape out of the station's film library and riff away. In those days, the rights were already sorted out since KTMA had licensed the films for broadcast. This was not the case with the new Comedy Central incarnation of MST3K. Instead, the show's producers needed to license films directly from distributors, an endeavor that came loaded with its own pitfalls. As Hodgson explained to *Wired*'s Brian Raftery, "Film distributors would do this trick where they'd license you several movies," many of which held no interest for the SoL crew.[19] According to

Corbett, the Best Brains would obtain a batch of films only to find that some were unusable due to poor image and sound quality while others proved too boring and talky for the showrunners' purposes. Other times they received films containing content deemed inappropriate for basic cable, as when they opened a box to discover a collection of Italian horror movies featuring copious amounts of sex and violence.[20]

Luckily, the crew had the backing of HBO and Comedy Central, and the two companies did their best to help untangle the legal issues surrounding the films. Even then, the process proved taxing for all involved. As noted by former Comedy Central executive Art Bell,[21] most of the films chosen to be riffed on MST3K were wrapped up in "crazy chains of ownership," making it difficult to track down the individuals or groups who held the licensing rights.[22] Additionally, the owners of said films "often didn't know how to price these things," meaning that network executives needed to haggle to get the best price since they wanted "to buy this stuff by the pound."[23] Adding to this problem, Comedy Central only had a small amount of money to spend on the show, meaning that purchasing film rights stretched MST3K's already thin budget.[24] Finally, many rights owners proved reluctant to allow the showrunners to use their films because they did not understand how their product would be used. The challenges continued even after licensing rights had been untangled and acquired; Bell explains that HBO would send Best Brains "10 films for every one they picked for the show," with the SoL crew rejecting numerous films as unsuitable for riffing.[25] However, Bell attributes this fussiness as a big factor in the show's quality, stating, "the fact that they were so picky helped make the show as good as it was. They honed bad-movie selection into a fine art."[26]

Along with features, the SoL crew also riffed on several short films (or "shorts" as they came to be known) during this period, most of which were provided by New York–based film historian and founder of the Prelinger Archives, Rick Prelinger. These shorts included serials about square-jawed heroes like Commando Cody (George D. Wallace) and Crash Corrigan (Ray Corrigan), as well as industrial and educational films produced by the likes of Coronet Films and the Centron Corporation. Interestingly, Centron's principal director, Harold "Herk" Harvey, would go on to direct *Carnival of Souls*, a cult classic horror film that received the riffing treatment courtesy of Michael J. Nelson and his cohorts at RiffTrax (see chapter 4). Sometimes, the shorts consisted of bite-sized segments of a TV show from the medium's golden age, as in the case of the long-running soap opera *General Hospital*. These shorts would become synonymous with MST3K (as well as its spinoffs RiffTrax and the Mads; see chapter 4), spawning a host of running gags and recurring characters that continue to delight loyal MSTies to this day.

See, for instance, *Mr. B Natural*, in which the title character (a puckish imp played by actress/singer/dancer Betty Luster) tries to inspire a young boy to play the trumpet, preferably one manufactured by sponsor C. G. Conn. Mr. B would become a fixture of MST3K, with Jones making multiple appearances as the character throughout the series. *Circus on Ice*, meanwhile, unleashes the horrors of the Toronto Skating Club's 40th Annual Carnival, which includes ice-skating clowns and a depiction of a graceful fawn (portrayed by Jacqueline du Bief) being gunned down by hunters. Joel and the bots labeled much of the ice-based antics as "nightmare fuel," an oft-repeated phrase used to describe anything they found terrifying (mostly clowns). Shorts such as these left an indelible impression on both the show's creators and viewers, inspiring everything from cosplay (fans frequently show up to MST3K events dressed like Mr. B Natural) to in-jokes (most MSTies will recognize the exclamation "BOING!" from the 1950 short *Are You Ready for Marriage?*).

Though MST3K's format and humor remained largely unchanged, the production process underwent a slight metamorphosis following the move to the Comedy Channel. Initially, the five original crewmembers spent the day writing and recording the host segments before cramming into a tiny studio to fire up a movie (many of which they were seeing for the first time) and improvise jokes as the narrative unfurled, all before the local pro-wrestling program took over the workspace in the late afternoon. Mallon, meanwhile, recorded the riffing session, which was then edited and broadcast to a small but loyal audience of Minnesotans. This lo-fi, do-it-yourself approach worked just fine for public access, but such tactics would not cut it in the wider world of basic cable.

As explained in *The Mystery Science Theater 3000 Amazing Colossal Episode Guide*, it took nine days to write and produce an episode of MST3K during the Comedy Central years.[27] The writers and performers spent day one watching (and rewatching) a movie while improvising jokes that were recorded on a Macintosh computer along with the corresponding time code numbers from the film. The next day, the crew took a break from the film to work on the host segments, humorous sketches that take place between the movie riffing segments. Day three involved watching the movie yet again to work out which jokes would be used in the show. Day four was devoted to composing music and building props and sets while a small group of writers revisited the film yet again to edit jokes and assign lines to the performers. Day five consisted of finishing props, handing in final script rewrites, and gathering the cast for a read-through. A full dress rehearsal took place on day six while the host segments and movie segments were shot on days seven and eight, respectively. Day nine was used to review the episode and give it a final polish (e.g., adding, removing, or rewriting jokes, reshooting segments, etc.) before sending it out into the world. Producing the show had become a much more involved process than it was at the beginning, when it consisted of five guys riffing on Z-grade movies in a tiny studio nestled inside a small UHF station.

The question of whether slightly increased production values would improve the product was answered on November 18, 1989, when the show made its Comedy Channel debut with episode 101, in which Joel and the bots riff on *The Crawling Eye* aka *The Trollenberg Terror*. While the show maintained the handmade appearance and casual tone established during the KTMA years, it definitely looked and felt more professional. Unfortunately, the somewhat bigger platform did not necessarily yield big ratings, at least not immediately. The Comedy Channel had only just launched and had yet to establish much of a presence on TV, much less an audience. As Weinstein explains, the cast and crew "had to go to an outer-ring-suburb bar on a Saturday morning to see a premiere, because none of our cable companies carried the Comedy Channel at that point."[28] Nevertheless, MST3K stood out from the reruns of old sitcoms and minor comedy flicks that comprised the bulk of the Comedy Channel's offerings at that time, thanks in large part to its quirky sensibilities, unusual format, and winsome cast. The series quickly developed a small-but-loyal cult audience, but more importantly it helped drive interest in the new network. According to Bell, MST3K "was the Comedy Channel's first attention-getting show, in a big way. And we really rode that to success in terms of getting better distribution and advertising sales, and keeping the network alive."[29]

MST3K would become one of Comedy Central's signature shows, developing a fervent and diverse fanbase that included Vice President Al Gore, avant-garde musician Frank Zappa, standup comic/pop culture junkie Patton Oswalt, and members of the Minnesota Vikings football team.[30] Network executives did everything they could to promote the show, including programming the annual Turkey Day marathons, airing twenty-four-hour blocks of MST3K every Thanksgiving Day from 1991 to 1995. These marathons included special bumper segments between episodes as well as the premiere of at least one new episode, and they proved quite popular with the show's most dedicated fans. Unfortunately, with great success came great change; MST3K would undergo numerous upheavals during the Comedy Central years, including Weinstein leaving to pursue a career writing for TV, landing gigs on such shows as *Malcolm & Eddie*, *Freaks and Geeks*, and *America's Funniest Home Videos*. More shockingly, MST3K would also experience the abrupt departure of its progenitor, Joel Hodgson, who exited the series in 1993. However, he stuck around long enough to change the landscape of television and inspire subsequent generations of amateur riffers, helping launch the era of participatory culture in the process.

"NOBODY CALLS THE ASHWAUBENON JAGUARS A BUNCHA GEEKY LOSERS!": THE JOEL ERA

Like most long-running shows, MST3K can be divided into different eras, with each one defined by the person wearing the Gizmonic jumpsuit. In that respect, MST3K recalls other long-running series such as *Doctor Who* or *Ultraman*, both of which spawned numerous incarnations and featured multiple actors in the title role at different points. In the case of MST3K, the period lasting from 1989 to 1993 is widely recognized as the Joel era, as it features Hodgson donning the red (and occasionally green) jumpsuit to play mellow custodial engineer and unwilling scientific guinea pig Joel Robinson. This era is marked by Hodgson's eccentric referential humor and sleepy-eyed persona, both of which appealed to Generation X audiences of the time. As discussed in chapter 1, postmodern irony was a hallmark of Gen-X humor, largely because, as author and journalist Darragh McManus puts it, "everything [Gen-Xers] say and do is lacquered with the bitter patina of sarcasm."[31] At the same time, many Gen-Xers possessed a deep knowledge and sincere love of popular culture, using (often obscure) intertextual references as a form of communication and cultural capital. Gen-X filmmakers Kevin Smith and Quentin Tarantino are prime examples of this phenomenon, as their films evoke everything from *Star Wars* to *Star Trek*, as well as 1980s teen flicks and exploitation cinema of the 1960s and 1970s.

Hodgson and MST3K tapped into that specific vein of satire starting with Hodgson's standup routine, which routinely saw him reference and poke good-natured fun at the popular culture of his youth through a lens of postmodernist irony. For instance, during an appearance on venerable pop culture institution *Saturday Night Live* in February 1984, Hodgson cracked jokes about *The Flintstones*, Mr. Potato Head, Rock 'Em Sock 'Em Robots, tin can telephones, and more. He regularly used his encyclopedic knowledge of pop culture and sardonic observations to generate both recognition and laughter in his audience. Though he may belong to the Baby Boomer demographic, Hodgson's ironic humor and abiding love of popular culture made him an honorary Gen-Xer.

MST3K served as another platform for Hodgson's peculiar brand of comedy, trafficking in the same sort of ironic detachment, bizarre non sequiturs, and allusions to popular culture. Hodgson adapted several of his standup gags for the show, often for the weekly "invention exchange," in which Joel and the Mads compete to see who came up with the best invention. Originally categorized as a prop comic (or, in his words, a "gizmocrat"), Hodgson alternately delighted and confounded audiences with his wacky, homemade inventions. These include the "Chiro-Gyro" (a helmet that appeared to make the wearer's head spin 360 degrees), the "Chalkman" (an inflatable airbag helmet for motorcyclists), and the "Cummerbubblebund" (a cummerbund with a working bubble machine attached).

They would all make appearances on MST3K during the Joel era, along with numerous new inventions created specifically for the show. When combined with the snarky, referential commentary over bad films, these nonsensical contraptions helped ingratiate MST3K to young adult viewers steeped in sarcasm and surrounded by consumer culture.

More importantly, perhaps, MST3K continued Hodgson's tendency to celebrate popular culture, especially that of the 1950s and 1960s, via scathing humor. The jokes of this era frequently seemed to originate from a place of love, both for the pop culture being referenced and the so-called terrible movies being mocked. Journalist Paul Brownfield notes that under Joel's leadership MST3K often felt like it was "part insult comedy aimed at the movies" but that there was also "something congenial in the show's tone," which he attributes to either the robot puppets or the series' Midwestern origins.[32] It is more likely a combination of the two; the bots' charmingly handmade appearance and adorable personalities likely softened the blow of cutting barbs such as "I'd like to shoot them with a 3mm Howitzer," which was Tom Servo's brutal opinion of the makers of the sleazy biker flick *Sidehackers* aka *Five the Hard Way*. As Beaulieu explains, "You can get away with saying a lot of things with a puppet that you can't say with a human."[33]

Joel, meanwhile, embodied the concept of "Midwest nice," which author Paul Kix describes as "the most sincere, malicious, enriching, and suffocating set of behaviors found in the English-speaking world."[34] According to Kix, these behaviors include humility, kindness, and simplicity, but also repression and passive-aggression. Urban Dictionary defines Midwest nice as "a manner of non-confrontationally addressing a situation that is somehow annoying in a passive-aggressive manner that is subtle enough to be considered friendly."[35] With his relaxed demeanor, genuine politeness, and sarcastic attitude, Joel epitomized the dichotomies of Midwestern niceness, seeming apologetic even when casually unleashing savagely funny observations like "I think a certain teen idol is hopped up on goofballs!" to describe Little Richard's manic performance in the beach flick *Catalina Caper*, riffed in episode 204. The bots' delightful dispositions and Joel's Midwestern attitude both contributed to MST3K's affability, thus helping the show appeal to viewers.

Joel's relationship with the bots was another factor in the show's success during this period. According to MST3K lore, Joel created Crow, Tom Servo, and Gypsy out of spare parts he found lying around the satellite. In many respects, Joel served as the bots' father, and this parental dynamic played out as he tried to teach them about different aspects of human society, often with humorous results. For instance, in episode 205, the trio suffer through the Soviet era "thriller" *Rocket Attack U.S.A.* In keeping with the spirit of the film, Joel tries to teach his little robot pals about the Cold War and McCarthyism. However, as explained in the *Amazing Colossal Episode Guide*, Joel describes this historical event as "the

Charlie McCarthy[36] Hearings on Un-American Activities, which targeted Howdy Doody,[37] as well as Gumby,[38] Pokey,[39] Kukla,[40] and Ollie,"[41] along with several other 1950s puppets.[42]

Later, in episode 321, the SoL crew celebrate Christmas by watching *Santa Claus Conquers the Martians*, a Z-grade family film from 1964 in which goofy looking aliens kidnap old St. Nick and a pair of annoying kids and abscond with them back to the red planet. This time around, Joel helps the bots get into the holiday spirit by singing carols (namely Crow's original composition, "A Patrick Swayze Christmas"), writing holiday essays (Servo pontificates about how Santa's reindeer will explode in the vacuum of space), exchanging gifts (Gypsy receives a framed photograph of her beloved Richard Basehart[43]), and decrying the evils of capitalism while browsing catalogs from Sears and Nieman Marcus. The relationship between Joel and his mechanical offspring provided MST3K's writers and performers with multiple opportunities to make wry observations about various aspects of contemporary society.

This relationship might also explain why MST3K resonated with kids, who likely saw themselves reflected in the bots and may have viewed Joel as a bit of a gentle father figure. In addition to being adorable puppets, Crow and Servo were also sarcastic agents of chaos who frequently made droll observations about the absurdity of the adult world. In episode 211, for example, during a break from watching the lavish international co-production *First Spaceship on Venus*—which boasts a screenplay by Polish sci-fi novelist Stanislaw Lem, author of such classic books as *Solaris* and *The Futurological Congress*—Servo narrates a fake holiday-themed advert for "Klack's Industrial Saladoos-based snacks and snippets." The mock advert ends with the line "Remember, if you're incapable of showing emotion but know how to cook, Klack has a snack idea for you!" Here, Servo highlights the inherent falseness of adverts that make it seem as though a product or brand can take the place of a genuine emotional connection with other people. Similarly, in episode 313, Crow draws inspiration from *Earth vs. the Spider* aka *The Spider* for his own original screenplay "Earth vs. Soup," in which humanity battles a giant bowl of soup. This silly premise serves as a perfect send-up of the low-budget creature features the SoL crew frequently endures.

Of course, jokes such as these are probably lost on most preadolescent viewers; kids undoubtedly find more enjoyment in Servo's silly songs, such as "Creepy Girl," an ode to the ethnically ambiguous heroine of *Catalina Caper*, or Crow's repeated use of the naughty-sounding exclamation "dickweed" to insult unpleasant characters like Luther Blair, the misogynistic hero of *Fire Maidens of Outer Space* played by Anthony Dexter. As Murphy observes, "For the kids who are sitting in front of the parents these jokes are going [right over their heads] and they're hitting the parents right in the foreheads."[44] Still, the bots' confusion about grownup society struck a chord with many young viewers, who no doubt enjoyed the puppets' frequently juvenile antics, as in episode 202: prior to heading into the theater to watch *Sidehackers*, a frazzled Joel warns the rowdy, overtired bots that he does not want to hear another peep out of them, prompting the mischievous pranksters to respond with a high-pitched "Peep!" just before the ad break begins.

Additionally, while Joel served as a father figure for both the bots and the youngest members of the audience, he also appealed to kids due to his own youthful exuberance and innocent outlook on the world. Throughout his time aboard the SoL, Joel often came across as a kid at heart due to his madcap inventions and his love (or at least appreciation) of cartoons, toys, and other pop culture artifacts aimed at children. Children regularly think up weird creations that they then construct out of LEGO bricks or cardboard boxes, so Joel's outrageous constructions likely appealed to preteen viewers of MST3K. Inventions such as an adding machine that prints out candy on a strip, a combination CD player/hair dryer, and a Polaroid camera that puts anyone's picture on US currency no doubt amused younger audience members who spent their own days dreaming up silly devices. At the same time, Joel frequently demonstrated a deep understanding of kid-friendly media through his riffs, which referenced everything from *Ricochet Rabbit & Droop-a-Long* to *Star Wars* to the toy line He-Man and the Masters of the Universe. As with the bots' numerous jokes, kids probably missed most of Joel's more obscure references—while watching the 1951 educational short *Alphabet Antics* produced by Castle Films, Joel jests that "P is for plagiarism from Ogden Nash!"[45]—but they nevertheless saw in him both a substitute dad and an audience surrogate. This may explain why the MST3K crew received so many letters from the under-ten set, many of which were read onscreen during the final host segment each week.

Sadly, long-simmering tensions between Hodgson and Mallon finally boiled over in 1993, leading to Hodgson's departure from MST3K that same year. According to Mallon, who had directed several episodes of the series by that point, "Joel operated under the idea that this was his show, and everyone was working for him," whereas the rest of the cast and crew were "into this sort of cooperative mode—that it's all of us working together."[46] Hodgson, meanwhile, claims that the conflict revolved mainly around a proposed MST3K movie, stating, "We had decided, oh, let's be like *Star Trek: The Next Generation* and do a movie. Instead of 22 movies a year, we'll do one really good one and be rich and famous."[47] However, in Hodgson's telling, Mallon appointed himself both producer and director of the planned film, a move that Hodgson felt failed to acknowledge his own position as the creator of MST3K, describing it as "kind of a power grab on [Mallon's] part."[48] While Hodgson viewed himself as the show's primary architect, he nevertheless considered MST3K an ensemble effort, asserting "We did everything as a group."[49] So, Hodgson told Mallon "If you direct this [film], I'm leaving," and the creative partnership fell apart soon after that.[50] Hodgson then left the show "to pursue a career in Los Angeles creating and developing television."[51]

Before his departure, however, Hodgson presided over what many fans consider MST3K's glory years, spanning from seasons two to five and encompassing numerous movies that more than earn the distinction of "so bad they're good." It was during this period that the SoL crew took on one of the world's biggest movie stars, riffing on *Godzilla vs. Megalon* in episode 212 and *Godzilla vs. the Sea Monster* aka *Ebirah, Horror of the Deep* in episode 213. Season three, meanwhile, saw the showrunners dust off the *Gamera* movies originally riffed during the KTMA years and mock them anew. This era also saw the MST3K debut of such fan-favorite flicks as *Pod People*, *Cave Dwellers* aka *The Blade Master*, *Time of the Apes*, and *The Amazing Colossal Man*. Then, in season four, Hodgson et al. rescued from obscurity *Manos: The Hands of Fate*, unleashing it upon an unsuspecting audience who had never seen anything quite like this ponderous regionally produced horror flick made by fertilizer salesman Harold P. Warren (who also stars). Other highlights of this era include the first appearance of Mr. B Natural, original songs like "Hike Your Pants Up" (episode 307) and "Oh, Kim Cattrall" (episode 403), and hilarious inventions such as Johnny Longtorso (an action figure sold in separate pieces introduced in episode 421) and Chinderwear (underpants for your chin cleft, as seen in episode 505). Aside from co-creating MST3K, Hodgson's time aboard the SoL proved an especially formative stretch in the show's history, one that featured a wealth of memorably bad movies and unforgettable comedy.

Hodgson ended his tenure on a high note; in episode 512, his final appearance as a series regular, Joel and the bots riff on the dreary cop flick *Mitchell*, starring beefy 1970s icon Joe Don Baker, best known for his roles in the films *Walking Tall* and *Charley Varrick*. The episode's host segments chronicle Gypsy's attempts to liberate Joel from the satellite and return him to Earth. The action kicks off when Gypsy overhears the Mads plotting to dispatch their new temp worker, the awkward but affable Mike Nelson, but mistakenly thinks they are discussing Joel. With Mike's help, Gypsy discovers an escape pod inside a crate marked "Hamdingers" hidden deep in the bowels of the satellite, and together they trick Frank into granting Gypsy control of the SoL. After the movie, Joel boards the escape pod and rockets back to Earth, leaving behind a plaque inscribed with an abbreviated quote from what he identifies as his favorite movie, *The Seven Faces of Dr. Lao*:

> The whole world is a circus if you look at it the right way. Every time you pick up a handful of dust, and see not the dust, but a mystery, a marvel, there in your hand. Every time you stop and think, "I'm alive, and being alive is fantastic!" Every time such a thing happens, you are part of the Circus of Dr. Lao.

Confused by the passage's lack of profundity, the bots briefly ponder what will happen next and whether the Mads will send a replacement before descending into panic. Meanwhile, way down in Deep 13, the Mads lament the loss of their favorite test subject before setting their sights on an oblivious Mike, who just wants them to sign his timecard.

Though Hodgson would later return to MST3K and movie riffing (see chapter 5), his departure in 1993 left MSTies shook, partly because the series' tone changed somewhat with the introduction of its new host. While Nelson also hailed from the Midwest (born in St. Charles, Illinois, he grew up in northwestern Wisconsin before moving to the Minneapolis-Saint Paul area of Minnesota) and was similarly imbued with Midwestern niceness, he seemed to hold less affection for popular culture than his predecessor. In fact, Nelson often seemed somewhat contemptuous of mass media, especially the low-budget, trashy movies regularly featured on MST3K. For instance, in his book *Mike Nelson's Movie Megacheese*, a collection of humorous essays and film reviews, Nelson refers to Keanu Reeves as "phenomenally below-average"[52] and compares Bruce Willis to a Jeep Cherokee with "a bad ABS pump, a snapped rear-door support, bead leaks on virtually every tire," and rust "spreading around all the sheet metal screws, making it look like the kind of vehicle an unsuccessful check-forger might drive."[53] Though exaggerated for comedic effect, Nelson's contempt for these pop culture touchstones comes through loud and clear.

Under his leadership, MST3K remained collegial, but the riffs often felt more vicious, as though they emanated from a place of cynicism rather than love. Of course, many fans (including one Mr. Matt Foy) enjoy watching Mike and the bots tear apart a terrible movie and find their takedowns funnier than the somewhat more restrained humor of the Joel episodes. Retrospectives usually privilege the Joel style, but the cult popularity of astoundingly inept films like *Werewolf* and *Hobgoblins*,[54] riffed in episodes 904 and 907, respectively (see chapter 3), prove that there are absolutely fans of Mike's somewhat more brutal humor. The change in hosts also divided many fans into factions devoted to celebrating (and occasionally deriding) one host or the other. Yet, despite the disruption caused by Hodgson's exit, longtime viewers took solace in the fact that MST3K's mission of mocking bad movies remained largely unchanged.

Mystery Science Theater 3000: The Movie (1996), directed by Jim Mallon.
GRAMERCY PICTURES / PHOTOFEST © GRAMERCY PICTURES

"YOU GUYS WATCH JOE DON BAKER MOVIES?": THE MIKE ERA

MST3K announced its new status quo via an updated opening credit sequence and a revised theme song that featured Nelson replacing Hodgson on vocals. The credit sequence and theme song would each change several more times over the ensuing years, usually to reflect a change in network—as when the show made the leap from Comedy Central to the Sci-Fi Channel (see chapter 3)—or the introduction of a new cast—as when Jonah Ray took over hosting duties of MST3K when it relaunched on Netflix in 2017 (see chapter 5). The door sequence—a POV shot of Cambot passing through a series of six doors that played whenever the theme song ended, the Movie Sign flashed, or when the crew left the theater—was also altered "to reflect the evolving art direction of the show itself."[55] The SoL set remained mostly the same, though it would likewise undergo several cosmetic changes throughout MST3K's lifetime starting with episode 609, which introduced a new, somewhat darker lighting scheme to the host segments that occurred between viewings of the tedious Coleman Francis flick *The Skydivers*. Ultimately, it seemed as though the post-Joel MST3K wanted to alert fans to the differences (new host, modified theme song, updated sets, different tone) while simultaneously comforting them that little had changed; the madcap humor, referential gags, and mockery of terrible Z-grade movies all remained untouched.

As Nelson explains, the crew endeavored to make the changeover as seamless as possible by avoiding "radical changes."[56] In other words, the more things changed the more they stayed the same.

Despite serving as head writer and occasional performer for much of MST3K's original run, Nelson's spot as replacement host was not assured. Initially, the showrunners "brought people in and auditioned them" for the position, something Nelson found "a little weird" as suddenly there were all these other performers "marching in and throwing on jumpsuits."[57] It was only after a camera test with Beaulieu and Murphy that involved a lot of improvising and messing around that Nelson finally landed the role. Nelson assumed hosting duties starting with episode 513, spending his inaugural installment riffing on the crude 1960s creature feature *The Brain That Wouldn't Die* alongside Crow and Servo, at this point still performed by Beaulieu and Murphy, respectively. Written and directed by neophyte filmmaker Joseph Green, the film follows Dr. Bill Cortner (Jason Evers), a creepy transplant specialist who keeps his decapitated fiancée's head alive in a laboratory while he tries to find her a new body. His search entails stalking and murdering voluptuous young women like Doris Powell (Adele Lamont), a glamour model whose beauty is marred by a facial disfigurement.

With its inane premise, hammy acting, leering camerawork, and ludicrous monster (a mutated man who looks like the love child of Richard Kiel and Beldar Conehead), *The Brain That Wouldn't Die* often feels like it was made solely to be mocked by the SoL crew. Indeed, the film proves so immediately punishing that Mike tries to escape from the satellite during the episode's second host segment. The movie also inspired numerous jokes about the seediness of its premise, as when Mike drolly observes that Dr. Cortner's lecherous and murderous actions render him unlikeable. Elsewhere in the episode, Servo comments on the sultry saxophone score by joking, "It's a sleazy morning out there. You're listening to K-PORN, Holmes and Reems in the morning. Sleazy, slutty music all morning long. Here's one from Skinny and the Sweat Beads." A combination of incompetence, tedium, and squalor makes *The Brain That Wouldn't Die* the perfect target for Mike's maiden riff.

Almost immediately, "fans divided into the Joel camp versus the Mike camp."[58] Nelson self-deprecatingly likens the transition to actor Ted Wass, who appeared in the sitcoms *Soap* and *Blossom*, "replacing Peter Sellers as Inspector Clouseau" in the widely reviled film *Curse of the Pink Panther*.[59] However, as Mallon observes, "at the end of the day, the bulk of the show was making fun of bad movies, and that didn't change at all."[60] Hodgson, meanwhile, thought Nelson was a good choice for his replacement, though he worried that they were perhaps too similar as they were both "white doughy [guys] from the Midwest."[61] Ultimately, though, Hodgson gave his stamp of approval to Nelson, stating after the fact that the showrunners' decision to stick with a proven formula "worked out great" and "they did a really good job" following his departure.[62] Still, longtime fans needed time to get used to the new situation. Foremost, the change in hosts led to new and unfamiliar cast dynamics; whereas Joel seemed more willing to go along with the experiment and felt a bit of affection toward the movies, Mike often appeared far more eager to escape from the SoL. This meant that fans likely identified differently with Joel than they did with Mike, who seemed to want no part of the movies being riffed.

In addition, Mike's relationship with the bots represented perhaps the biggest change from the Joel era. As Beaulieu explains, "Joel's character created the robots," and therefore "his relationship with them was kind of parental."[63] Whereas Joel felt like the bots' father, Mike was more like an uncle or a stepdad, and he often endured hazing, both good-natured and otherwise, orchestrated by his new robot companions. Beaulieu compares the dynamic between Mike and the bots to that of "a pizza restaurant manager who is only like maybe a couple of months older than the staff is."[64] Nelson also brought a distinct type of humor to MST3K, one that may be best described as misanthropic, especially when compared to Hodgson's more pleasant, easygoing brand of comedy. During the Mike era, jokes seemed to stem more from an attitude of scorn or derision for the films being watched, and the riffs truly dripped venom throughout this period. Compare Joel's lighthearted jab of "Aw, she's the ginchiest. Life does begin at 40!" to describe the middle-aged teen heroine of *Ring of Terror* in episode 206 to Mike's "*More* ordinary? Man, he'd have to work at that" to describe the bland hero of *Laserblast* in episode 706. Throughout the Mike era, the writers' and performers' contempt for the films became far more apparent.

The invention exchange represents another adjustment that took place during Nelson's tenure as host. Initially, the SoL crew intended to continue the tradition of the invention exchange when Nelson took over, resulting in such imaginative fabrications as the gutter-bumber-chute (an umbrella with an attached gutter system), the Waiter Baiter (a mechanical arm designed to signal waitstaff), and the Razor Back (a giant razor for people with especially hairy backs). However, the showrunners quickly abandoned this recurring bit because of its close association with Hodgson. As Murphy explains, "Joel was the gizmocrat, the one who brought that invention exchange spirit on board."[65] Nelson, on the other hand, "is not an inventor."[66] Murphy teasingly explains that while Nelson is creative, artistic, innovative, clever, and resourceful:

> The sight of a screwdriver puts him in a cold sweat. He used to hire kids to build his car models. I had to explain to him what a lawnmower does. We wrote the instructions on how to change the toilet paper roll right on the wall so he wouldn't be embarrassed. Mike is many things, but he is not a tinkerer.[67]

The SoL crew would stop doing the invention exchange segment with episode 519, in which Mike and the bots riffed their way through the fantastical sword-and-sandal flick *Outlaw* aka *Outlaw of Gor* aka *Gor II*.

In 1993, shortly after Nelson took over hosting duties, Comedy Central expressed reservations about MST3K's two-hour-long runtime and asked if the show could be shortened to an hour. In response, the Best Brains came up with *The Mystery Science Theater Hour*, splitting episodes from the Joel era into two parts that were hosted by Nelson in character as Jack Perkins, who referred to himself simply as "your host." Each episode began with a modest title sequence accompanied by a piano version of the MST3K theme song "Mighty Science Theater," while the host stood in an austere studio festooned with images from whatever film was being lampooned in that episode. In the first half-episode, the host introduced the movie, providing a brief description of its plot. In the second half-episode, the host recaps the previous installment via clips. Every episode ended with the studio lights dimming and the silhouetted host performing some comical action inspired by the final segment. Best Brains produced sixty episodes of *The Mystery Science Theater Hour* edited from thirty episodes of MST3K. *The Mystery Science Theater Hour* failed to replace the standard two-hour-long version of MST3K, but it proved useful for syndication purposes; in 1995, Tradewinds Television syndicated *The Mystery Science Theater Hour* to local broadcast stations unwilling to devote a two-hour programming block to reruns of MST3K.

The Mike era also saw the departure of adored performer Frank Conniff, who played Dr. Forrester's second bumbling sidekick TV's Frank. Conniff left the series in 1995, making his last appearance as a series regular in episode 624, in which Mike and the bots watch the Mexican wrestling-themed horror film *Samson vs. the Vampire Women* aka *Santo vs. the Vampire Women*. In this episode, Torgo the White (Nelson, reprising a recurring character from *Manos: The Hands of Fate*) appears and escorts Frank to Second Banana Heaven, leaving a despondent Dr. Forrester without a victim. Like Weinstein and Hodgson before him, Conniff would embark on a career writing for TV shows, working on such beloved series as *Sabrina the Teenage Witch* and *Invader Zim*. From 2008 to 2018, he also appeared as Moodsy the Clinically Depressed Owl in the stage show *Cartoon Dump*, a monthly comedy/music revue devoted to showcasing some of the worst cartoons of all time. Following this, Conniff reunited with original cast members of MST3K to co-create the live movie riffing shows *Cinematic Titanic* and *The Mads Are Back* (see chapter 4). Conniff may have left MST3K, but he never abandoned his movie riffing roots.

Not long after Conniff's exit, the Best Brains team turned their attention to making *Mystery Science Theater 3000: The Movie*, the first (and, at the time of writing, only) attempt at translating the series to the big screen. The film, which featured Mike and the bots mocking the Cold War classic *This Island Earth*, entered production in spring 1995, though it had been in the planning stages since at least 1993, when Hodgson initially floated the idea of making an MST3K movie. By 1994, Best Brains had entered negotiations with Paramount Pictures to distribute the movie, but that deal fell through when the studio demanded the film be used to explore the characters' backstories rather than recreate the show's premise of heckling movies. Later that year, Universal Studio executives attended the first ConventioCon ExpoFest-A-Rama to watch the cast perform a live riff on *This Island Earth*, which was a Universal production. The suits liked what they saw and offered to distribute *Mystery Science Theater 3000: The Movie* through Universal's subsidiary, Gramercy Pictures.

Production commenced at the Best Brains studio in Eden Prairie, Minnesota, far from the glitz and glamor of Hollywood. However, this did not stop Universal executives from meddling with the film, first by demanding the removal of one of the host segments (in it, the SoL crew deals with a meteor shower), and then changing the film's ending; instead of Mike and the bots triumphantly sending a Metaluna Mutant (the film's primary monster) to enact revenge on Dr. Forrester, the finale instead sees Forrester inadvertently teleport himself into the bathroom of a previously introduced Midwestern Metalunan while back on the SoL the crew realizes they will never escape from the satellite. The film debuted on April 19, 1996, playing in just twenty-six theaters throughout the United States and grossing a mere $1,007,306 against an estimated five million dollar budget. Though it failed commercially, *Mystery Science Theater 3000: The Movie* received generally positive reviews; for instance, John Kelly of the *Washington Post* declared the film "painfully funny in places: painfully because you nearly herniate yourself stifling laughs to keep from missing the next bon mot."[68]

Mystery Science Theater 3000: The Movie bombed at the box office at least partly due to a lack of advertising and promotion on the part of distributor Gramercy Films. The Best Brains team contend that Gramercy opted to focus all their marketing efforts on the Pamela Lee vehicle *Barb Wire*, an action movie inspired by the comic book of the same name published by Dark Horse Comics. History has shown that Gramercy apparently made the wrong choice, as *Barb Wire* ultimately proved to be a resounding critical and commercial failure, earning just $3,793,614 against an estimated nine million dollar budget along with a reputation as a "convoluted mess."[69] The SoL crew have since expressed frustration with how *Mystery Science Theater 3000: The Movie* was released, claiming that Gramercy marketed it as a "rock and roll" film, meaning "a movie that slowly goes from city to city, plays one-to-three weeks, depending on the money it brings in, and moves on."[70] While *Mystery Science Theater 3000: The Movie* failed to make much of a dent at the box office, it nevertheless pleased longtime fans and developed a rabid cult following once it hit home video.

On May 18, 1996, just under one month after the movie premiered, MST3K aired its last episode on Comedy Central. After seven years making fun of trashy movies such as *Robot Holocaust*, *The Giant Gila Monster*, and *Kitten with a Whip*, the network finally decided to cancel the series. By this point, MST3K was being overshadowed by other Comedy Central shows like *Politically Incorrect*, *The Daily Show*, and *South Park*, all breakout hits that left executives wondering "where MST3K fit on the network's increasingly crowded schedule."[71] In episode 706, the final one to air on Comedy Central, Mike and the bots riff on an edited version of *Laserblast*, a cheap sci-fi quickie about an ostracized teenager who embarks on a rage-fueled rampage after stumbling upon a super-advanced alien laser gun in the California desert.

The film was co-produced by exploitation impresario Charles Band and featured visual effects by legendary effects artist David Allen. Band, the charismatic founder of Empire Pictures and Full Moon Features, helped usher in the home video era of the 1980s thanks to his involvement in hundreds of genre classics including *Parasite*, *Metalstorm: The Destruction of Jared Syn*, *Ghoulies*, *Trancers*, *Re-Animator*, *From Beyond*, *Troll*, and *Puppet Master*, among others. Many of these films spawned numerous sequels and spinoffs, launching franchises that continue well into the twenty-first century. Several of them also received the riffing treatment courtesy of MST3K and its various offshoots. Allen, meanwhile, launched his visual effects career in 1970, providing stop-motion effects for the sixteen-millimeter student film *Equinox* before creating the Pillsbury Doughboy. He would go on to become one of leading effects artists in the film industry, working on movies such as *Flesh Gordon*, *The Howling*, *Caveman*, *Q: The Winged Serpent*, *The Hunger*, and *Willow*. Allen also oversaw visual effects on several of Band's productions including *Dolls*, *Puppet Master*, *Robot Jox*, *Subspecies*, *Demonic Toys*, and *Doctor Mordrid* (riffed by Emily and crew in season thirteen of MST3K; see chapter 5). Allen spent much of his career developing *The Primevals*, a passion project that pays homage to adventure films such as *Jungle Goddess* or *The Mole People* (both featured on MST3K), but he sadly passed away in 1999 before its completion.

Laserblast proved an ideal match for MST3K thanks to an unappealing hero played by Kim Milford, a pair of goofy looking but impressively animated aliens, appearances by slumming acting legends Keenan Wynn and Roddy McDowall, and an exceedingly silly story involving a bullied teen fighting back with extraterrestrial weaponry. The film proved perfect for riffing, with Mike joking that it looked like it was "composed entirely of second unit footage," while an interminably long shot prompts Crow to declare, "I think they were going for a *Touch of Evil* feel, but they got a touch of something else." For reference, *Touch of Evil*, directed by Orson Welles and widely considered the last true film noir, follows Mexican narcotics officer Mike Vargas (Charlton Heston) as he interrupts his honeymoon with new wife Susan (Janet Leigh) to investigate a murder committed in a border town ruled by the corrupt police captain Hank Quinlan (Orson Welles). The film is famous for its opening sequence, a three-and-a-half-minute-long tracking shot that follows Heston and Leigh as they cross the Mexican border. Later in the episode, Mike wonders "what the 'flaw' was that prevented Leonard Maltin from giving this the full three stars?" Despite the dark cloud of cancellation hanging over the proceedings, *Laserblast* ensured that MST3K went out with a, uh . . . blast.

The episode's host segments were filled with a sense of finality, as Dr. Forrester announces that his funding has been cut. He then disconnects the umbilicus, a 370-mile-long cable connecting Deep 13 to the SoL that first appeared in episode 601, which features the salacious teen flick *Girls Town*. Forrester explains that he sabotaged the SoL so that its orbit will decay and send the whole thing crashing down to Earth, killing everyone aboard, before he calmly resumes packing his stuff with the help of his mother, Pearl (a recurring character played by Pehl). Servo and Gypsy manage to fix the satellite's thrusters, allowing the crew to escape Earth's orbit and head into deep space. During their voyage into the unknown, Mike and the bots encounter an annoyingly literal space robot named Monad (a parody of the Nomad MK-15c from the original *Star Trek* episode "The Changeling"), change a fussy star baby's diaper (a nod to the classic 1968 sci-fi film *2001: A Space Odyssey*), and avoid a black hole thanks to Mike cosplaying as Captain Kathryn Janeway (Kate Mulgrew) of *Star Trek: Voyager*. The episode ends with the SoL crew reaching the edge of the universe and transforming into non-corporeal beings of pure energy. Meanwhile, back in Deep 13, Dr. Forrester is reborn in a sequence that sends up the ending of *2001: A Space Odyssey*. Pearl embraces her now-infant son and expresses joy over getting a second chance to raise him right, prompting Forrester to utter the final line of the Comedy Central version of MST3K: "Oh, poopie!"

"THIS MUST BE A PARAMOUNT PICTURE": THE EVOLUTION OF RIFFING

Despite the series' abrupt cancellation, the Comedy Central years proved vital to the legacy of MST3K, as they comprised an effervescent period in which the cast and crew perfected the art of movie riffing. As mentioned, the Best Brains team routinely spent up to two full days watching a movie, riffing on it while a stenographer transcribed the improvisational sessions. This process allowed the writers and performers to determine which jokes worked while also granting them time to revise or remove those that did not, allowing for a much higher ratio of successful riffs per episode. Indeed, throughout the Comedy Central years the MST3K crew honed the timing and speed of the riffs, increasing the number of jokes to roughly seven hundred per episode, a far cry from the KTMA years when the cast often struggled to come up with gags due to improvising while watching a movie for the first time ever. During the Comedy Central years, riffing evolved from simple observational jokes like "This must be a Paramount picture," spoken by Servo when he sees the opening shot of a mountain peak in *The Crawling Eye*, to wry gags like Crow's "She undercut the subtle nuance of my wiener joke!" to describe the effect of a young woman's riposte to a pushy guy's come on in *Laserblast*.

The performers also learned to play off each other during the Comedy Central years even as they avoided ad-libbing, which Hodgson compares to "a traffic jam."[72] Nevertheless, the cast found plenty of opportunities to develop their characters' personalities and relationships and use them to generate humor, as when Crow and Tom would poke fun at both Joel and Mike for their Midwestern upbringings. For instance, in episode 621, the SoL crew watch *The Beast of Yucca Flats*, in which a defecting Soviet scientist turns into a rampaging monster following a nuclear blast. During one of the host segments, an RV full of drunk Wisconsin rednecks shows up outside the satellite leading Mike to muse that it reminds him of "something out of . . ." and before he can finish his thought Servo interrupts with "out of your youth, perhaps?" The Comedy Central years also saw the performers increasingly utilize callbacks to previous riffs, past episodes, and a host of films, thereby tapping into the memetic power of riffing. During this era, characters like Mr. B Natural and Torgo made several appearances on the show, while repeated exclamations such as "Hi-keeba!" (lifted from director Arthur C. Pierce's 1966 dud *Women of the Prehistoric Planet*) and "Switcher!" (a reference to the 1987 film *Mannequin*) became catchphrases for the series' characters and its most devoted fans.

Throughout the Comedy Central years, MST3K also encouraged a culture of active fan participation and dynamic media consumption. The advent of home internet providers helped the show build its audience via UseNet newsgroups such as rec.arts.tv.mst3k.misc and alt.tv.mst3k, both of which allowed fanatical MSTies across the United States to connect and discuss their favorite show.[73] In addition, the Best Brains team encouraged fans to record episodes and share them with others via their repeated mantra of "Keep circulating the tapes," a directive that appeared in the end credits of every episode produced during the Comedy Central era. The combination of the internet and a relaxed attitude toward piracy helped MST3K cultivate an enthusiastic audience comprised of faithful, participatory admirers.

Mallon contends that MST3K mainly appeals to people who are "above-average smart—you know, B-plus students and higher."[74] He argues that the show's intelligent, pop-culture-savvy fanbase suggests that "audiences are not as dull as Hollywood might think they are."[75] Truly, MST3K packed a plethora of intertextual references into every episode, skewering all aspects of American society and post–World War II culture while also making allusions to art and trash in equal measure. For instance, episode 301—Joel and the bots take on the ultra-low-budget Italian sword-and-sandal flick *Cave Dwellers*—includes jokes about playwright Harold Pinter, poet Robert Frost, philosopher Niccolò Machiavelli, sportscaster Curt Gowdy, and theologian John Calvin. While the blending of high and low culture has come to feel commonplace in the internet era, it was rare to see such blurring of lines during the early years of MST3K, which helped popularize the practice in many ways.

The series also operates as a form of culture jamming, a type of protest used to disrupt media culture and its attendant cultural institutions such as corporate advertising. Larry Closs, former senior editor of *TV Guide*, contends that one of the reasons MST3K resonates with viewers is because the series dares to mock the tropes and conventions of TV itself, something most shows tend to avoid.[76] Yet MST3K did more than take a stand on TV: it took aim at the entirety of American culture, using humor to peel back the curtain on the social mores, cultural customs, and ideological standards that support and accelerate everything from economic disparity to racial discrimination to gender inequality. This may explain why Matt Roush, a former television critic for *USA Today*, describes MST3K as an "outlaw show, kind of a maverick show."[77]

For example, in episode 317, Joel and the bots riff on *The Home Economics Story*, essentially a twenty-five-minute-long advertisement for Iowa State College (which Joel describes as "the high school after high school"). The short follows Kay and her friends as they learn about the benefits of enrolling in the home economics program offered by Iowa State. The riffs in this episode call attention to the gender roles of the 1950s, highlighting the limitations imposed upon women in the postwar United States. The short posits that women should aspire to jobs that revolve around cooking, interior decorating, or teaching, and that they should eventually settle into motherhood while their husbands support the family. At one point, the narrator intones that "a general home economics course" can prepare women for "that very important career of being Mrs. Johnson," to which the SoL crew respond with a resounding "Boooooooo!" Later, Joel gives voice to the thoughts of a young girl who learns of the societal limitations facing women in the United States, exclaiming, "What?! We have to be subjugated to men?!" Through such humor, MST3K helps viewers recognize how media help sustain all manner of communal traditions and societal imbalances.

MST3K also (likely indirectly) helped its viewers develop their media literacy via silly jokes about all aspects of popular culture. For instance, the show introduced many viewers to the tropes and techniques of cinema itself. In episode 203, Joel explains the concept of gobo, a matte-box system often used to create the effect of looking through a pair of binoculars or a gun sight, after the bots express confusion about its use in the turgid adventure film *Jungle Goddess*. Similarly, in episode 301, Joel spends one of the host segments teaching the bots about the art of Foley, or the reproduction of everyday sounds that are then added to a film during post-production. He accomplishes this by shaking a box full of hamsters to recreate the sound of a rampaging herd of buffalo, and then adds milk to simulate the sound of a herd of water buffalo. Such comedic reflections elicit laughs, but they also help to educate viewers about how movies are made. In this way, the show empowers audiences by helping them to build a vocabulary they can use to dissect the media in their own lives.

At the same time, MST3K draws attention to the thematic and stylistic tendencies of respected directors by referencing "good" films during "bad" movies, all while obliterating such artistic distinctions. When a samurai warrior shows up in *Cave Dwellers*, Servo jests that "they've jumped right into a Kurosawa film!" Later, in episode 407, Servo observes that a long take in the campy monster movie *The Killer Shrews* is "a planned sequence, like the opening of *Touch of Evil* or the Copacabana scene of *Goodfellas*." With these witticisms, the performers offer insight into the techniques employed by widely revered filmmakers like Akira Kurosawa, Orson Welles, and Martin Scorsese, but also by schlocky B-movie directors such as Joe D'Amato and Ray Kellogg. Such intertextual references help to reveal that little separates high art and low trash beyond critical consensus and arbitrary taste hierarchies. When the MST3K crew mentions a "good" movie like *Casablanca* while watching a "bad" movie like *Overdrawn at the Memory Bank*, the artificial distinction between which texts are disposable and which are deemed sacred threatens to crumble.

The SoL crew also frequently highlights the aesthetic and subtextual inclinations of less-esteemed filmmakers; for instance, whenever a voluptuous woman appears onscreen, the SoL crew can be counted on to make a reference to director Russ Meyer, known for showcasing large-breasted women in his films (e.g., Servo describing *Kitten with a Whip* as "Russ Meyer's Goldilocks"). Similarly, when trying to gauge the badness of a given film, the performers also frequently invoke Edward D. Wood, Jr. and Roger Corman, often considered the patron saints of bad movies thanks to directorial efforts like *Plan 9 from Outer Space* and *It Conquered the World*, respectively.[78] Not only did Joel and the bots riff on Wood's *Bride of the Monster* and Corman's *Teenage Caveman*, but they also frequently referenced these icons of trash cinema when mocking movies made by other people, as when Crow admonishes the makers of *The Creeping Terror* to be careful because "Roger Corman needs to use this set later!" Over the years, the various MST3K crews also riffed the Wood (or Wood-adjacent) flicks *The Violent Years* and *The Sinister Urge*. In addition, they poked fun at the Corman-directed pictures *It Conquered the World*, *The Day the World Ended*, *Swamp Diamonds*,

Gunslinger, The Undead, and *The Saga of the Viking Women and Their Voyage to the Waters of the Great Sea Serpent,* along with numerous films that he produced.

While not the first show to appropriate and ridicule mostly forgotten B- and Z-grade movies from the 1950s, 1960s, and 1970s, MST3K is largely responsible for introducing the art of movie riffing to contemporary audiences and establishing many of its practices. As Pehl notes,

> The idea of riffing, of mocking, of commenting on things is very prevalent nowadays. Obviously, it was happening before *Mystery Science Theater* codified it. But it just seems to have pervaded a lot of the way comedy is done now—it's its own genre now.[79]

Indeed, while MST3K failed to connect with a wide audience during its first run on Comedy Central, the show still inspired an entire generation of riffers, and its mission of using highly referential humor to mock bad movies lives on in the form of podcasts such as *The Flop House* and *How Did This Get Made?* which are devoted to the discussion and ridicule of bad movies like *Foodfight* and *The Apple.* In addition, YouTubers like TotalBiscuit, the Angry Video Game Nerd, and the Game Grumps have all adapted MST3K's style of comedy to the world of video games, poking fun at such inferior digital games as *B-17 Bomber* and *House Party.* Comedy Central may have cancelled MST3K prematurely, but the show's legion of fans has kept its spirit alive for more than twenty years.

Like a zombie in one of the hokey horror films riffed on the show, MST3K would claw its way out of the grave following its sudden cancellation by Comedy Central. In 1997, the series reemerged on the recently launched Sci-Fi Channel with a new cast of villains and even a different voice for Crow, as comedian Bill Corbett took over for Beaulieu, who left to pursue other writing opportunities following the show's cancellation. Around this time, the world was changing along with the show, particularly with the emergence of the World Wide Web. MST3K was one of the earliest television shows to build a passionate fanbase online, and the internet's unprecedented access to fast knowledge empowered fans to explore movie riffing on their own terms. Chapter 3 considers how MST3K continued to expand and explore the potential of riffing in this new interconnected age. The chapter demonstrates how movie riffing works by looking at the tropes and techniques the performers employed to critique both film and culture, as well as how viewers at home appropriated and adapted these tactics. Chapter 3 reveals that MST3K provided fans with a model for twenty-first-century media criticism, making it more than just an entertaining diversion.

CHAPTER THREE

"CROOOOOOOOOOOOOOW! (I'M DIFFERENT!)"

The Sci-Fi Channel Years

On February 1, 1997, *Mystery Science Theater 3000* fans' harrowing 259-day wait for the return of their favorite show ended when MST3K debuted on its new television home, the Sci-Fi Channel. Mike Nelson and the bots returned to the Satellite of Love (SoL) and resumed existence as material beings after transcending corporeality and becoming pure energy at the end of season seven. Life on the SoL had returned to normal. Well, sort of. Crow was, by his own account per the new theme song, different. With Trace Beaulieu having departed the show, Crow was now voiced and articulated by Bill Corbett, a New York native whom observant MSTies may have noted for his credits as a contributing writer in the final episodes of season six. Beyond the jolt of a different voice, Corbett's Crow was demonstratively more temperamental than Beaulieu's take on the character. Throughout season eight, Crow proved more prone to rage in the theater and demonstrated increased inhospitality toward Mike, whom Crow claims not to recognize in the early Sci-Fi episodes. Crow's new personality, coupled with Corbett's admittedly less-than-graceful puppetry,[1] was attributed to the bot apparently suffering "a stroke during the 500 years he hung out on the Satellite"[2] alone prior to the return of Mike, Tom, and Gypsy.

MST3K's three-season run on Sci-Fi kicked off with a series of jarring changes that left MSTies both exhilarated and, at times, disoriented. The changes were as immediate as they were abundant. For the first time in show history, Dr. Forrester was not the SoL crew's chief antagonist. For the first time in MST3K history, the show would also feature a season-long story arc unifying season eight's twenty-two episodes. This development came by decree from network higher-ups, described by Kevin Murphy as "bitter, dry, humorless trolls"[3] whose influence fans generally consider to have negatively impacted MST3K's time on Sci-Fi. In an ominous reprise of Gramercy's tragic mishandling of *Mystery Science Theater 3000: The Movie*, once again the show whose ethos had always been "the right people will get it" was in the hands of executives who clearly did not get it. Season eight's emphasis on plot stands out because it is such a dramatic outlier in the show's history. At the heart of its unifying plot is the SoL being pursued across the universe by a vengeful new antagonist. This pursuit takes the crew to a series of locations that are ultimately blown up or destroyed through various mishaps.

Season eight begins with the SoL pulled to an unknown planet revealed to be Earth in the year 2525—complete with obligatory reference to "In the Year 2525" by 1960s pop-rock duo Zager and Evans—now inhabited by apes evolved from men. Trapped above what fans have dubbed "Deep Ape," Mike and the bots meet Earth's most articulate and intelligent (this is not high praise) spokesape, Professor Bobo (Murphy). Bobo, flanked by even-dimmer sidekick Dr. Peanut (Nelson), informs their captives it is Ape Law, as decreed by the mysterious Lawgiver, that they must watch a bad movie. In a surprising twist, episode 801 featured a film with a level of cultural cachet unusual for the show: *Revenge of the Creature*, sequel to Universal's iconic *Creature from the Black Lagoon*. Lest enthusiasts of cinematic incompetence fret that MST3K would double down on a pivot to "classics" like *This Island Earth*, riffed in MST3K's sole big screen outing, *Revenge* is every bit as cheesy as the riffing fodder of the Comedy Central era with its cheap locations, ham-fisted melodrama, and actor John Agar[4] earnestly setting up punchlines that Mike and the bots swat down with ease.

Episode 801 closes with the dramatic introduction of the Lawgiver, MST3K's new lead villain Pearl Forrester, with Mary Jo Pehl reprising her role from the Comedy Central years. Last seen in a supporting role cradling son Clayton following his transformation into a star baby at the end of season seven, Pearl reveals that she never got around to raising baby Clayton right as she had intended, eventually smothering him to death. Claiming that Clayton's dying wish was for her to continue his experiment, Pearl had herself cryogenically frozen until such time that she could continue to torment Mike and the bots in the future. Pearl and her ape minions do just that from the comfort of Deep Ape until episode 804, when Mike inadvertently helps a cult of bomb-worshiping human mutants (a reference to the 1970 film *Beneath the Planet of the Apes*) blow up the Earth. Vowing revenge and promising to dog the SoL crew "to the ends of the universe," Pearl and Bobo hop into the Widowmaker, a space-traversing Volkswagen van, and set off to pursue Mike and his robot companions. The loop is thus closed and another Forrester endeavors to break Mike's will in the name of mad science.

The crew next winds up on the Observer planet, inhabited by a race of om-niscient, self-sufficient brains, played by Corbett, Nelson, and Paul Chaplin, who have acquired all knowledge in the universe and appear as pale-faced ghouls carrying their brains in pans.[5] The Observers subject their captives, whom they demean as "those who are of an amoeba," to a battery of humiliating activities such as intelligence testing, fighting to the death, and eventual dissection, along with terrible movies for Mike and the bots, of course. The four-episode arc on the Observer planet ends when Mike, commanding the SoL's nanites (tiny robotic helpers first introduced in episode 801) to save Pearl and Bobo from dissection, accidentally explodes the planet. Corbett's Observer (aka Brain Guy) joins Pearl and Bobo as a second lackey.

Across the rest of the season, Pearl, Bobo, and Brain Guy continue to pursue Mike and the bots through time and space, with Observer beaming movies to the SoL via his brain. The characters' adventures take them to an unnamed "camping planet" (also exploded by Mike) and back in time to ancient Rome (burned down by Bobo). After surviving encounters with omniscient space children, "renegade warlike robots," and execution-happy Roman empress Flavia (Bridget Jones), the interplanetary pursuit story arc is effectively resolved with the opening of season nine, which begins with Pearl returning to her ancestral Castle Forrester on pres-ent-day Earth to continue tormenting Mike and the bots from solid ground.

Mystery Science Theater 3000 (Comedy Central), 1988 to 1999. Shown: Crow, Michael J. Nelson, Tom Servo.
COMEDY CENTRAL / PHOTOFEST © COMEDY CENTRAL

Fans have debated whether season eight's interplanetary pursuit arc was an asset or a liability, with negative assessments tending to linger over the discussion with hindsight. For many, including the show's creators, season eight's emphasis on story and continuity was superfluous: "What the hell do you want with a story arc? This is a puppet show," Murphy told *Wired*.[6] In the end, the lesson learned from Mike and the bots' odyssey through time and space is that which defines MST3K has always been movie riffing, not episodic storytelling. Regardless of who assumes hosting duties, MST3K's legacy and true contribution to television and culture lies in how it innovated the craft of movie riffing. Rather than traditional comedic storytelling, MST3K's elaborate and ever-evolving vocabulary of riffing tropes, references, and callbacks to previous episodes rewards fans' repeat viewership.

"REMEMBER TO BELIEVE IN MAGIC . . . OR I'LL KILL YOU": RIFFING AS CREATIVE COMMENTARY

If it were merely funny and quirky, MST3K would still deserve a reputation as a cult classic, a 1993 Peabody Award winner, and an icon of the early days of cable television. But MST3K transcends being funny. MST3K taught generations of viewers raised on TV, home video, and later streaming video how to talk back to the screens in their own lives. The show provided its devoted fandom with the key to a toolbox of creative techniques for reading and responding to not just movies but any mediated text: TV, music videos, commercials, memes, or anything else that elicits a response from consumers. It is this utility that sits at the heart of MST3K's cultural legacy: the series established not only an ethos for responding to media but a vocabulary for articulating that response. Through consistent and active engagement with its riffing vocabulary and techniques, MST3K becomes heuristic for its audience, which is a fancy way of saying MST3K presents viewers with the building blocks that they can adopt, adapt, and experiment with in future viewing situations. Barry Brummett suggests that such building blocks are a necessary function of good criticism, stating, "Theory and method need to explicate this example, this object of study, but they also need to explicate the next example, to teach us how to understand the next rhetorical event that comes along."[7] MST3K accomplishes this lofty goal from its perch in popular culture without ever skimping on the funny.

There may be readers skeptical that MST3K and movie riffing constitute legitimate criticism (we should really just relax, in other words). Yet to deny that pop culture informs and compels people's everyday lives ignores both history and the profound influences of fiction and fantasy on those who consume such genres.

Scholar and critic Kenneth Burke suggested that literature (as well as other storytelling forms) functions as equipment for living, with storytelling forms like satire and comedy aiding readers to "size up situations in various ways and in keeping with correspondingly various attitudes."[8] Along those lines, MST3K's highly adaptable riffing vocabulary is equipment for riffing, and one must understand how a tool works before they can use it.

Even casual MST3K viewers know movie riffing when they see it. The movie unfolds, and riffers respond to the onscreen action, dialogue, or setting by mocking it with words or gestures. This simple pattern cannot capture the essence of how MST3K "raised talking back to the TV into an art form."[9] Those who do not enjoy or understand MST3K may reduce the show to simple snark and ridicule, but the show's creators understood that a deluge of negativity would quickly alienate the audience. As Corbett explained to NPR, "I think it does get really tiresome to just hear three guys be jerks about something."[10] He continues, "You can't just be a voice of generic sarcasm, you have to be funny and clever and occasionally a little more generous, and shift your point of view here and there so you're not always making fun of the movie so much."[11] Corbett confirms what discerning viewers already know: the MST3K school of movie riffing was never about taking a hatchet to some well-meaning but inept cinematic relic. Rather, beneath the show's performance of mockery lies an essential element of sensemaking and speaking back to the messages within the movie. Movie riffing is directed at the screen, but it is performed for the audience.

Though much has been written about the style of MST3K—the do-it-yourself aesthetic, the sci-fi trappings, the intertextual humor—significantly less has been written about the show's riffing techniques. According to the tallies on the MST3K fansite Project: Riff,[12] Joel, Mike, and the bots made over eleven thousand unique riffs during seasons one through ten (not counting shorts), so it is a towering task to make sense of it all. The jokes range from high-brow cultural allusions to contemporary pop culture references to angry outbursts to self-consciously juvenile scatology. However, one overarching truth clearly emerges: one should not minimize the riffing ethos of MST3K to mere ridicule or negativity toward a movie. It is more accurate to summarize MST3K's distinctive riffing as an isolation and magnification of a film's problematic elements. Rather than simply denouncing what they see, MST3K's riffers comment on something problematic on the screen, thereby drawing the audience's attention to it, then using it as a tool to build a response to the movie.

The Cambridge Dictionary defines problematic as "full of problems or difficulties."[13] Merriam-Webster's online dictionary defines problematic as something being not definite or settled.[14] These definitions illustrate how MST3K's style of riffing becomes impactful speech. To be problematic does not mean something is inherently bad or wrong; rather, it means that the thing requires attention and action. Riffing on the problematic elements of media is a form of persuasive speech that asks the audience to accept the riffer's perspective toward onscreen elements that contain multiple possible meanings. By repeatedly reframing what is on screen over the course of a film, MST3K's riffers effectively challenge and potentially dismantle the meanings foregrounded by the film, replacing them with the riffers' preferred interpretations. Meaningful criticism need not be the riffer's objective: when the riffing is insightful and smartly articulated, the effect is cumulative.

By expertly riffing on a film's problematic elements, the SoL crew draws the audience's attention to specific elements of the film, such as dialogue, characterization, plot, setting, effects, costumes, sound design, etc. Producers and artists assemble these elements in ways meant to fully immerse viewers in the viewing experience. When MST3K's riffers draw attention to problematic elements of the film's construction—off-putting characters like Torgo or Mitchell, incomprehensible plots like those found in *The Beast of Yucca Flats* or *Cry Wilderness*, ineffective appeals to whimsy as in *Pod People* or *Munchie*—the audience focuses on the problematic elements and resists immersion in the film's universe. Done well, riffing transforms a film into a completely new viewing experience, one that more closely fulfills the interpretive goals of the riffers. Once experienced, riffing cannot be simply undone or unexperienced. Riffing opens any film to inspection of what it says and does not say, what it includes and what it leaves out. This is a different and more invitational outcome than blunt snark or negativity.

"THESE TOOLS ARE MY FRIENDS!": EQUIPMENT FOR RIFFING

Elizabeth Ellsworth suggests that mediated texts compel viewers to accept certain values and to identify with some characters and against others. Viewers ask themselves, "Who does this film think I am, and am I willing to be that person?"[15] Through elements like plot, characterization, cinematography, and other purposeful artistic choices, media implore their audience to accept specific articulations of good and evil, right and wrong, heroic and deplorable. One of MST3K's most effective riffing techniques is subverting a movie's invitation to identify with or against its characters by introducing shades of gray into simplistic portrayals of good and evil. MST3K's riffers routinely challenge the virtues of protagonists and smooth the evil edges off antagonists, responding to Ellsworth's question of whether they are willing to be the person the film envisions with a firm "no, and get bent for asking."

MST3K's oeuvre offers several examples that illustrate how the SoL crew subverts cinematic depictions of heroism. For instance, when riffing *The Mole People*, Mike and the bots often react defiantly to know-it-all windbag Dr. Bentley (Agar). Though the film presents Bentley as an intelligent and intrepid explorer, Mike and the bots reframe the character as self-important and blathering. When Bentley is lowered into the underground world of the mole people by his comrades, Servo riffs, "I've got to believe that right now, the other guys are contemplating cutting the rope," implying the audience ought to feel the same way. Mike suggests verbosity is a product of insecurity, adding in the persona of Bentley's inner monologue:

> Why do I talk so much in front of those guys? Every time I open my mouth, I just act like I know it all. I just want to tell them how much I like them and stuff, but then when I talk, I say this stupid junk. I don't know, maybe I'm just kind of insecure. But I do know a lot; why shouldn't I talk?

Agar's pompous performance ultimately breaks Crow: "Oh, movie, I'm not a praying man, but if you can hear me, please kill John Agar!" Though *The Mole People* clearly invites audience members to identify with Bentley as a sensitive, courageous hero, Mike and the bots reject any inclination to do so, instead taking the opposite stance.

One of the most prominent heroic values embodied by popular cinema is rugged masculinity: moviegoers are regularly force-fed heroes who kick ass, woo women, and save the day singlehandedly with their own physical prowess and assertion of their will in every situation. Joel, Mike, and the bots regularly push back against a film's framing of aggressive, virile masculinity as ideally heroic. This often includes the tactic of mocking the physical or sexual prowess of the hero. For instance, while watching *Eegah*, Joel and the bots completely reject the film's presentation of Arch Hall Jr. as suave teen heartthrob Tom, instead pointing out that he makes for a rather unappealing lead. Impersonating the actor, Joel quips, "Sorry about my face," while Servo observes that Hall, Jr. resembles "a Cabbage Patch Elvis." Later, while enduring *Mitchell*, the crew mock the physique and hygiene of Joe Don Baker's abrasive, hard-drinking anti-hero with such venom that it spawned a legend of Baker planning to violently retaliate against the writers (see chapter 2). What MSTie could forget Mike and the bots' comprehensive episode-long deconstruction of the uber-beefy Dave Ryder (Reb Brown), hero of *Space Mutiny*? After reducing the buff, headstrong Ryder into a loud, stupid dolt worthy of mocking monikers like Butch Deadlift and Big McLargeHuge, Mike drives the point home by rejecting the film's equation of hypermasculinity with sexual virility. When *Space Mutiny* depicts a spaceship blasting off as a visual metaphor for triumphant intercourse, Mike responds incredulously: "I think Chunkhead's more of a shuttlecraft if you know what I'm saying."

MST3K's riffs reject brainy heroes every bit as strategically as they do brawny protagonists. Crow immediately forecloses on the heroic potential of time-traveling genius Nick from *Time Chasers* by humorously demanding, "Can I see your supervisor, movie? This will not stand." Likewise, in *The Giant Spider Invasion*, the crew ridicules NASA scientist Dr. Vance (Steve Brodie) for his middle-aged physique and prominent neck wattle, with Crow suggesting Vance is "carved out of lard." Of course, Joel, Mike and the bots do not just poke fun at central characters; they also mock supporting characters and sidekicks. Alan Hale's lovable, wisecracking sheriff in *The Giant Spider Invasion* is reframed as both a "doughy has-been" and an ineffective, gluttonous "pork vacuum." When the kindly cook in *I Accuse My Parents* assures on-the-lam Jimmy that he never sends any down-on-their-luck customer away hungry, Crow quips, "Got 'em piled out back." Meanwhile, the aw-shucks Southern folksiness of Buffalo Bill Joe Hickens (Jim Stafford) in *Riding with Death* is received with hostility, transforming the affable sidekick into an incoherent "cracker" whose country charms become emblems of threatening violence ("This [song] goes out to my friends in the *Posse Comitatus*") and ignorant racism ("America for Americans. Let's send all the Indians back to Africa").

On the opposite end of the moral spectrum, the SoL crew often undercuts the menace of a movie's antagonists, short-circuiting the film's capacity to align the audience against them. For example, the underground slave-driving Sumerians of *The Mole People* are mocked as non-threatening, instead deemed "a pride of Dr. Smiths"[16] by Crow and "a civilization of elderly great aunts" by Servo. The menace of Coleman Francis' merciless anti-hero Griffin in *Red Zone Cuba* is repeatedly kneecapped by the crew's revelation that Francis resembles Curly Howard of the Three Stooges. Meanwhile, the intergalactic alien invaders of the laughable Japanese superhero flick *Prince of Space* are mocked (and clucked) mercilessly for resembling chickens, as well as for their campy costumes and soft physiques. No less a threat than the Devil himself has his menace undercut by the crew's ridicule of director Roger Corman's slow-moving fantasy flick *The Undead*, as Mike and the bots dismissively refer to the campy Lord of Flies as both "Peter Pan: Antichrist" and "Satan, the prince of cabaret."

Inverting either end of the spectrum of good and evil is a handy trick, but flipping both has twice the potency. Joel and the bots demonstrate this technique when riffing the post-apocalyptic thriller *Warrior of the Lost World*. The film follows an unnamed nomadic mercenary who, with the aid of his annoyingly voiced high-tech motorcycle, helps to dismantle the Orwellian government known as the Omega, led by the evil Prosser (Donald Pleasence). Joel and the bots forcefully reject the film's unnamed anti-hero, rejoicing in his pain, bristling at his abrasiveness, and denying him the dignity of a name, dismissing chipmunk-cheeked actor Robert Ginty as "*The Paper Chase* Guy." When *The Paper Chase* Guy rescues the resistance leader but abandons his daughter Nastasia (Persis Khambatta) in enemy territory as he escapes by helicopter ("Let see what this baby can do," he mumbles), Servo says incredulously, "This baby can sit right back down and pick up his daughter." With this joke, Servo reframes *The Paper Chase* Guy's rugged individuality as cowardice. Later, when *The Paper Chase* Guy shares a triumphant, passionate kiss with Nastasia, Crow recoils, "Oh, just drape a piece of liver over her face, for heaven's sake. It'll have the same effect!" Left with no one to cheer for, Joel and the bots instead bestow their affections on the dystopian ruling party's motorcycle-crushing armored vehicle MegaWeapon, whom Joel calls after the film to appease the fawning bots (Nelson voices MegaWeapon during the host segment).

MST3K demonstrates that movie riffing empowers riffers to reject or modify a film's constructed binaries of good and evil. Villains can become laughable, just as heroes can become loathsome or ineffective. This deconstruction of heroic mythologies becomes useful when reading problematic films such as *Space Mutiny* or *Mitchell*, which glorify mindless aggression and violence as world-saving strategies. MST3K's rejection of simple yet seductive binaries of good versus evil keeps the film and its characters open to reevaluation and audience self-reflection. When a film presents viewers with Perfect Good versus Perfect Evil,[17] it effectively bars them from questioning the values they represent. Murphy captures this quandary in his noted hatred of *Forrest Gump* and its angelic hero, explaining "The experience is like being forced to eat heavily sugared whale blubber. Worse, it's emotional propaganda. The film is set up in such a way that you are not allowed to dislike it."[18] Utilizing riffing techniques to lower heroes and raise villains is more than being contrarian: it prevents the movie from foreclosing on the viewer's agency to decide for themselves with whom or what they side.

The theme of dramatic subversion extends beyond heroes and villains. MST3K's riffers often recognize a film's foregrounded tone (dramatic, melodramatic, horrific, humorous) and contradict it. When a film attempts to assert a dramatic or horrific tone, the riffers will contradict it by inserting whimsy or domestic themes. As such, murderous rampaging monsters can be recast as non-threatening pests or pets. For example, when riffing on *Revenge of the Creature*, Mike likens the iconic Gill-Man's deadly rampage to being pounced by the lovable Dino from *The Flintstones*. In *The Giant Spider Invasion*, being devoured by a giant spider from outer space becomes grotesquely comical. At one point Servo jokes, "Does it matter that the spider ate him with his butt?" to which Mike responds, "You know, I think it seems suitable for this guy." While watching *Agent for H.A.R.M.*, Servo brands the villains' deadly spore gun, which horribly kills and mutates its target, "the booger gun" and reframes its projectiles as bird poop. Such observations help the riffers diminish the emotional impacts of the onscreen action and encourage viewers to engage with any element of the film they choose.

Similarly, MST3K's riffing subverts themes of domestic or personal angst, rejecting a film's efforts to make viewers identify with the characters and themes through pathos. In *The Leech Woman*, for instance, titular character June Talbot has descended into alcoholism due to her unhappy marriage and launches into a melodramatic rant against her husband, wailing, "You've got what you want. Why can't I have a little one for the road? Just enough to make me numb?" Rather than accepting the film's melodramatic framing, Mike replies with banal consumerism: "Uh hum. Would you like to supersize it?" During *I Was a Teenage Werewolf*, when a vigilante squad of locals—a terrifying image that taps into cultural memory of lynch mobs—hunts the titular monster, Mike and the bots transform the mob into yokel buffoons. Crow jests, "Say, Cletus, how much pork gravy do you use to make toast?" Mike, meanwhile, impersonates lovable dimwit Ernest P. Worrell to joke, "Hey, Vern, looks like they killed the dog, huh?" While watching Troy McGregor (Christian Malcolm) being pursued by evil cultists in *The Final Sacrifice*, Crow spies a small detail on the vehicle of a cultist and says, "I think his menace is undercut by the 'baby on board' tag."

Conversely, MST3K riffers introduce the specters of terror or morbidity into lighthearted moments. During *The Deadly Mantis*, when soldiers search a nondescript pile of snow, Servo declares in the tone of a dire newscaster, "Frosty the Snowman's partially melted body was found at the site, a victim of a pistol whipping. Herbie the Misfit Elf is wanted for questioning." Watching *Riding with Death*'s climactic stockcar race, Servo introduces the threat of harm when he takes on the role of the track announcer to offer enthusiastically, "If a driver is killed, Section 31b gets a free Hormel hotdog!" In *Catalina Caper*, during an exuberant teen song-and-dance number, Joel and the bots reframe the cast's ethnic homogeneity (i.e., overwhelming whiteness except for Little Richard) by referencing Apartheid and the National Front.

The most impactful examples of this tactic often come when the riffers both reject the film's suggestion of whimsy and replace it with a tone of stark realism. Mike and the bots illustrate this powerfully in *The Horror of Party Beach* when the film introduces two drunk pilots who leave a bar after a night of drinking. These characters are introduced only to be killed by monsters, and the film presents their stumbling, slurring drunkenness as comedic. Through riffing, Mike and the bots cover the two drunks in seven shades of grotesque wretchedness. When the film has one of the drunks ask, "What's that sound?" to establish the monster's presence, Servo answers, "Oh, I'm urinating." Crow, meanwhile, concludes that "Otis of Mayberry had a quiet dignity compared to these guys." Mike joins the pile-on by slurring, "Are we going to raise the specter of wife swapping?" Mike and the bots' stance against these disposable characters becomes so pointed—at one point Servo savagely asks, "Can the monsters kill these guys three or four times?"—their riffing doubles as both a contradiction of the film's attempts at comic relief and a commentary on the wretchedness of alcoholism.

Movie riffing can also turn the fantastic into the mundane. When the archae-ologists of *The Mole People* discover a five-thousand-year-old stone tablet, "one of the oldest public records," Crow trivializes the reveal by suggesting it reads "no matter where I serve my guests, they seem to like my kitchen best." Later, when our adventurers discover an ancient oil lamp, the Sumerian equivalent of the Holy Grail, Crow similarly dismisses the wonder of their historical find with "It's either an offering to the gods or . . . a gravy boat." Whenever riffing transforms the dramatic into the mundane or vice versa, the effect for the viewer is the same: the riffers assert their interpretive agency to contradict the film's intended ef-fect. Doing so allows viewers to roam outside the emotional experience provided by the producers. Audiences can reject obvious interpretations and engage more deeply with events onscreen. They come to understand that multiple interpreta-tions are always possible, and they need not accept the terms presented by a film's producers.

Identifying and making light of errors and flaws in a film's creation is synon-ymous with movie riffing in the public consciousness. Any given MST3K episode features dozens of riffs on problematic acting, storytelling, costuming, setting, and other essential elements of film production. Rather than simple mockery, the SoL crew's trademark riffing on the kinks and seams in the filmmaking process fulfills a crucial role in the process of interpreting media: recognizing the ele-ments of mediated storytelling (characters, tropes, techniques) and making sense of how and whether they fit into what the filmmakers are attempting to convey to the audience.

When riffing *The Leech Woman*, for example, Mike and the bots frequently highlight the use of stock footage, recycled from Universal's 1954 adventure movie *Tanganyika* to approximate an African setting. "Oh, the matte paintings of Africa are beautiful," Mike states with mock awe. Servo highlights this con-trast, stating "Meanwhile, thousands of miles away in actual Africa . . . and now back to our set." Crow scathingly observes, "It's not stock footage, it's more like stock mileage at this point." The act of drawing the audience's attention to the common cost-saving incorporation of stock footage or cheap sets seems simple: a liberal use of stock footage signifies that a film is low-grade or less-than. Yet this is not simple derision, and if any TV producers can empathize with making art on a budget, it would be MST3K's showrunners. Drawing attention to the liberal incorporation of stock footage fulfills an important purpose: it draws attention to the fact that the film is constructed from distinct elements rather than standing as a singular, sovereign work of art.

MST3K routinely educates audiences on where to look for loose seams in a film. There may be poorly assembled sets, such as in *Gunslinger* when Joel and the bots repeatedly point out that the door to villain Cane Mero's inn room opens inward rather than outward, concluding that he must be staying in the hall. Upon hearing a knock at Mero's door, Joel announces, "Come out . . . or in." There may also be onscreen incongruities, such as *Riding with Death* prompting Mike to observe incredulously that lead character Sam Casey (Ben Murphy) has been bandaged so totally after an underwater explosion his head wrapping has no air holes. MST3K's riffers notice poor or inconsistent lighting or cinematography, as when Crow suggests that the producers of *The She-Creature* "tried to light this, but this movie is like a super-absorbing black hole." *The Horror of Party Beach* likewise features several shots that switch between day and night, inspiring Servo to declare, "Meanwhile later yesterday afternoon, I guess?" while Crow observes "They must have gone the speed of light because they can see themselves arriving."

Among the most glaring (and most fun to riff) continuity errors are when a film fails to keep track of key plot changes such as characters' deaths. *Red Zone Cuba*, *Space Mutiny*, and *The Incredibly Strange Creatures Who Stopped Living and Became Mixed-Up Zombies!!?* all include supporting actors or characters who are killed in one scene but reappear after their deaths. While watching *Space Mutiny*, Mike and the bots have great fun riffing on the reemergence of Flight Lieutenant Lamont, who is killed only to reappear at her station on the bridge *in the next scene*, with Crow joking, "I think it's very nice of you to give that dead woman another chance" and Mike calling out, "Alright, look alive everyone—oh, sorry Susan."

Problematic casting and acting choices are often fair game for riffing. Joel, Mike and the bots often comment on the incongruous age of actors playing presumably much younger characters. For example, Joel and the bots spend nearly the duration of *Ring of Terror* riffing on the cast appearing to be the oldest student body ever filmed. Mike combines mocking *The Horror of Party Beach*'s casting of Alice Lyon (then thirty years old) to play love interest Elaine with the filmmakers' choice to crudely dub her voice, riffing, "I don't like slumber parties now that I'm in my forties" in a flat, robotic voice. Servo sums up this idea while watching *Terror from the Year 5000* when he suggests in the tone of a commercial disclaimer, "Remember, when making a dramatic film, be sure to use genuine actors."

Beyond obvious onscreen shortcomings, MST3K educates viewers on how stories are crafted through stock elements and tropes. In *Parts: The Clonus Horror*, when protagonist Richard (Tim Donnelly) discovers a videotape that explains the purpose and history of the secret clone farm where he resides, Servo jokes, "Convenient he happened to wander into the department of backstory." Crow immediately recognizes Ed Wood's purpose for introducing the character Strowski in *Bride of the Monster*, announcing in character as Strowski, "Hello,

I'm the worthless ancillary character waiting to be killed off, hello?" When *The Incredibly Strange Creatures Who Stopped Living and Became Mixed-Up Zombies!!?* portrays protagonist Jerry (played by director Ray Dennis Steckler) in a surreal fever dream, Mike interprets a shot that combines camera zoom with a thudding bass as the camera operator hitting the Steadicam against the performer's head. When a clattering sound effect is inserted via foley, Mike wonders if Jerry just dropped marbles onto the floor.

MST3K's riffers often seize on something in the background of a film's action or dramatic focus to draw the audience's attention away from the intended focal point. In *The Horror of Party Beach*, a monster stalks two young women who pass by a meat shop's sign with the advertisement "Look Polish" with the bottom of the sign obscured by foliage. Mike and the bots subvert the dread of the impending monster attack by instead speculating on what "Look Polish" could be advertising. They pull a similar trick twice in *Devil Doll*. After heavy-smoking protagonist Mark (William Sylvester) is dumped by spellbound love interest Marianne (Yvonne Romain), the film cuts to a scene in which evil magician the Great Vorelli (Bryant Haliday) prepares to transfer Marianne's soul into a ventriloquist dummy. Rather than participate in the unnerving scene, Servo notices in the background a suitcase with a British European Airways logo and says, "Look up there, he flies Aunt Bee airlines." Mike, channeling the distinctive voice of Aunt Bee Taylor (Frances Bavier) from *The Andy Griffith Show*, says, "We'll be flying at a cruising altitude of 30,000. You may experience some turbulence, oh Andy." The next scene depicts a despondent Mark drinking in a pub. Rather than accepting identification with the lovelorn hero, Crow notices in the background a reflected image that includes the word "midgets," prompting him to ask, "What is that, a menu item?" Mike replies, "As long as they're boiled and come with chips, sure."

One memorable instance of dragging an incidental image into the foreground of consciousness features the infamous "Hitler building" as seen in the juvenile Japanese sci-fi spectacle *Invasion of the Neptune Men*. During the film's spirit-crushing ten-plus-minute air battle, stock footage is inserted from *World War III Breaks Out*, which features the destruction of a building with a large mural of Adolf Hitler. Unlike the film's characters, Mike and the bots recoil in shock from the sudden image of one of history's greatest monsters, then humorously mourn the loss of the Hitler building:

Servo: They took out the Hitler building! Where is everybody going to go to see Hitler memorabilia?

Crow: All the Hitler rides and games, the Hitler salt and pepper shakers.

Mike: That great restaurant The Bunker, it's gone. You sons of a . . .

Crow: What's next, the Mussolini mall?

Servo: Followed by the Pinochet petting zoo?

In addition to serving as a reminder not to unwittingly feature Hitler into a movie ostensibly aimed at children, the Hitler building sequence serves as a much-needed reprieve for the riffers to escape the misery of the film through purposeful self-distraction.

On the surface, riffing on a movie's gaffes and problematic choices may come across as shallow mockery rather than critique. However, riffing on botched elements of a text's craft should not be dismissed as mean-spirited because it fulfills a crucial and underappreciated function in active media consumption by keeping the constructed nature of cinematic storytelling in the foreground. Such riffs reveal that a movie (or whatever is being riffed) is a product crafted by artists and producers with purpose. Films are generally engineered to immerse viewers into a manufactured universe, one crafted intentionally in the service of art, profit, or both. Keeping the text-construction process visible highlights the truth that films are always crafted through a series of purposeful artistic choices that are executed with varying degrees of purpose, skill, and care. Isolating and magnifying any element of film—obvious or subtle goofs produced by stress, indifference, or lack of skill—draws the audience's attention to a film's construction and invites audiences to question not only how it was made but why.

Mystery Science Theater 3000 (Comedy Central), 1988 to 1999. Shown: Crow, Tom Servo.
COMEDY CENTRAL / PHOTOFEST © COMEDY CENTRAL

"HEY, IT'S GLORIA ESTEFAN AND
THE CATALINA DEUS EX SOUND MACHINA":
INTERTEXTUALITY IN MST3K

Upon receiving its Peabody Award, MST3K was cited as "an ingenious eclectic series" that references "everything from Proust to *Gilligan's Island*."[19] This ability to recall and deploy numerous cultural references and alter the reading of a film is another product of MST3K's vaunted intertextuality (see chapter 1). No show can boast MST3K's vast and eclectic array of references to other pop culture texts to aid them in making sense of the dramatic scenario at hand. The show's peerless use of intertextual references taught dedicated viewers how to make sense of one viewing situation by tapping into other viewing situations, glorifying intertextuality as an indispensable tool in any media consumer's kit for surviving even the most challenging or confounding nights at the movies. The ability to recall and utilize references to other pop culture texts, and to transfer meaning associated with that text to the movie being riffed, empowers audiences to venture outside the confines of the film being riffed. With a wide arsenal of intertextual references, a riffer can greatly expand their vocabulary of references with which to skillfully respond to any text.[20]

MST3K's intertextuality can be divided into two recurring strategies: references to other cultural texts and figures, and callbacks to previous episodes. An example of the former occurs in episode 506; while watching *Eegah*, Joel and the bots chant "Eegah-chaka! Eegah-Eegah-Eegah-chaka!" in reference to the phonetically similar "Ooga-Chaka! Ooga-Ooga-Ooga-Chaka!" chant heard in the Blue Swede song "Hooked on a Feeling." If a viewer knows the song, they are likely to get pleasure from recognizing the reference and a chuckle from the cleverness of the wordplay. Other intertextual references require more sensemaking from readers to figure out what the riffer is saying about the film. When riffing *The Beast of Yucca Flats*, a character runs frantically from an attacking low-flying plane, causing Mike to declare that director Coleman Francis "steals from only the best." Without specifically naming it, Mike is referencing an iconic scene from Alfred Hitchcock's *North by Northwest* in which Cary Grant's character runs from a low-flying crop duster. Here, viewers both take pleasure from recognizing the reference and gain critical insight from Mike's rejection of the scene's artistic merits on the grounds of plagiarism.

MST3K is frequently lauded for its intertextual chops, and rightfully so. The sheer breadth and range of references from the obscure to the iconic, from highbrow to low-brow, is unparalleled in popular culture. Consider the crew's riff of *Overdrawn at the Memory Bank*. While riffing the 1984 made-for-public-TV movie, Mike and the bots make references to political singer Mark Singer, grunge group Nirvana's 1992 single "Come as You Are," the 1992 Jack in the Box *E. coli* outbreak, the 1964 British horror film *Children of the Damned*, Canada's single-payer healthcare system, venerable British TV series *Dr. Who*, actors Oliver Reed and Peter O'Toole (specifically, their alcohol consumption), Spinal Tap keyboardist Viv Savage, LensCrafters' "glasses ready in about an hour" advertising campaign, the notorious box office bomb *Ishtar*, the 1980s moral panic over Satanic messages backmasked on vinyl records,[21] the Rolling Stones' song "You Can't Always Get What You Want," furniture vendor Pier 1 Imports, David Lynch's surrealist masterpiece *Eraserhead*, and, of course, *Overdrawn*'s film-within-a-film *Casablanca* (as Servo states, "Never show a good movie in the middle of your crappy movie").

Yet the practice of intertextuality itself is not inherently funny or insightful. If the simple act of making an intertextual reference was itself humorous, the internet would not be littered with polemics against the non sequiturs found in the long-running animated series *Family Guy*. It is MST3K's creativity and talents for articulating critical meaning through intertextual references that makes its riffing special.

As equipment for riffing, MST3K's mastery of intertextuality works thanks to the writers' talent for choosing the right reference in response to the right film element, as well as the performers' talent for delivering it in a manner that facilitates audience understanding. While MST3K draws liberally on references to other films and cultural artifacts, the show is also noteworthy for its callbacks, in which the SoL crew riffs on dialogue or characters from previously riffed movies, or even refers to jokes from earlier in the same film. The history of MST3K is rich with callbacks made iconic through repetition and fan appropriation. Such callbacks include "Hi-keeba!" (probably MST3K's first and longest-running callback), the phrase "Time for go to bed!" uttered by imposing actor Tor Johnson in *The Unearthly*, the admonition "He tampered in God's domain" from *Bride of the Monster*, violent delinquent Mooney (Peter Breck) shrieking "I killed that fat barkeep!" in *The Beatniks*, and the oft-repeated "Watch out for snakes!" from *Eegah*. Fans will no doubt recognize each of these callbacks as catchphrases that hearken back to the most absurd moments of the Joel years.

MST3K kept manufacturing instant classics throughout the Sci-Fi era, including *The Giant Spider Invasion*'s beloved rallying cry of "Packers!"[22] Mike and the bots directly reference Wisconsin's publicly owned NFL team no less than fourteen times, calling out some permutation of the riff ("Packers!' "Packers, woo!" "Packers won the Super Bowl!") whenever a crowd assembles or during moments when a character cries out in spider-induced terror. The inspiration for the recurring Packers riff is obvious: *The Giant Spider Invasion* is set in rural Wisconsin, ground zero for Green Bay Packers fandom. Yet the riff goes beyond geographic coincidence; the phrase "Packers!" plays a role in Mike and the bots' systematic riffing of the film's cast as drunk, "repulsive and stupid" individuals unworthy of the audience's sympathy. Rather than accepting the film's portrayals of its Wisconsinites as agents of vigilante justice or sympathetic victims of an alien attack, calling out "Packers!" whenever they gather reframes these portrayals of panic or vengeance as dimwitted drunks bleating for their favorite football team. Mike, Crow, and Servo combine this rallying cry with more eloquent riffs, including Servo embodying a desperate carnival patron who hopes a ride "will build up enough speed to launch us into Minnesota so we can start a real life" and later needling Wisconsin native Mike with "Greasy guys carrying unconscious girls. Comfortable 2 p.m. beer buzz. Ya homesick yet?" Yet "Packers!" condenses a litany of jokes at the expense of Cheeseheads everywhere into a two-syllable trope that is as much fun to shout as any reference in the MST3K library. Thus, any time Corbett, Murphy, or Nelson need a quick riff on drunk, slovenly Midwesterners, calling out "Packers! WOOO!" brings it all back with hyperefficiency.

Season eight turned out to be a watershed year for manufacturing callbacks. One episode after minting "Packers!" Mike and the bots hammered out another callback-worthy reference, having a field day with *Parts: The Clonus Horror* star Peter Graves' role as host of the A&E documentary series *Biography*. The trio references *Biography* directly nineteen times, reveling in Corbett, Murphy, and Nelson's respective Graves impressions while also distracting the audience from Graves' antagonistic portrayal of evil US president-to-be Jeffrey Knight. When riffing *Riding with Death* three episodes later, Mike and the bots set out to punish whoever scripted Ben Murphy to refer to two thugs as "turkeys" by making fourteen riffs plus a full skit about turkeys: "One of those airborne turkeys," Mike riffs in his best laconic Murphy impression as a helicopter hovers overhead. Last but not least are the forty (!) beefy, chunky names bestowed upon Dave Ryder in *Space Mutiny*, of which your authors' favorites are Blast Hardcheese and Stump Chunkman. *Space Mutiny* is a masterclass of creating internal callbacks, with riffs on Sherry's birthday card (made during the multiple scenes of celebration), Captain Santa Claus (referring to the appearance of the husky, bearded Commander Alex Jansen, played by Cameron Mitchell), and railing kills (remarked upon whenever a character falls to their death over one of the many safety rails in the ship's cavernous basement) dotting the entire episode.

Sometimes MST3K's cast indulged in purely idiosyncratic riffs whose inclusion is less concerned with conveying attitudes toward the film being riffed and more about simply expressing the riffer's attitude toward an unrelated phenomenon. This type of riff often takes the form of a negative or insulting outburst, as the riffer eschews commenting on the film in favor of denigrating a cultural text or figure they apparently resent. For example, during *Beginning of the End*, Graves becomes another target of mockery when his etymologist says "I hope you have a strong stomach" before projecting a film. Servo responds with the non sequitur

"Gabe Kaplan's performing" seemingly to lash out at the comedian and star of 1970s sitcom *Welcome Back, Kotter*. In episode 813, when Ivan, hero of Soviet fairy tale *Jack Frost* aka *Frosty*, chases a lone feather through the forest, Servo evokes the opening of *Forrest Gump* and lashes out, "Go find Forrest Gump, stick him in the eye AND KILL HIM!" adding "stupid movie" under his breath. When two sailors dump a sealed barrel of toxic waste into the water in *The Horror of Party Beach*, Servo says, "I hope that's Paula Cole in there," conveying surprising hostility toward the singer of "Where Have All the Cowboys Gone?" When aliens attack in *Invasion of the Neptune Men*, Mike pleads, "Shoot at Earth all you want, just get Bill Maher." Finally, in *Time Chasers*, when GenCorp employee Matthew Paul (aka Pink Boy) marvels that Nick's time transport could be used to change the past, Crow does not hold back his ire, announcing "We could use this to prevent Newt Gingrich, Jim Carrey, and the Smashing Pumpkins!"

Though MST3K's idiosyncratic references tend to be negative, there are instances when the riffer references a beloved text or performer with only a tangential connection to the film at hand. Throughout the show's history, the Best Brains expressed appreciation for rockers The Replacements and Frank Zappa as well as obscure biker series *Then Came Bronson*. These examples mark relatively rare instances of MST3K's riffs offering cultural criticism that barely, if at all, impacts the audience's interpretation of the film being riffed. Such jokes reflect an earnest interjection of the writers' and performers' idiosyncratic tastes into the interpretive process and assert agency over the viewing scenario.

Intertextuality has become one of the defining literacies of twenty-first-century media participation. Switch on a popular YouTube personality, podcaster, or online critic, and chances are they will drop a bevy of intertextual references. Furthermore, if they've been around enough and built up a significant back catalog, chances are they will dip back into their history with callback references. Intertextual riffing is both versatile and impactful as a form of cultural reference. When strategically deployed, an intertextual riff can connect onscreen action to offscreen phenomena with rhetorical wit and precision, empowering the riffer to persuade and educate the audience as far beyond the parameters of a single film as they can conceive.

Beyond just constituting a form of series continuity and rewarding repeat viewers, callbacks help make MST3K's vast library of references coherent in ways that unbridled eclecticism cannot. By harnessing intertextuality, MST3K talks back to culture with the same impact it talks back to the screen. Joel Hodgson, the father of modern movie riffing, once explained, "jokes are a straight line between a comic and an audience. A riff is a triangle: it's between the person riffing, the screen, and the audience."[23] With all due respect to Joel, your authors would like to offer a supplemental geometric metaphor: a riff as a prism. When riffers expose their ideas to the light of an audience—each member possessing their own perceptions, vocabularies, and experiences—the light refracted is the unique, unpredictable product that results when people's ideas and perceptions collide in real, brilliant time.

"LOOK, IT'S TAMMY FAYE BAKKER!": FAMOUS FACES AND CULTURAL (IN)SENSITIVITY IN MST3K

A form of intertextual riffing worthy of its own distinction, remarking upon a performer's resemblance to other celebrities is one of MST3K's most prominent and beloved tactics. When a film stars familiar actors, the SoL crew acts swiftly to link those stars to their more familiar past or future works, effectively adding new avenues for intertextuality and piercing the veil of film as a sovereign, self-contained work. As MST3K rarely features films for which otherwise iconic actors are remembered, the process of evoking more beloved and well-known films often serves to undercut the epic posturing of the film being riffed. Movie riffing privileges media literacy: the more pop culture literate riffers are, the more potential references to actors' other roles they can summon to craft their response to the film.

Whenever a famous or respected performer pops up in a film featured on MST3K, the riffers evoke that person's more respected roles, diminishing the film being riffed as inferior. For example, Elinu, chief antagonist of *The Mole People*, is played by Alan Napier, better known as kindly butler Alfred Pennyworth in the 1960s live-action *Batman* TV series. "No one is to tell Mr. Wayne about our little soiree," Crow jokes, emulating Napier's dignified English accent. Michael Landon's presence in *I Was a Teenage Werewolf* inspires multiple references to the actor's role as Little Joe in the Western series *Bonanza*. When Landon's hotheaded protagonist Tony is interrupted during a fistfight, Servo impersonates Landon to lament, "I thought it was all right if I picked a little fight, *Bonanza*?" referencing the show's famous theme song. Similarly, the presence of Hugh Beaumont and Cesar Romero in *Lost Continent* triggers plenty of riffs on *Leave It to Beaver* and *Batman*, respectively.

In a similar vein, Mike and the bots riff on familiar actors Alan Hale in *The Giant Spider Invasion* (Crow marvels "Professor made a toaster out of coconuts?" when Hale answers the phone), Dick Sargent in *Parts: The Clonus Horror* (not only referencing his role as Dick York's replacement on *Bewitched* but suggesting an inferiority complex for the former), William Sylvester in *Devil Doll* (Servo sarcastically suggests, "Kubrick saw this scene and said we found our Heywood Floyd" in response to a scene of Sylvester's Mark dozing), and Raul Julia in *Overdrawn at the Memory Bank* (the crew riffs on his role as Gomez Addams in the 1991 film *The Addams Family* without venom due to a combination of esteem for Julia's acting and his then-recent death from cancer). Along those lines, when Clint Eastwood makes his film debut in a small role in *Revenge of the Creature*, the bots jump on his brief appearance with Servo quoting the *Dirty Harry* line "seeing as how I've got a .44 magnum," and Crow stating ironically, "This guy's bad. This is his last movie."

Stellar actors are in short supply in MST3K fare, but this dearth cannot deter the SoL crew. When no celebrity actor is present, the riffers manufacture their own simulacra of celebrity, noting a character's physical resemblance to a celebrity unrelated to the film and accordingly superimposing that celebrity's presence into the narrative, opening new avenues for intertextual riffing. Season eight, for example, features characters being transformed via riffing into actors and filmmakers (Michael Nesmith, Donny Most, Chuck Connors, Michael Moore), musicians (Henry Rollins, Rick James, Bob Dylan, Johnny Mathis), athletes (Dan Fouts, Cecil Fielder), political figures (Jimmy Carter, Gloria Steinem, Ross Perot, George Stephanopoulos), media figures (Phyllis George, Joe Bob Briggs, Dr. Demento), and murderers named Charles (Whitman, Manson).

MST3K's riffers often riff on celebrities as a one-off observation, as when Servo briefly notes a saxophonist in *Revenge of the Creature* resembles Shemp Howard of the Three Stooges without further reference. Other times, Mike and the bots riff on celebrities in bursts. During one of *The Mole People*'s ritual dance and sacrifice scenes, the crew suggests the presence of Linda Hunt, Björk, Helen Mirren, and Shirley Manson. As part of Mike and the bots' thematic riffing on the 1970s during *Parts: The Clonus Horror*, Mike suggests a pack of bike riders includes Cheryl Tiegs, Shelley Hack, Willie Aames, Lance Kerwin, and the DeFranco Family. Later in the episode, a single unnamed biker becomes Peter Fonda, Gary Busey, Malcolm Forbes, and Michael Parks of *Then Came Bronson*. Crow supplies an early highlight of *Space Mutiny* when he identifies Commander Jansen, his daughter, and his right hand as "Sting, Debbie Reynolds, and God." In a legendary performance, Servo elevated celebrity simulacra to unprecedented heights during *Warrior of the Lost World* by riffing celebrity names for fifty-three cheering observers[24] in forty-eight seconds before poetically sticking the landing by forgetting *The Paper Chase* Guy's name.

Other times, Joel, Mike, and the bots manufacture celebrity for more extended and strategic intervals. For example, while riffing *Agent for H.A.R.M.*, Mike and the bots decide that one of the villains resembles musical icon Prince, resulting in references to Prince songs "Kiss," "Raspberry Beret," and "I Would Die 4 U," capped by Crow's scandalous suggestion that "Prince" would "like to spend the night inside [a character's] sugar walls." While riffing *Jack Frost*, Mike and the bots make multiple jokes at the expense of Nastenka's (Natalya Sedykh) unattractive (according to the film, anyway) stepsister Marfushka (Inna

Churikova). Mike and the bots refer to Marfushka as Tom Petty, Penny Marshall, Danny Bonaduce, and Anthony Michael Hall; except for perhaps Marshall, each reference can be interpreted as the riffer amplifying the film's stance that Marfushka is ugly and therefore wretched. Later in the film, Crow acknowledges the film's problematic attitude toward Marfushka by observing that it considers "slightly unattractive people are evil," though perhaps his criticism of the film comes too late in the game after the SoL crew has verbally recast Marfushka as a man three times.

All comedy is transgressive, but what separates incisive comedy from the regressive is whether the transgression reveals critical truth. Though MST3K will never be mistaken for cruder contemporaries such as *Beavis and Butt-Head* or *South Park*, it has at times traded in risqué commentary that can in hindsight be criticized as harmful, misleading, or xenophobic. For example, season eight's two Japanese features—*Prince of Space* and *Invasion of the Neptune Men*—bring out a barrage of crude riffs on Japanese culture, including mockery of Japan's educational system ("Due to the apocalypse, cram school will be delayed by 45 minutes this morning"), cuisine ("More squid eyes?"), fashion ("Put on your upsetting shorts"), and media ("So is this going to be a super violent porn cartoon?"), to name a few. Things even get downright racist during *Prince of Space* when Crow riffs on an exterior shot of an apartment with an exaggeratedly ethnic scatting of the *Seinfeld* theme or when Servo articulates a dog's bark as "*a-rufaroo-bow-hawow*" in a faux Japanese patois.

To its writers' credit, MST3K is the rare 1990s comedy that eschewed misogyny and hatred of homosexuality without losing the edge of its humor. Yet Japanese people were not the only population to be singled out as other. *The Incredibly Strange Creatures Who Stopped Living and Became Mixed-Up Zombies!!?* features a series of transphobic jokes at the expense of actress Carolyn Brandt, whom Servo jests is "Renée Richards is Wendy Carlos in *Glen or Glenda*." Crow, meanwhile, refers to Brandt as "the most masculine man I've ever seen" while Mike declares that her "little sizzler" has been hidden by duct tape. In addition, like its contemporary *The Simpsons*, MST3K regularly took shots at retirement-age adults, often peppering older actors with riffs about Metamucil, gravy skin, asking about one's grandchildren, and unflatteringly comparing the titular Leech Woman in her aged state to Irene Ryan's "Granny" (cue Servo: "JEEEEEEED!") from 1960s sitcom *The Beverly Hillbillies*. The Joel era also featured its share of problematic riffing, including a whole skit of crude Mexican stereotypes in *The Black Scorpion* ("Fun with ethnocentrism!" the *Amazing Colossal Episode Guide* acknowledged in a mea culpa years later)[25] and Joel misnaming Ator's East Asian sidekick Thong as "Dong" or "Wong" while riffing *Cave Dwellers*, suggesting Ator will bake Thong a rice cake with a saw in it to escape prison.

There is little point in adjudicating whether such riffs are racist, transphobic, or ageist, but there is potentially great insight to be gained in exploring how those riffs contribute to or detract from the riffers' cumulative message to the audience. Transgressive humor should not be dismissed outright because it can contribute to incisive social commentary. When utilized skillfully, it can expose truth through exaggeration and overperformance of a problematic attitude, helping the audience realize that the real non-exaggerated attitude is also problematic.

Often, rather than directly denouncing a film's problematic content, Joel, Mike, and the bots temporarily co-opt its problematic attitudes and magnify them to a degree that an earnest acceptance of the film's perspective becomes absurd. One of the most memorable examples of this occurs during *Santa Claus* when the film unfurls a procession of crude racist stereotypes of children working in Santa's workshop (e.g., sombreros and ponchos for Mexican children, bone jewelry and tribal paint for African children, turbans and bhindis for Indian children). Crow responds by overperforming xenophobic with mischievous glee, noting that kids from France "stink to high heaven" and English children "have rotten teeth." Later in the episode, he half-heartedly attempts to atone for his bigotry by dismissing kids from the United States as "too spoiled and lazy to help Santa." To their credit, Mike and Servo appear outwardly offended by Crow's behavior, suggesting the at-home audience ought to feel the same way. Even without Mike and Servo's guidance, it is clear from Crow's tone he is criticizing the film's racism by belting it to the back row. It is unlikely that viewers would interpret Crow's adoption and exaggeration of the film's racism as earnest bigotry.

The riffers engage in a similar activity when they overperform sexism and misogyny. Consider the abundance of 1950s sci-fi and monster movies riffed on MST3K, many of which star a know-it-all manly scientist who possesses a subordinate feminine love interest. It is a safe bet that the riffers will deploy anti-women rhetoric that, interpreted literally, would be incredibly sexist. During *Revenge of the Creature*, for example, Mike, in character as John Agar, refers to love interest Helen Dobson (Lori Nelson) as "Professor Honeytush"; a later riff suggests Helen understands her instructions for dealing with the creature as "do my makeup and talk about boys, right?" During *The Leech Woman*, when Neil's fiancé demands an explanation after he has succumbed to the villain's feminine wiles, Crow jokes, "This is the fifties. Why am I explaining things to a woman? Get in the car!"

Mike and the bots often riff on issues that are rarely acceptable targets for mockery in the twenty-first century. Such issues include disordered eating ("I'm so upset I might binge on a saltine"; "Oh no, I couldn't [eat], I just had a half a cling peach yesterday"), anti-feminism ("They've only been together for a couple hours, but they're already on the same [menstrual] cycle"), and unhealthy body weight ("I can still fit in the dress I wore to my baptism"; "She might breathe in some fog and gain weight"). The SoL crew's riff of *Angels Revenge* includes a sprawling list of exaggerated anti-feminist jokes, riffing on the film's bootleg Angels by calling them "The T&A Team" and suggesting they are distracted by makeup, shopping, hair dye, and shampoo. Taken out of context, such jokes are misogynistic and problematic by the standards of 1990s television and even more so today. Yet they can be read as working against misogyny if the viewer interprets them as magnifying and rejecting the slightly less blatant misogyny embedded by the filmmakers. Only an obtuse or ungenerous interpretation of Crow's checklist of bigoted ethnic stereotypes during *Santa Claus*, or Mike and the bots exaggerated tittering at the idea of a woman photographer doing her job in *The Deadly Mantis* would conclude they are earnest statements that reflect the attitudes of the writers. A complete reading reveals a comedic critique of such attitudes by exaggerating them to the point that they are warped beyond validity.

Whether one interprets such riffs as ironic overperformances or earnest statements of problematic attitudes will be influenced by having a positive parasocial relationship with the show's writers and characters. Fans of the show, of the characters and the performers behind them, will likely be more inclined to read such risqué riffs as something more than mere cheap shots at vulnerable populations. Even then, though MST3K's writers deserve credit for keeping their comedy humane and decent, being a fan does not entail remaining willfully ignorant of the fact that sometimes experiments in verbal atom cracking[26] simply blow up in a performer's face.

"WHERE, OH WEREWOLF": CLEVER WORDPLAY AND PUNNING (BOOOO!) IN MST3K

A riff may be conceived of the cleverest reference or most incisive critique, but if the riffer botches the delivery or picks vague or questionable language to craft the riff, it will most likely be met with a shrug or a cringe. This is rarely a problem for MST3K's adept writers and performers. It would be an oversight to celebrate MST3K's riffing without celebrating the role of creative wordplay, which infuses the riffers' message with a joy and playfulness that makes criticism fun and memorable.

Among MST3K's favorite forms of riffing wordplay is playing with homophones. When the SoL crew hears a piece of movie dialogue or reads onscreen text, they may respond with a riff that evokes the meaning of a soundalike word with different meaning. For example, when *The Deadly Mantis* introduces a newspaper headline reading "Fear of mantis mounting," Servo responds, "I'd fear mantis mounting, too," deliberately misreading the intended meaning of the headline and replacing it with this more hilariously, horribly sexualized reading. When *The She-Creature* villain Carlo Lombardi meets resistance in trying to hypnotize his subject, Lombardi assures his audience, "Ladies and gentlemen, my subject is not herself tonight. She is too tense." Crow responds, as Lombardi, "She's a tipi and a wigwam," cutting through the film's intended tension with an absurd mishearing of "too tense" as "two tents." Close enough counts for this language game, too: when *Prince of Space* introduces the minor character Captain Munakata (Tadashi Minamikawa), Mike responds, "I understand you're stuffed with cheese," intentionally mishearing the pilot's name as "manicotti." Many episodes begin with a riff on the title card, such as in episode 405, when Servo remarks during the opening of *Being from Another Planet* aka *Time Walker*, "Being from another planet, I didn't have a lot to do with this film." There may be no finer riff of an actor's name in recorded history than Joel and Servo setting the tone for *Cave Dwellers* with, "How much Keeffe is in this movie anyway?" "Miles O'Keeffe."

Another technique involves MST3K's riffers "answering" the film, often in the persona of a character being addressed, offering an ironic or incongruent response spoken over the movie's dialogue. Mike and the bots illustrate this technique twice in *Devil Doll*. When protagonist Mark says, "You know, I've got to hand it to that Vorelli. His act is certainly different," Mike finishes his thought: "than a good act." Later, when Vorelli meets and ogles his new assistant (complete with a male gaze camera reveal Crow dubs "leer-cam"), he growls lasciviously, "Ah, Grace," to which Mike responds, "That's what I'm not living in a state of." In *Space Mutiny*, Mike employs this trick with great comedic impact when Ryder yells out "MacPherson!" to warn Lea of the traitor's presence. Mike, mimicking Ryder's panicked cry, calls out, "That's a really good strut suspension!" thus diffusing any tension possible with incongruent auto repair advice.

Yet another favorite technique of MST3K's riffers is ironic misdirection, which consists of the riffers beginning a statement that suggests appreciation or approval of something onscreen only to pause and reverse course with a statement of disapproval. In *The Incredibly Strange Creatures Who Stopped Living and Became Mixed-Up Zombies!!?*, Servo riffs on one incompetent police officer with the cop drama cliché, "He's a cop gone bad" before sheepishly adding, "I mean he's just a cop who's really bad at his job." When shifty Dan Kester (Robert Easton) is eaten by the Volkswagen-sized spider in *The Giant Spider Invasion*, Crow begins dourly, "I hate it when a movie kills off a beloved character" before announcing enthusiastically, "This is great, though." During *Space Mutiny*'s pathetic climactic cart duel between the heroic Ryder and the villainous Elijah Kalgan (John Phillip Law), Mike gestures toward thoughtful film criticism, "You know a lot of people have compared this scene to the climactic chariot scene in *Ben Hur*" before shifting gears and revealing his true opinion, "Yeah, you know, they usually say '*Ben Hur* was really good. This movie totally sucks.'" In addition to playing with irony, Mike toys with the notion of film criticism itself, fooling the audience with what sounds like traditional film criticism before foreclosing on the idea that *Space Mutiny* could be compared to *Ben Hur*.

In the lexicon of movie riffing, the antithesis of clever wordplay is the lowly pun.[27] Shunned by comedians as the cheesiest of wordplay, puns are deployed on MST3K not out of lack of imagination but with gratuitous self-awareness that elevates the form: the riffers are drinking from the bottom shelf and want everyone to know it. "Now there's a man out standing in his field," Crow quips during *Monster a Go-Go* as a character meanders through a field, eliciting exasperated groans from Joel and Servo. When *The Mole People* cuts to the broken head of a statue, Mike sings the chorus of the old standard "I Ain't Got Nobody" (changing "nobody" into "no body"), drawing a "shut up" from Servo. When Hank removes the cursed amulet from Jessica's neck in *The Thing That Couldn't Die* Mike becomes a repeat offender, riffing "Isn't it a Denver amulet?" ("amulet" sounding vaguely like "omelet"), which draws another "shut up" from Servo and an "I hate you, Mike" from Crow. In an alternate timeline, puns are even punishable with physical violence, as during *Time Chasers* when Mike's time-displaced older brother Eddie knocks Crow out of his seat for taking punning too far by responding to hero Nick Miller (Matthew Bruch) by declaring he "shaved this morning and got a nick."

Yet MST3K also has a soft spot for this most rudimentary form of wordplay. In *Invasion of the Neptune Men*, long after the movie has plunged the riffers into despair and left them sobbing, Servo sees a bridge onscreen and quips, "Mr. and Mrs. Bridge!" a reference to a 1990 Merchant Ivory film. Predictably, Mike and Crow respond disapprovingly ("Shame on you!" says Crow), but there is no anger behind their chidings. "I feel better now," Servo says, having lightened the mood, if only temporarily. There are many roads to salvation from horrible movies, and MST3K suggests that a bad pun can be one, too.

If clever wordplay and intertextuality reside near the top of the hierarchy of skillful riffing and puns sit squarely at the bottom, MST3K also reminds viewers that sometimes it is okay, even necessary, to forsake riffing altogether and simply express inner turmoil (while riffing on the 1956 Roger Corman Western *Gunslinger*, Joel laments "Man, this movie is just sitting on my head and crushing it") or lash out at the movie as an emotional safety valve. When a film becomes unbearable or sinks low enough to forfeit the right to be viewed evenly, MST3K's riffers are not too proud or self-conscious to avoid expressing themselves with direct, visceral statements of anger, resentment, or disgust toward a movie or character.

Any season of MST3K is bound to include its share of movies that descend beneath "cheesy" to become uniquely insufferable. This is, of course, the goal of Dr. Forrester's experiment: to find a movie so wretched it can bring the world's population to its knees. During the show's Comedy Central years, Joel and the bots suffer mightily through the intolerably boring rock climbing and sandstorm scenes during *Lost Continent* and *Hercules Against the Moon Men*, respectively, the latter gifting the world the concept of Deep Hurting. Mike and the bots similarly suffered through the Coleman Francis trilogy of *The Sky Divers*, *Red Zone Cuba*, and *The Beast of Yucca Flats* (in response to *Red Zone Cuba*, Crow declares, "I want to hurt this movie, but I can never hurt it the way it hurt me").

During the Sci-Fi years, the dreariness of *The She-Creature* proved a punishing adversary, with Mike stating at the end that "if I ever wanted to put a movie in a stump grinder, this is the one." Mike and the bots so dislike *Space Mutiny* that Servo proposes the film's dénouement should involve the attorney general explaining "how you can join in a class action suit against this movie." Similarly, the crew so despises *Hobgoblins* that Servo brings in a cardboard cutout of director Rick Sloane for an extended insult session in which he speculates that Sloane had his brains replaced with rat droppings.

At times certain scenes or characters become so offensive that only vitriol will suffice to push back. In season four, Joel is so offended by Torgo (John Reynolds) salaciously ogling Margaret (Diane Adelson) through a window as she changes in *Manos: The Hands of Fate*, he covers Crow and Servo's vision and chastises the Mads for lacking decency. In season eight, Mike and the bots aggressively reject the singing and antics of Buffalo Bill Joe Hickens in *Riding with Death*, culminating with Servo suggesting, "Listening to him is like flossing with a razor blade." The relationship between Nick and journalist Lisa Henson (Bonnie Pritchard) in *Time Chasers* is so uninspiring that Servo hopes they end up together "at the bottom of a well, torn apart by animals." A scene in *Devil Doll* in which Vorelli is implied to molest a hypnotized Marianne plunges Mike and Crow into ontological crisis, with Mike concluding, "Look, there's no God. There's the proof: not a single God."

No movie in MST3K history brings our heroes to the brink like *Invasion of the Neptune Men*.[28] A banal, turgid, and terminally repetitive piece of dreck that is somehow the same movie as *Prince of Space* with all the fun extracted, *Invasion of the Neptune Men* has Crow begging off within seventeen minutes and eventually breaks Mike and Servo, too. Mike gives up on life and leaves the theater despite there being no oxygen outside when the movie is playing. Servo loses all composure during the nadir of this "stupid little cockroach of a movie," a ten-plus-minute slog of stock battle footage and repeated shots whose only point of interest is a few seconds of the previously mentioned Hitler building. Unable to carry on, Servo breaks down into sobs and hallucinates that the movie has become *The Magnificent Ambersons* while the others beg him to stop. "To be dead, to be nothing, to watch *Neptune Men* no more," Crow mutters into the void. Only laughter can save the day, it seems, and it says much about the in-universe wretchedness of *Invasion of the Neptune Men* that Mike and the bots' spirits can only be buoyed by a visit from *Prince of Space*'s Krankor (played by Corbett), whom Mike forcefully expelled from the SoL just three episodes earlier.

"The only logical response to this movie is pure unbridled hate," Crow says matter of factly of *Agent for H.A.R.M.*, summing up the idea that the purifying power of anger can hold when rational thought and comedic goodwill are not enough. Though expressions of anger are often considered degraded speech in contrast to rational dialogue, cultural critic Neil Nehring suggests that visceral reactions such as anger, tedium, and frustration should be recognized as "essential political emotions."[29] MST3K suggests that there is room in the riffer's toolbox for carefully crafted references to Douglas Adams' *A Hitchhiker's Guide to the Galaxy* and the 1967 Beatles song "A Day in the Life" as well as angrily demanding that a movie like *Overdrawn at the Memory Bank* "jump up [one's] butt."

Coming off dramatic changes and the storytelling experiment that spanned season eight's twenty-two episodes, seasons nine and ten each consisted of thirteen episodes, but shorter runs did not stop the Best Brains team from producing a series of classics. Season nine includes all-timers such as *Hobgoblins*, *The Pumaman*, *Werewolf*,[30] and *The Final Sacrifice*, aka "the worst thing to ever come out of Canada" (here we presume Brain Guy meant "greatest"). Season ten featured the long-awaited returns of both Joel and Joe Don Baker (the latter via the 1984 "action" flick *Final Justice*) and even saw Mike and the bots square off against their most formidable text yet: the "greatest drama of all time" *Hamlet* (though in the form of a lifeless German TV production from 1960).

Sadly, the good times would not last. Season ten, and ultimately MST3K's run on cable television, concluded with episode 1013, with the SoL crew riffing the hip Italian crime caper *Danger: Diabolik*.[31] The episode begins with Pearl inadvertently initiating reentry protocol for the satellite. After one last movie, Pearl ends an era when she pulls the plug on the SoL ("Look, Nelson, move on. I am"), sending MSTies' favorite interstellar dog bone crashing back to Earth. Miraculously, everyone survives. Gypsy becomes a millionaire thanks to her successful company ConGypsCo while Mike, Crow, and Servo, having rejected Gypsy's offer to buy stock in her new venture, share a garden-level one-bedroom home in Wisconsin.

MST3K's fate on Sci-Fi had already been long sealed before Pearl's fateful joystick malfunction. On February 24, 1999, six weeks before season ten premiered, Best Brains Inc. announced it would produce no more episodes for Sci-Fi. "Ten years is a great run for any series," Jim Mallon said in a press release announcing the cancellation. "We've had a tremendous ride and it's time for Mike Nelson and the 'Bots to come down to Earth." With the benefit of hindsight, and with the knowledge that the future held more movie riffing than was conceivable at the time, there is much inspiration to be gleaned from season ten's conclusion. MST3K's final moments can be read as the culmination of an allegory for the power (and necessity) of becoming literate, critical media consumers. Ultimately, the riffing techniques explored in this chapter are more than building blocks for comedy: they cross over from the realm of fiction into our world and our own adventures in responding to the myriad media in our lives.

Throughout MST3K's run on cable, Joel, Mike, and the bots are subjected to terrible movies against their will, only to riff their way through them (with varying degrees of whimsy and ease) thanks to their vast knowledge of popular culture. They endure captivity and transform difficult audiencing experiences with creative riffing tactics. Tracing MST3K's development from the novel but primordial riffing of the KTMA era to the hilarity of late-era classics like *Space Mutiny* or *Werewolf* suggests that riffers can progress from novice to master with practice.

When first subjected to Dr. Forrester's experiment during the KTMA era, Joel and the bots are unequipped to respond to the films with the dexterity that would eventually come to characterize MST3K. The KTMA episodes are appealing for their low-fi charm, but one need only compare the five *Gamera* riffs on KTMA and their long stretches of in-theater silence to their redone versions during season three to know that Best Brains' writers and performers would get much better at every observable aspect of movie riffing. As Servo, Crow, Joel, and later Mike endured as captive audience members, their vocabularies expanded with both intertextual references and an ever-expanding kit of internal callbacks. Long pauses between riffs disappeared. Increasingly clever and insightful riffs replaced those that simply stated what was on the screen without making a joke (known as "state park" jokes in the MST3K writing room).[32] Every now and then a film brought them to their knees (or where their knees would be if they had legs, as in the case of Servo) but through endurance and will, the crew struggled on, refusing to succumb to nihilism or passivity.

Back here on Earth, the prevalence of mediated messages has only increased in the decades since MST3K first left the airwaves. The advent of smartphones and social media brought heightened anxiety and an unprecedented wave of distractions and disinformation that erodes people's ability to separate reality from propaganda. Always-on technology corrodes boundaries between work and home, between public and private. Each new technological doodad brings both wonders and burdens on body, mind, and heart, and it is becoming increasingly difficult to tell the difference.

It is no exaggeration to suggest that there are times when people immersed in the always-on, always-connected cultures of the media-saturated twenty-first-century need to unplug and power down but cannot. It is not only the bulk of the mediated messages encountered; new technologies make it difficult to make sense of what we are being asked to accept, believe, or do with the information surrounding us. Mediated misinformation, disinformation, and partisan propaganda place an unprecedented burden on consumers of media to respond in informed, ethical ways—not only for their own personal wellbeing but for the health of friends, families, and communities. These days, life can often feel like being subjected to a dozen mad scientists' experiments with media at once.

MST3K dramatizes the urgency of critical media consumption, a practice that has become essential to health and happiness in the twenty-first century. Should Joel, Mike, or the bots fail and succumb during Phase One of their captors' experiment, Phase Two is to unleash that perfectly bad movie onto the world to dominate its subjects. MST3K does more than make people laugh at cheesy movies. It presents the audience with the fully realized image of the ultimate evolution of the critical media consumer: the riffing trickster who integrates media into their life willingly as equipment for living to wield no matter what demands media place on them.

The final scene of season ten ends on a powerful note, and if the story of MST3K had to end there, it would be hard to imagine a more poetically perfect dénouement. Mike, Crow, and Servo gather on their couch in front of the TV to watch a movie, which happens to be *The Crawling Eye*, the same movie Joel and the bots riffed ten years earlier in episode 101. Back in season one, as *The Crawling Eye*'s opening credits announce Forrest Tucker as the movie's leading man, Joel responds, "Oh, Forrest Tucker. He's from *F-Troop*," an accurate reference to a more well-known Tucker role but a classic "state park" joke, merely an acknowledgment of an objective fact. It is clear throughout season one that Joel and the bots are still figuring movie riffing out not only as performers but as characters in their universe, as dramatized by season one's skits in which Joel patiently explains humanity to Servo and Crow. Within two seasons, Joel and company were flourishing as riffers and producing all-time classic riffs like *Cave Dwellers*, *Pod People*, and *The Unearthly*.

Mike, Crow, and Servo ultimately escape captivity, yet they do not escape mediation because by 1999 there is no escape. In a simpler tale, they may have absconded to their own Walden, a cabin in the woods far away from the tendrils of the movies that they endured for years. With the agency to choose, they embrace cheesy movies willingly, only now their riffing toolboxes are bursting with symbolic equipment to handle the job. "Oh, Forrest Tucker," Mike riffs in a lighthearted tone, "he's the guy who makes sure all trees' shirt tails are in." Crow remarks to Mike and Servo that the movie is familiar, and MST3K's end credits roll for what seemed like the final time. From their own couches, fans were left to wonder what the crew could do with a movie as bad as *The Crawling Eye* if only there was more time. They only had to wait two decades and multiple revolutions in media production and distribution to find out.

CHAPTER FOUR

"THEY WATCH MOVIES AND THEN MAKE UP JOKES ABOUT THEM"

The Spinoffs

"**F**or once, Mystery Science Theater 3000 fans aren't laughing," wrote television critic, future *Gone Girl* author, and MSTie[1] Gillian Flynn in the April 16, 1999 edition of *Entertainment Weekly*.[2] There should have been much to celebrate in 1999 with the start of a momentous tenth season, but despair crept in after February's announcement that season ten would be MST3K's last for the foreseeable future. Despite passionate and organized collective action from MSTies that spanned print and web writing campaigns, including a full-page ad in the trade publication *Daily Variety* pleading for another station to pick up the unmoored series,[3] MST3K would not be spared from cancellation. Critical acclaim, a passionate cult following, and robust home video sales were no longer sufficient to keep MST3K in orbit.

The series had been foundational in the history of not one but two successful upstart cable networks, but the die had been cast when Barry Schulman, Sci-Fi's vice president of programming and MST3K's internal booster, resigned from the network in 1998 amid a flurry of personnel changes at USA Networks.[4] Bonnie Hammer replaced Schulman, and within one year of the handoff MST3K was canceled, neither the first nor the last series to suffer such a fate despite boasting a devoted cult audience clamoring for more. MST3K having its umbilicus yanked for the second time in a few years was too cruel not to be emblematic of a larger trend in mass media at the turn of the century. In the unique media landscape of 1999, characterized by rapid conglomeration following the Telecommunications Act of 1996 but not yet ready for viable web-based distribution as an alternative to cable, corporate media harbored no sustainable outlet for MST3K's production model.

When Comedy Central axed MST3K in 1996, the station cited falling ratings.[5] In hindsight, the death knell more likely involved shifting priorities as the cable industry evolved. MST3K was born during the wild west days of cable, when programmers filled their lineups with whatever they could to establish an identity, and an offbeat UHF cow-town puppet show fit right into the Comedy Channel's motley lineup next to *Tommy Sledge, P.I.* and reruns of *The Abbott and Costello Show*. Once the crown jewel of a ramshackle lineup, MST3K was deemed expendable when Comedy Central went all in on its second phase, which was defined by shows like *South Park* and *The Daily Show*. "You get an anomaly like *South Park* that just blows the barn doors off any preconceived ratings expectations and shows you how high the bar can be and where everything else needs to strive for," Comedy Central executive Eileen Katz reflected after the announcement of MST3K's 1999 cancellation.[6] "The reality now is that every show we put on the air has ratings goals that we need to hit."

When Sci-Fi picked up MST3K after its 1996 cancellation, the network, born in 1992, was still in its primordial phase just as the Comedy Channel had been in 1989. MST3K gave Sci-Fi marquee original programming to tout while filling its lineup with reruns of *Lost in Space*, *The Twilight Zone*, and *Dark Shadows*. Yet when Sci-Fi announced MST3K's cancellation, the cable channel had no original programming in the same orbit of success as *South Park*. Predictably echoing Comedy Central's cancellation rationale of low ratings, Hammer also acknowledged what appeared to be MST3K's ultimate Achilles' heel: the rising cost of licensing movie rights. In 1988, Joel Hodgson and the original MST3K crew could simply raid KTMA's film vaults to find cost-free, severely marginalized riffing fodder. Once cable television expanded, distributors of film rights demanded more in exchange for their suddenly attractive assets. A movie in MST3K's wheelhouse cost as much as seventy-five thousand dollars,[7] giving the show a much higher bar to clear in terms of generating revenue through ratings and ad sales. MST3K's raison d'être had facilitated its own ironic demise. If the cheesy movies of yore had accumulated value beyond what networks were willing to license as MST3K's proverbial punching bags, the series surely played a role in rehabilitating those films' value to the point that being publicly ridiculed was no longer distributors' last and best option.

With corporate overlords no longer willing to pay for movie riffing's raw materials, MST3K seemed fated to drift into oblivion as episode after episode fell out of syndication when existing movie rights expired. Yet far away from corporate media mergers, Nielsen ratings, and ravenous film distributors, a post-MST3K movie-riffing cottage industry was slowly emerging. A new media landscape would herald a triumphant return for movie riffing for those who knew where to look, one characterized by technological innovation and new modes of media production and fan engagement that marched in stride with a coming explosion of online cultural expression.

Cable television may have been ready to move on from movie riffing, but fans weren't. It would take seven years for the architects of MST3K to crack the code of a new business model that would revolutionize movie riffing in the twenty-first century. This journey to riffing's new age began with the former members of Best Brains as they strove to extract their roots from the soil of traditional media with simultaneously tantalizing and frustrating results.

"INSIDE TIMMY": THE BRAVE NEW WORLD OF TIMMY BIG HANDS

Visiting www.timmybighands.com today through the magic of the Internet Archive's WayBack Machine[8] transports readers of a certain vintage back to an intoxicating epoch in the history of the so-called Information Superhighway. MSTies online since the days of bulletin boards, UseNet groups, and chat rooms will recall with some degree of nostalgia that the internet of the mythical year 2000 was a radically different world, one predating the proliferation of networking websites today commonly lumped under the heading of social media. It was an unconquered frontier still six years away from the Web 2.0 revolution ignited by the impacts of sites such as Facebook and Twitter. At that time, building and maintaining an online presence demanded vision and knowhow. It required passion, creativity, and dedication. It necessitated learning to love clunky frames, low-resolution visuals, walls of Times New Roman text, and frequently clipart.

Timmy Big Hands is unambiguously a product of this unique blip in the internet age when primitive websites featured retina-shocking backgrounds, questionable if not downright hostile font choices, and irritating animated banner ads. Launched in 2000 and debuting just over a year after the public demise of MST3K, Timmy Big Hands was an online humor magazine published by five MST3K alumni: Patrick Brantseg,[9] Paul Chaplin,[10] Bill Corbett, Kevin Murphy, and Michael J. Nelson. As did so many of its contemporaries, Timmybighands. com violates every aesthetic principle of modern web design. Its pages suffocate the eyes with dense paragraphs of text surrounded by a piercing cerulean background, dotted liberally with Corel clipart images for click navigation. Garish even for its day and very much in the spirit of MST3K's do-it-yourself aesthetics, Timmy Big Hands updates the creators' self-aware style of riffing on pop culture for a new medium. As MST3K often riffed on the act of film criticism itself,

Timmy Big Hands meta-riffs on the then-fashionable propagation of online magazines following the seismic 1995 launch of Salon.com.

A cheeky spoof on the all-things-to-all-readers coverage that was popular with online magazines of its era, Timmy Big Hands' articles pontificate on a shotgun blast of topics such as literature, travel, the outdoors, and consumer products, all covered with a thick syrup of satirical irreverence, absurd Midwestern humor, and, well, syrup. Its style of humor will be familiar to anyone with a worn-out copy of *The Mystery Science Theater 3000 Amazing Colossal Episode Guide* or who spent hours clicking through its online equivalent on Sci-Fi's website. This time, though, instead of spoofing the hammy dialogue of John Agar or Peter Graves, Timmy Big Hands effectively spoofed the self-important musings of contributors to early online magazines.

Among the recurring features on Timmy Big Hands are satirical consumer product-style reviews of non-products such as saliva, happiness, and "guys who are about five-eight, five-nine":

> Most problematically, these guys are neither tall nor short, and so project none of the automatic élan associated with either of those more interesting options. . . . If you're not too picky, guys who measure just above five-nine or so are fine. You'll always be able to find one, and they are guys. They fill the bill. But once you get a taste of something a little more idiosyncratic, with more pizzazz, I'm betting you'll want to move up, or down.[11]

Timmy Big Hands also features a series of mock comic strips visually composed entirely of clip art as well as absurd ads for dystopian GMO Frankensyrups featuring a spokesman with a consistently mutating head.

A highlight of the site is a mock serial novel called *The Tort*, the conceit of which is that each chapter is written by a different author.[12] Chapter IV begins:

> The sun broke through the sweaty haze, lightly poaching the quiet residential streets of Oakdalle as Jake Sharp parked his previously-owned [*sic*] Seville next to the yellow crime scene ribbon. He couldn't help but think of the lyrics of that song:
>
> > What's so special,
> > About Special Dinners,
> > It's got the special taste of milllk [*sic*].
>
> He filed it away in his mind. Angus Silverstein was trundling over to his car.
> "Angus."
> "Sharp." They exchanged meaty handshakes. My God, thought Sharp, his hand is beefier than ever. Angus. Beef. He wondered.

"More of you to love than ever to love, Angus." Sharp patted Angus'
bulging tummy, then jiggled his ample man-breasts.[13]

In some ways, *The Tort* recalls both the literary technique of "cut-up" and the
surrealist drawing game known as Exquisite Corpse. Developed by the Dadaists
in the 1920s and later utilized by Beat writer William S. Burroughs, cut-up is a
literary technique in which an existing written text is cut up and rearranged to
generate a new text created by chance. Exquisite Corpse, meanwhile, is a drawing
game conceived by the Surrealists André Breton, Yves Tanguy, Jacques Prévert,
and Marcel Duchamp, who would take turns drawing different sections of a body
on a sheet of paper that was folded to hide each individual contribution. *The Tort*
echoes each of these techniques in that the individual authors wrote their chapters
independently of one another and created a humorous legal thriller almost entirely
by chance. Regardless of its influences, *The Tort* served as yet another outlet for
the former MST3K crew to continue practicing their specific brand of humor.
With joyful tears in their eyes and season five's "Doughy Guy" song in their
hearts, riff-deprived MSTies could take comfort in knowing the crew was still out
there riffing on beefy guys, inane commercial jingles, and self-serious dramas.
The venture would, however, be fleeting.

Timmy Big Hands lasted about a year before being shuttered in 2001. In a
2003 interview, Nelson attributed the website's demise to logistics and straight
cost-benefit analysis:

Timmy Big Hands, you know, it was great fun, it was successful for what
it was. We got unbelievable press, and we were really proud of the product.
But (it was) a really bad time to start a website and we just couldn't—we all
had our separate things going on. We were producing it together, but in the
end, it ate up too much time and wasn't making any money, so we just had to
fold it. We thought about perhaps turning it into a book or doing this or that,
but it was just too complicated by that time. So, we just folded it down.[14]

Once again, Nelson and company were ahead of their time, though this time not to
their advantage. The dot-com bubble had burst. A model for reliably monetizing
internet content was still materializing. As print media practitioners were shocked
to learn, consumers accustomed to newspapers and magazines were not ready
to pay for online writing, and advertisers were not convinced the World Wide
Web was worth their investment. If the internet of 2001 was not yet ready for a
self-consciously basic website like Timmy Big Hands, it certainly was not ready
to replace cable TV for delivering riffing to the masses.

"I'M GOING TO SINK THIS BITCH": KICKING AGAINST THE PRICKS OF OLD MEDIA DISTRIBUTION

Among the palpable limitations of cable-era MST3K were constraints on which movies could be riffed. Recent films, as well as those of any commercial or critical appeal (with rare exceptions like the 1969 astronaut drama *Space Travelers* aka *Marooned*) were prohibitively expensive, and by the time of MST3K's second cancellation even movies such as *Final Justice* or *The Horrors of Spider Island* were becoming too rich for Sci-Fi's taste. Fans could only fantasize about what MST3K would be able to make out of legendary bombs like *Ishtar* or *Howard the Duck* let alone whether movie riffing could even work when faced with the best of what Hollywood could offer.

Full-length riffs of Hollywood standouts were never in the show's twentieth-century business model, but MST3K memorably flirted with contemporary Hollywood in 1995 with the "MST3K Little Gold Statue Preview Special." For twenty-two minutes, Servo and Crow satirized Oscar-season prognostication specials by drawing hasty conclusions on that year's best-of contenders based on cursory viewings of screeners and irrelevant criteria (e.g., awarding Best Director based on physical attractiveness: Robert Redford wins, naturally). Between clips, Crow and Servo conduct faux interviews with prerecorded snippets of Kenneth Branagh and John Travolta in the tradition of "Weird Al" Yankovic's fake celebrity interviews and take a pointed shot or two at high-brow prestige cinema. Undressing critical darling and Best Screenplay nominee *Three Colours: Red*, Servo explains, "See, this is one of those 'important' films, which means it's boring and you see it in a theater full of people with B.O. and you pretend that you get it."

Best Brains updated the bit in 1998 on Sci-Fi with the "Academy of Robots' Choice Awards Special" in which Mike and the bots finally realized fans' dream of riffing genuine Oscar fodder, albeit in clip form. The result was riffing magic. Any reductive assertion that movie riffing only works on B-grade fare was dismantled as Mike and the bots relished in delivering "glancing blows at the titans of Hollywood" (to quote Crow as he speaks on the phone to "future president Al Gore") with hilarious results. Highlighted by five minutes of riffing on *Titanic* that is as relentlessly funny as any MST3K episode of the era—anchored by Servo's immortal "I'm going to sink this bitch"—the dream of a full-on MST3K riff of Hollywood's finest was more intriguing than ever. If only there was a way to circumvent the financial and logistical roadblocks . . .

Following MST3K's cancellation, Nelson and Murphy set about sinking various Hollywood . . . ahem, let's say "fare" . . . via the printed page. Trading in audiovisual riffing for timeless print, Nelson and Murphy modified MST3K's characteristic humor for traditional film reviews and cultural commentary in a medium in which the First Amendment guarantees no film or filmmaker is off limits. The result is writing that is funny and at times inspirational. Yet the limitations of the medium revealed that though film criticism and movie riffing are both essential functions, they are not one in the same.

Nelson published *Mike Nelson's Movie Megacheese* in 2000, one of his six humor books released during the period between MST3K's cancellation and the 2006 launch of his most enduring project. Of the six,[15] *Megacheese* hews closest to MST3K-style movie riffing, featuring biting commentary on a range of 1990s films and TV series as well as the actors who populate them. Nelson offers sweeping comments on a selection of "bloated, star-gorged production[s] with a lousy script that relied on special effects and sinful advertising budgets"[16] of the period such as *Broken Arrow*, *Twister*, *Independence Day*, *Face/Off*, and most famously *Batman & Robin*, of which Nelson writes: "it's the single worst thing that we as human beings have ever produced in recorded history."[17] Nelson comically skewers prominent actors and filmmakers of the time, mocking in his distinct voice the talents of Steven Seagal, John Travolta, Jason Lee, David Fincher, Shane Black, and Jim Carrey ("Personally, I believe there is no hell foul enough to contain [Carrey's] fetid soul"[18]). It is easy to read prose such as Nelson comparing 1998's *Lost in Space* movie to "a fairly discreet sausage burp: It's somewhat reminiscent of the original yet not altogether welcome"[19] and imagine it seamlessly delivered via Shadowrama.[20]

In 2002, meanwhile, Murphy published *A Year at the Movies: One Man's Filmgoing Odyssey*, one of the most ambitious and funniest books ever written about contemporary moviegoing. Murphy endeavored in 2001 to see one theatrical movie every day for the calendar year. His travels take him from local multiplexes to the exotic locales of Sundance and Cannes, a drive-in tour along Route 66, the smallest movie theater in the world in Australia, and Quebec City's Hôtel de Glace, a hotel constructed entirely of ice. Along the way, Murphy attempts to eat only theater food for a week, smuggles an entire Thanksgiving dinner into the theater, rips tickets at his local theaters, beholds the transition from film projection to digital exhibition, and solemnly reflects on the communal power of cinema from New Zealand on September 11, 2001.

A Year at the Movies appeals to readers as a celebration of moviegoing before multiplexes and corporate conglomeration flattened the experience. Murphy laments that moviegoing has become an act of passive consumption rather than engagement with art, writing, "what have we lost in the process? Only passion, risk, and community—in short, the things that make a public art like cinema both public and art."[21] As Nelson explored in *Movie Megacheese*, Murphy trades movie riffing for more traditional film criticism laced with humor to convey attitudes toward the movies and actors that then dominated Hollywood. Murphy rejects the merits of Adam Sandler, Rob Schneider ("Schneider offends me on so many levels it's hard to know where to begin"[22]), and everyone complicit in the loathsome *Town & Country*, offering the artistry of Joel and Ethan Coen, Jean-Luc Godard, Buster Keaton, and Terrance Malick as counterpoints. Murphy even tags in Nelson for the tall task of suffering through *Corky Romano*, reflecting on the epistemology of "bad movies" along the way.

The books of Nelson and Murphy serve as an important post-MST3K bridge for the once and future riffing partners, whetting readers' appetites for the duo to apply their humorous critical approach to contemporary Hollywood fare. As insightful and entertaining as Nelson and Murphy's books are, they nevertheless put into focus how riffing is distinct from ex post facto criticism. Riffing as a form of communication stands apart from traditional criticism for its capacity to confront and disrupt the discrete elements of films at the moments they unspool, reaching the audience before those elements coalesce into a coherent whole. Astute criticism can and always has made sense of films and specific elements of filmmaking, but it does so in hindsight rather than as the film plays out before the audience. In print Nelson and Murphy can, for example, clearly and compellingly convey their disgust for Carrey and Schneider so that readers can consider the validity of their criticisms. Riffing their acting as it plays out onscreen is a different experience altogether that unfolds in real time. Riffing can problematize and contextualize acting and other cinematic elements while the audience watches the performance unfold on the screen, showing rather than telling the riffers' critical arguments.

Five years after MST3K's cancellation, fans were greeted with the first new post-MST3K movie riffing troupe when Corbett, Murphy, and Nelson debuted the Film Crew. Though only briefly active, the Film Crew serves as another formative bridge to guide movie riffing across the changing media landscape—and as another illustration of the painful limitations of traditional distribution models. The Film Crew flashed promise but tragically died so that movie riffing could forge its way forward through the unconquered terrain of online distribution.

First establishing its premise in brief web clips and appearing in broadcast media such as National Public Radio, American Movie Classics, Starz, and Encore, the Film Crew ventured into the expanding world of DVD commentary tracks by recording a humorous commentary for Legend Video's 2005 DVD release of *The Three Stooges in Color*. With Nelson keeping the flame of movie riffing alive by recording post-MST3K riffs of Legend's colorized releases of *Night of the Living Dead*, *Reefer Madness*, *Plan 9 From Outer Space*, and *The Little Shop of Horrors*, the possibility of reconstituting the Sci-Fi-era riffing trio of Corbett, Murphy, and Nelson was big news for fans. The Film Crew struck a deal with Rhino Video, distributor of MST3K's first wave of VHS and DVD releases, to release Film Crew episodes on DVD.

With one foot firmly planted in the classic MST3K ethos, Corbett, Murphy, and Nelson played fictionalized versions of themselves hired by dingbat media magnate "Bob Rhino" to record commentary in the name of "preservation of Hollywood's forgotten gems." The premise itself is a riff on the early days of DVD when releasing a movie or TV series with commentary or other special features signified a degree of cultural value in the text. Rather than celebrating or intellectualizing the movie to instill it with artistic capital, however, the Film Crew riffs each film in classic MST3K style—in hindsight a wonderfully clever inversion of DVD's function in industry-sanctioned paratextual production.[23]

The Film Crew completed only four episodes, riffing on the salacious Rue McLanahan vehicle *Hollywood After Dark*, the goofy atomic-age schlockfest *Killers from Space*, the sleazy jungle flick *The Wild Women of Wongo*, and the sword-and-sandal epic *The Giant of Marathon*—all four films more forgotten than hidden gem and fitting comfortably in the MST3K wheelhouse of quality and affordability. Like MST3K, our characters appear onscreen in host segments to set up the premise, banter with their benefactor foil, and engage in hijinks during film breaks. Unlike MST3K, the riffers are not visually present in the theater, only as disembodied voices.

The Film Crew's riffing techniques are classic MST3K and represent what should have been the first viable transplantation of the show's iconic riffing tropes and techniques to a post-MST3K enterprise. Picking up where they left off in 1999, Corbett, Murphy, and Nelson's commentary on *Hollywood After Dark* (think *Girl in Gold Boots* crossbred with *The Sinister Urge*) subverts the film's appeals to prurience by riffing on the incongruity of McClanahan (of future *Golden Girls* fame) as an object of erotic desire. The Film Crew compares McClanahan to Art Garfunkel and Roger Daltrey, suggesting "She turned Melissa Ethridge to men" in service of rejecting the film's offering of McClanahan's Sandy as both protagonist and sexual object. The Crew relishes in burlesque riffing of the film's grotesque depiction of sexualized dancing ("Good show tonight, not a flat lap in the house") while mocking the film's hackneyed portrayals of sexual mania (Kevin asks, "Is he humping a tree?" to which Bill replies, "Yeah, he's getting a little wood"). The Film Crew's intertextual chops are as sharp as ever when riffing *Killers from Space*, making humorous references to *The Outer Limits*, *Apocalypse Now*, singer Glen Campbell's then-recent DUI, journalist Walter Winchell, and of course a full quota of *Biography* references with Peter Graves in the starring role.

Though the riffing was sharp as ever, the limitations of distributing movie riffing through traditional home video suffocated the project. The Film Crew's DVDs were shelved when Rhino declined to distribute them for reasons not publicly disclosed and heatedly debated among the fandom online. Regardless of who pulled the plug on the Film Crew and why, the project withered on the vine before Shout! Factory distributed the existing four episodes in 2007 after Corbett, Murphy, and Nelson had moved on. All references to Bob Rhino are noticeably edited to "Bob Honcho" to scrub Rhino's involvement from the project.

Ultimately, the cause of the Film Crew's failure as a venture was bigger than any one movie, producer, or distributor. DVD replacing VHS did not change the fact that even if riffers accepted the limitations of dirt-cheap or even rights-free movies, distributing movie riffing by twentieth-century means (e.g., TV, home video) both constrained the films available and put the riffers at the mercy of executives who could say no or enforce arbitrary restrictions based on profits or politics. The premature snuffing of the Film Crew, followed in 2006 by two consecutive Rhino-distributed MST3K DVD boxsets (volumes nine and ten) being suddenly yanked from shelves due to rights snafus,[24] made clear that twenty-first-century movie riffing was not going to thrive under archaic production models.

"THIS IS NO TIME TO QUOTE TIRED INTERNET MEMES, SIR!": RIFFTRAX AND THE REBIRTH OF RIFFING IN THE DIGITAL ERA

On July 20, 2006, Nelson ushered movie riffing into the internet age with the launch of RiffTrax, a web-based riffing project producing pre-recorded audio commentary tracks distributed digitally and independently of the movies being riffed. Consumers could download and sync the MP3 file to their copy of the movie, at last circumventing the shackles of copyright and traditional media distribution. RiffTrax began with Nelson performing solo, first riffing his beloved *Road House*, followed by *The Fifth Element*, *Cocktail*, *xXx*, and the Britney Spears road movie *Crossroads*. Nelson was soon joined by Murphy, then Corbett, with the three forming the core of RiffTrax and riffing hundreds of movies as a trio. Later, MST3K alums Bridget Jones-Nelson and Mary Jo Pehl came on board as Bridget and Mary Jo, as did occasional celebrity guests such as Yankovic, Fred Willard, Joel McHale, and Neil Patrick Harris.

To analyze RiffTrax's riffing on a micro level could span its own tome due to the sheer scope of films riffed and the abundance of creativity on display. Corbett, Murphy, and Nelson join forces hundreds of times, utilizing riffing techniques discussed in chapter 3 while experimenting with the form. Corbett, Murphy, and Nelson take on new and risqué genres (blaxploitation, R-rated slashers) and work too blue for TV (during the orgy scene from disco-era musical *The Apple*, Murphy opines, "I wonder if the cinematographer intentionally put that Vaseline on the lens or if it just sort of happened"). They both revisit the glory days of MST3K (producing new riffs of classics such as *Manos*, *Space Mutiny*, *Time Chasers*, and *Merlin's Shop of Mystical Wonders*) and developed their own lexicon of references separate from the MST3K oeuvre, taking on new challenges ranging from riffing "good" movies (e.g., *The Wizard of Oz*, *Casablanca*, *It's a Wonderful*

Life) to sub-*Manos* Z-grade schlock seemingly beneath contempt such as *Things*, *Feeders*, or the dregs of Joe Estevez's filmography (such as the mind-boggling atrocity *Rollergator*).

As with any successful spinoff of a beloved classic, RiffTrax has both developed its own dedicated fanbase while leaving some longtime MST3K fans pining for the more appreciative, less dismissive tone of the show's earlier era (i.e., the Joel years). RiffTrax's distinctive voice and aggressiveness in dismantling the films they riff inspires reflection and discussion online about the roles of appreciation and generosity in riffing bad movies. Does a soulless Hollywood blockbuster like the worst of Michael Bay's *Transformers* movies equally deserve to be riffed with fondness as Ed Wood's pugnacious-yet-lacking *Bride of the Monster*? As critics, do passion projects that fall to pieces on screen (e.g., *The Room*, *Birdemic: Shock and Terror*, *Miami Connection*) deserve respect and charity based on the merits of their spiritually grandiose conceptions? Do fans want to see sacred cows like *Night of the Living Dead*, *Halloween*, *Doctor Who*, or *Mothra* riffed in the first place? These ongoing conversations contribute to critical conversations of the goals and techniques of not just riffing but broader media criticism.

At the time novel from a technological and distribution perspective, RiffTrax in hindsight liberated movie riffing as a potential performance space. Thanks to the convergence of technological advances in home media and consumer practices, the innovations of RiffTrax allowed riffing to flourish in a twenty-first-century performance space. At the time of RiffTrax's launch, MP3 players, led by Apple's iPod, were becoming increasingly popular; accelerated by Apple debuting the iPhone in 2007, mobile phones were evolving into versatile tools for storing and playing digital audio files the size of full-length movie riffs. DVD was peaking in popularity, having recently overtaken VHS as the United States' home video medium of choice.[25] Blu-ray had just launched, offering consumers another easy (if initially expensive) method for accessing movies. DVDs became easier to locate and had significantly decreased in price since the turn of the century, and by 2005 a disruptive company called Netflix, not yet involved in the streaming video game, was shipping over a million DVDs per day to customers hooked on its rental-by-mail subscription service (R.I.P. 2023).[26] RiffTrax was as ready to capitalize on the new technology as fans were to embrace it, and when RiffTrax cracked the code, no mediated text was out of reach for professional or amateur riffers with a microphone, internet, and something to say.

The movie riffing sphere, once constrained by economic and technological limitations, proliferated. Still producing riffs at an astounding pace over fifteen years later, RiffTrax has published more than 530 full-length riffs and over 460 shorts. Nelson and company took professional riffing to places it had never gone with "Just the Jokes" audio commentaries of previously untouchable films such as *The Lord of the Rings: The Fellowship of the Rings* and *Star Wars: Episode IV—A*

New Hope while honoring MST3K's legacy of riffing low-budget and public-domain fare through production of video-on-demand riffs of *Reefer Madness*, *House on Haunted Hill*, and *Carnival of Souls*. RiffTrax continues to produce audio-only commentaries for Hollywood royalty like *Jurassic Park*, *Harry Potter and the Sorcerer's Stone*, and *Twilight*, later applying the technique to prestige TV series like *Game of Thrones* and *Stranger Things* while skewering all-time stinkers such as *The Room*, *Santa and the Ice Cream Bunny*, and *Battlefield Earth*. RiffTrax also helped save movies previously unreleased (*Birdemic* auteur James Nguyen's scrapped 2005 fiasco *Replica*), previously lost (1934's *Maniac*), and media previously available cash-only at fan conventions (1978's *The Star Wars Holiday Special*, complete with commercials).

Though Nelson and RiffTrax are often recognized for their innovation in full-length commentary, they also deserve recognition for rekindling the flame of riffing short films. Riffing shorts was a regular feature on MST3K since season one when the Mads inflicted nine episodes of the drab 1950s Commando Cody serial *Radar Men from the Moon* as a lead-in to the episode's featured films. With many of season one and two's films having shorter runtimes, adding a short proved an effective way to fill out the episode's runtime.

By the end of season two and throughout the end of the Comedy Central era, Best Brains added educational and industrial shorts to the occasional Great Depression–era serial (the 1936 Crash Corrigan saga, *Undersea Kingdom*) or clip from *General Hospital*. Several shorts have taken their place among fans' favorite segments of the series, none greater than the icon of all MST3K shorts, *Mr. B Natural*, in which a prancing androgynous imp awakens the spirit of music inside a young child by visiting him alone in his bedroom.

Shorts play a significant role in a study of the art of movie riffing due to how they draw out more explicit political commentary from MST3K's writers. Shorts tend to appeal to viewers on more overt, frequently preachy terms than films intended for theatrical release, thus providing riffers an opportunity to directly challenge and contradict the film's politics. A review of MST3K's shorts library reveals how the writers and performers interwove comedy with critical commentary. For instance, during season three's *Alphabet Antics* and especially *Catching Trouble*, Joel and the bots articulate an ideology of anti-exploitation in their undiluted disgust and hostility toward the films' lighthearted depictions of animal abuse. "O is for the obscene treatment of animals . . . T is for tormented, tortured, and teased," Servo suggests at *Alphabet Antics*' depictions of creatures dressed in costumes and forced to drag a plow for the purposes of whimsy. Joel and the bots react even more aggressively in defiance of *Catching Trouble*, in which herpetologist Ross Allen brutally captures wild animals to be interred in a zoo. As Allen hunts and captures helpless crying black bear cubs, Joel declares, "Man, would I love to see that cub's mom come through the woods right about now." Joel and the bots frame Allen as nothing less than the ultimate evil. "Let's not forget who the evil serpent is," Joel says as Allen captures a diamondback rattler. The overtness of Joel and the bots' commentary leaves little question that MST3K's writers are speaking from the heart against animal abuse and exploitation.

MST3K's politics come out again during *Aquatic Wizards* in which the riffers grow angry at the narrator dubbing a water-skier a "Mexican jumping bean." "This time," Crow reacts with escalating rage, "the white fascist narrator will make a racial slur!" Joel and the bots likewise speak out against labor exploitation and environmental destruction under capitalism when riffing *The Truck Farmer*, a breathless celebration of exploiting migrant labor in agriculture. "In recent decades, truck farming has become big business," the narrator explains to which Joel responds, "but not for these people." "Oh, that's cheerful," Servo says sarcastically as the narrator rhapsodizes about the speed at which trees can be cleared and burned thanks to heavy machinery. During season six's *Progress Island U.S.A.*, a short film celebrating the effects of Operation Bootstrap in Puerto Rico, Mike and (especially) the bots aggressively reject the film's neoliberal propaganda and its invitations for the industrial exploitation of Puerto Rico's adult population, taking out their frustrations on the entire commonwealth of Puerto Rico.

Throughout its initial run, MST3K employed humor while articulating its generally left-leaning politics—"We were proudly woke before it was called being woke" Frank Conniff confirmed in response to Elon Musk during one of the billionaire's numerous "anti-woke" Twitter screeds[27]—but particularly when riffing more problematic shorts, the show's writers made their opinions against racism, sexism, environmental destruction, and exploitation explicit. MST3K was among several successful media entities of the 1990s to channel political commentary through irony, parody, and humor, joining influential shows and publications such as *The Daily Show*, *The Onion*, and AdBusters in using comedy to say what otherwise would be shunned by profit-first TV executives and advertisers.

Media scholars such as Robert Hariman[28] and Jamie Warner[29] have written that the performance of humor can function as an effective vessel for subversive or political critique and thus is an essential form of political commentary. Similarly, influential scholar Mikhail Bakhtin suggests that the critical deployment of humor "demolishes fear and piety before an object,"[30] making the exploration of complicated political issues accessible for the audience and opening the possibility of engagement with issues they may otherwise find intimidating or incendiary. Though MST3K sparingly dove headlong into overt politics, whenever they took the plunge they eschewed polemics in favor of tactics such as ridicule, parody, and humorous contradiction. The message to the aspiring riffer is clear: comedy and politics are very much capable of mixing.

Shorts were rarely featured during the Sci-Fi era, but they became perfect additions to RiffTrax's business model as fun-sized and inexpensive downloads by which customers could purchase a fresh riff for about a dollar. RiffTrax began its foray into the world of shorts with one-off Christmas shorts in 2006 and 2007 before regularly unearthing some of the strangest short films in the annals of the public domain, an alarming number of which feature people harming themselves at work or at home (*Shake Hands With Danger*, *More Dangerous Than Dynamite*), sentient objects chastising oblivious operators (*Paper and I*, *The Talking Car*), and a full spectrum of retrograde educational, industrial, and mental hygiene shorts (*If Mirrors Could Speak*, *Drugs Are Like That*). Several shorts became RiffTrax standouts for their ability to bewilder with their very existence, such as the twenty-seven-minute *Setting Up a Room*, the moribund misadventures of Norman Krasner trying to exit a parking lot or use a pay toilet, or the mind-bending quandary of whether corn is grass and the cornucopia of handcrafted garbage that exists at one's fingertips from the library of ACI Films.

Whether riffing shorts from the public domain or Hollywood blockbusters, RiffTrax represents an important cultural touchstone not only for movie riffing but more generally for the creation and circulation of media commentary and criticism in the twenty-first century, an age history will record as decentralizing the performance of cultural criticism. MST3K is rightly lauded for conceptually paving the way for anybody to be a critic in the 1990s, but those who accepted the invitation during that decade had dim prospects of their criticism reaching a significant audience. Joel, Mike, and the bots may have paved the way for a generation of amateur movie riffers, wisecracking Beavises and Butt-Heads, and aspiring *Talk Soup* hosts, but prior to the expansion of online participation during the Web 2.0 shift of the mid- to late 2000s, cultural criticism was still primarily reserved for those with high degrees of cultural capital and the resources of business owners who spied profit in sponsoring them.

Though there was and remains much discussion of the early internet as an uncolonized meritocracy where everyone's voice was equal, this promise was oversold. As political scientist Matthew Hindman suggested in his 2009 book *The Myth of Digital Democracy*, many of the same barriers that precluded everyday people from vying for space in the discursive and economic areas of the brick-and-mortar world also existed in the digital world.[31] The myth that everybody's voice online is as loud as everyone else's remains overstated, but the convergence of new and more accessible means of recording, editing, and distributing information and intellectual property, commonly placed under the umbrella of Web 2.0, enabled a new generation of critics and thought influencers to vie for space in a constellation of significant conversations, including the sphere of media criticism. RiffTrax is emblematic of this shift through its innovation of the isolated full-length commentary track.

Audio commentary tracks flourished in the early 2000s as DVD overtook VHS as the home media of choice. Audio commentaries were produced for

Laserdisc as far back as the 1980s, but DVD's capacity for multiple audio tracks and the ability to quickly switch between them invigorated the art of the commentary track. As added value, commentary tracks appealed to consumers with an appetite to know more about their favorite films and to producers enticing those consumers to upgrade from VHS during a period when DVDs remained relatively expensive. As media scholar Matt Hills wrote in 2007, DVD commentary tracks work to intensify the audience's relationships with the filmmakers,[32] creating the feeling of being in the room with the creators, experiencing the movie alongside them as they enlighten viewers, evoking a sensation of privileged togetherness. This sensation recalls the feeling evoked through MST3K's use of Shadowrama, which creates the illusion of sharing theater space with the riffers.

Access to this early wave of commentary tracks came with cost and constraint: commentaries were married to the physical possession of the DVD and commissioned by and subject to the whims of their producers or rightsholders. Commentary tracks most frequently feature directors, actors, production personnel, or industry-approved film historians telling stories about the film's production and/or explaining the motivations behind artistic choices. The results are at the best of times greatly informative, wildly entertaining, or both. Memorable commentary standouts of the early DVD era include Arnold Schwarzenegger's legendarily loopy commentary for *Conan the Barbarian* (Arnold: "exactly"), John Carpenter's effortless banter with Kurt Russell and Roddy Piper on their respective collaborations such as *The Thing* and *They Live*, and Harold Ramis and Ivan Reitman going full MST3K (complete with Shadowrama) for a "live" commentary of *Ghostbusters*. Yet for every memorable commentary, there are several others that are dull, overly technical, or both.

Regardless of their entertainment or informational value, DVD commentary tracks were and largely remain beholden to the power of filmmakers to influence public perception of their work. Hills observes that commentary tracks present the producers as "objects of fascination, and authority, for the audience"; they "enable producers to discuss their 'intentions' and offer up their favored interpretations."[33] Officially produced DVD commentaries are bound to be essentially paratextual: a supplement to and in service of the text and its owners. There are certainly commentary tracks critical of elements of the film or even mocking its quality, but it is a solid bet that if something is uttered during commentary that makes it to an official DVD release, those who stand to profit from it are comfortable with what is said about their asset. Unlike the scenario satirized in the Film Crew's framing device, critics seeking to contradict the preferred readings of a film's producers or rightsholders typically were not invited to the party.[34] Those dedicated enough to try endeavored by maintaining personal review websites with most toiling in relative obscurity until they tuckered themselves out and moved on.

RiffTrax is a vanguard to a new age in which media commentary can be produced and distributed by outsiders who operate counter to or independent of the goals of the film's producers while poaching from the rights holders of the media property being criticized. As digital media distribution expanded in the 2000s, RiffTrax was at the forefront of a cultural shift that disentangled movie commentary from physical media, one which even film insiders sometimes used. When directors Darren Aronofsky and Tom Holland were prohibited from recording commentaries for DVD releases of *The Fountain* and *Child's Play*, respectively, they recorded their commentary tracks independently and offered them to fans via download. Director Kevin Smith even experimented with a live in-theater commentary (e.g., *Clerks II*) that was recorded and later made available for download—a model that both RiffTrax and Cinematic Titanic, another collective of MST3K alumni, would embrace and perfect shortly after.

This agency was theoretically afforded to anyone with access to the technology used to record and distribute audio and later video, though reaching a wide audience was no guarantee. Though relatively few would gain a large audience, a seismic shift in media criticism was nevertheless underway. To forge one's way as a critic no longer required being sanctioned as an authority or securing permission to record and circulate a commentary track. Arguably no individual or organization has utilized their agency to do so more than the producers and performers of RiffTrax. One only need compare the project's longevity and cultural impact to those of the Film Crew to appreciate the iron claw old media held on movie riffing prior to 2006.

RiffTrax did more than democratize which movies could be riffed; it opened a new discursive space for people from all walks of life to publicly participate in riffing. In 2008, RiffTrax established a groundbreaking public marketplace dedicated to amateur riffing with its iRiffs forum, an open-access web shop through which anyone could post and sell their recorded commentaries, with RiffTrax and the riffer dividing the profits. "People are constantly doing it [riffing] themselves and wanted an outlet so we let people make their own and post them and compete with each other," Nelson said in 2009.[35] "That makes it possible for us to check out things we'd never do because the movie is too obscure for us. There are people out there who think we're just picking on the mainstream and so they do films we'll never get to."

Before RiffTrax's creative utilization of internet distribution, amateur movie riffing was alive but remained largely local and ephemeral. Hotspots for MST3K-style riffing existed in spaces such as Northwestern University's annual twenty-four-hour B-Fest (which predates MST3K). Riffing troupes such as Doug Benson's Movie Interruptions, Atlanta's Cineprov, and Austin's Master Pancake Theater built dedicated local followings through live performance and eventually streaming video. Yet before RiffTrax and iRiffs there was no dedicated forum for sharing one's riffing in an enduring format that did not require live synchronous attendance. The age of the YouTube critic was slowly starting; individuals such as James Rolfe (The Angry Video Game, neé Nintendo, Nerd), Doug Walker (Nostalgia Critic), and Michael Buckley (What the Buck!?) were among a select few building large online followings for their personality-driven media commentaries. Video-capture and editing software were still relatively expensive and less intuitive than they would become, requiring significant investment and technical know-how to produce reviews of passable quality. iRiffs promised not merely the possibility but the low-barrier invitation of going on the record and engaging a film before an audience fluent in and appreciative of movie riffing. Though the potential to earn modest income for one's riffing was an attractive feature, the legacy of iRiffs would be the establishment of a recognized and accessible public forum for riffing—a genre that would soon flourish as technological barriers lowered and YouTube exploded in popularity. Megan Condis suggests:

> iRiffs are the ultimate outgrowth of convergence cultures in that they allow audience members to participate in (and profit from) the production of new texts and the creation of new readings of old texts, as some of them are simply new takes on the films that MST3K and RiffTrax have already riffed.[36]

A survey of available iRiffs posted to the RiffTrax website reveals a cornucopia of feature-length riffs, as well as riffs on educational shorts, TV episodes, and music videos, including riffs by notable internet personalities of the era such as Chad Vader and Walker of Nostalgia Critic fame. Some performers, such as psycho-and-zombie couple Gary and Erin Slasher of Hor-RIFF-ic Productions, develop elaborate personae, tapping into the grand tradition of horror hosts such as Vampira or Zacherley. Others project the relaxed stream-of-consciousness vibe of an individual, a screen, and a microphone. Some riffs are professionally produced whereas others are low-fi and apparently improvised like KTMA-era MST3K.

One of the more intriguing possibilities of iRiffs is the potential for performers to approach riffing from specific standpoints or with distinct critical perspectives. Prior to the Netflix era, MST3K's core writers and performers had been predominantly Midwestern, white, masculine, and educated—all standpoints bound to powerfully influence the riffer's perspectives and values. iRiffs presented a space for performers from varying backgrounds and perspectives to riff media of their choice for their own goals, which in theory did not need to be driven by the prime directive of generating laughs. Riffers were afforded a venue to experiment with riffing's capacity for alternate or political critique, exploring the art of riffing's potential as a vehicle for purposeful cultural criticism with potential to be as enlightening as it was funny.

One interesting experiment in riffing as a vehicle for ideological criticism came from Matthew Filipowicz and Josh Bolotsky, comedians and activists who teamed up on "Atlas Riffed," a decidedly leftist riffing of 2014's much-maligned *Atlas Shrugged: Part One*. Filipowicz, a Milwaukee-based comedian and activist, and Bolotsky, an activist specializing in new media, utilize familiar MST3K-influenced riffing techniques to confront and reject the movie's heavy-handed "objectivist screed," deploying an arsenal of contemporary political intertextual references while isolating and magnifying inconsistencies in the film's embedded Randian philosophy.

To execute their critical goals, Filipowicz and Bolotsky lean heavily into intertextual references to political figures from both sides of the political spectrum. When referring to right-wing political figures—Joe Arpaio, Glenn Beck, Dick Cheney, James Imhoff, Alex Jones, Charles and David Koch, Ted Nugent, T. Boone Pickens, the cast of *Fox and Friends*—Filipowicz and Bolotsky evoke negative stigma associated with the individual (Jones' obsession with false flag operations, the Koch brothers' dark money manipulations, Pickens' environmentally hazardous fracking). Here, the duo attempts to transfer audiences' negative perceptions of these figures to the movie's exaggerated portrayals of libertarian heroism. Filipowicz and Bolotsky save enmity for political figures from the center-left and center-right such as Barack Obama and Michael Bloomberg, criticizing their use of drones in the Middle East and brutality toward Occupy protestors in New York, respectively, while also overperforming right-wing scapegoating of Obama for comedic effect, suggesting with tongue in cheek that *Atlas Shrugged*'s fictional financial apocalypse was the result of Obama repealing the Twenty-Second Amendment and socialists outlawing science. Because the film's plot centers on trains, there are plenty of references to future US President Joe Biden and his prodigious use of Amtrak.

Beyond intertextuality, Filipowicz and Bolotsky tug at the seams of the movie's incoherent attempts to reconcile author Ayn Rand's novel with a contemporary setting, riffing on libertarian protagonist Dagny Taggart incongruously taking public transportation to work or the film's portrayal of banker Midas Mulligan going Galt: "Bank CEOs: definitely the people who benefit least from government handouts." Filipowicz and Bolotsky riff frequently on lead actress Taylor Schilling's wooden portrayal of Taggart, comparing her unblinking gaze to David Cronenberg's *Scanners*, while crafting a recurring bit in which Taggart and fellow business idealogue Henry Rearden are emotionless libertarian robots.

"Atlas Riffed" is familiar MST3K-inspired riffing but with its politics boldly on the sleeve. Overall, Filipowicz and Bolotsky's experiment in overtly political riffing produces intriguing results. Each viewer's mileage will vary on whether the riff is funny—practicing objectivists and Fox News devotees will not likely appreciate the joke. Yet to the question of whether MST3K's brief forays into political riffing in shorts like *The Home Economics Story* and *Progress Island U.S.A.* can be cranked up all the way to the front of the mix without totally drowning out the humor, "Atlas Riffed" answers to the affirmative.

As of this writing, the iRiffs marketplace endures but appears to no longer be thriving. In 2011, the iRiffs shop had 650 riffs posted for sale; in 2023, it has 850. This does not mean that the project of promoting amateur riffing online failed or has concluded. Several of the more prolific iRiffs contributors maintain personal websites or have migrated to other formats. Some began on iRiffs only to branch out to new audiences on other platforms. Others gave riffing a shot or two and moved on without garnering much recognition. Once again, the enterprising minds behind RiffTrax were ahead of their time. By the time iRiffs peaked in activity, online review troupes like Red Letter Media, Screen Junkies, and Cinema Sins were among a new generation of media reviewers and critics consciously or unconsciously employing riffing techniques pioneered decades before on MST3K, with a handful building fanbases of millions on their own channels. In 2022, for weekend-warrior riffers who would rather play along at home without recording an iRiff, RiffTrax released *RiffTrax: The Game*, a multi-platform video game based on *What the Dub?!* that allows players to assemble riffs based on existing RiffTrax jokes or script their own. As of this writing the game enjoys a 94 percent positive review score on the digital game distribution service Steam and is regularly updated with new content.

"THAT'S THE REASON WE'RE HERE, TO EXPLOIT EXPLOITATION": LAUNCHING CINEMATIC TITANIC AND THE MADS

By 2007 a new generation of performers was embracing the art of riffing, but key voices from riffing's pioneering age had been absent too long. December 2007 saw the riffing marketplace expand with the launch of Cinematic Titanic, a riffing troupe comprised of MST3K alums Trace Beaulieu, Frank Conniff, Joel Hodgson, Mary Jo Pehl, and J. Elvis Weinstein. A joyous reunion, Cinematic Titanic was Hodgson's public return to riffing following his bitter 1993 split from MST3K; Weinstein had been absent from the riffing game since 1990; Beaulieu and Conniff departed MST3K in 1996. Fans and journalists warmly embraced Cinematic Titanic, heralding it as the century's closest analog to classic MST3K. Fans could have their riffing both ways: RiffTrax targeting Hollywood films and epically bad movies; Cinematic Titanic focusing exclusively on more obscure and schlocky fare, riffing B-grade horror flicks such as *The Oozing Skull* aka *Brain of Blood* and *The Wasp Woman* along with exploitation movies like *East Meets Watts* and *Dangers on Tiki Island*. Whereas RiffTrax's performance was almost entirely verbal, Cinematic Titanic's riffing was more conspicuously embodied: performers appeared on the periphery of the screen in revamped Shadowrama and interacted liberally with the film through visual comedy while breaking into mid-film skits.

Like RiffTrax, Cinematic Titanic embraced independent digital distribution along with self-released DVDs, releasing twelve riffs from 2007 through 2012. The first seven episodes incorporate an MST3K-esque framing narrative in which the Titans must riff movies against their will in an underground bunker, held by decree of an unnamed organization toward the mission of preserving films in a time tube after cinematic preservation has been threatened due to a tear in the electron scaffolding. The time tube framing story was ultimately extraneous, though worthwhile for regular cameos from comedian Dave (Gruber) Allen as Todd, the Titans' liaison to the organization holding them captive. The time tube was abandoned when Cinematic Titanic found its ideal niche in the riffing marketplace: live performance.

As triumphant as Cinematic Titanic was in Shadowrama, the Titans were truly in their element as a touring live performance troupe. With its communal energy, immediate audience response, and banter between performers, live movie riffing is a unique experience from which the five seasoned comedians spun magic. "We're all stand-up comics and performers at heart," Beaulieu told AV Club, "and to get in front of an audience that likes what we're doing—there's nothing better than that, as opposed to doing the TV show where you might wait weeks or months to hear anything. I prefer the live-show format. It's immediate, and it's much more gratifying."[37]

MST3K had dabbled in live performance, first in 1992 with Mystery Science Theater Alive! in which Joel and the bots riffed *World Without End* at the Uptown Theater in Minneapolis. In 1994, MST3K live returned at the MST3K ConventioCon ExpoFest-A-Rama, where in addition to episode screenings and fan sessions, the MST3K cast riffed *This Island Earth*, which they would later revisit in *Mystery Science Theater 3000: The Movie*. Two years later, about twenty-three hundred MSTies reconvened for ConventioCon ExpoFest-A-Rama 2: Electric Boogaloo.[38] In 2009, RiffTrax took its act on the road with a live riff of "the Citizen Kane of Bad Movies,"[39] *Plan 9 From Outer Space*, the first of many live performances at Nashville's Belcourt Theater simulcast to theaters across the United States. As of this writing RiffTrax has over thirty simulcast live performances, many of which were later made available as video on demand and physical media; those that could not be cleared for release beyond the livestream received Just the Jokes MP3 commentary tracks based on the live performance.

Cinematic Titanic was the first riffing troupe to tour the United States, performing on both coasts, in the South, and in the Midwest. Hodgson said he was inspired to pursue live riffing after seeing composer Philip Glass's live scoring of 1931's *Dracula*: "[T]hat resonated with me. It suddenly dawned on me, 'Hey, it's okay—we could just stand there and riff on a movie, and do it like a concert.'"[40] Live Cinematic Titanic performances offered far more than movie riffing, often beginning with warm-up comedy from Allen, Hodgson performing excerpts from his one-man show Riffing Myself, or Weinstein covering Elvis Costello's "Alison" or the "MST3K Love Theme" while playing bass guitar. After the movie's conclusion, the Titans greeted long lines of fans in the lobby to chat and sign autographs. There was genuine interpersonal warmth and a sense of community in being there live that transcended the art of riffing B-movies.

Fortunately for those unable to see the show live, Cinematic Titanic captured five live performances on DVD and video on demand. Best in show, and one of the funniest riffs ever committed to video, is the Titans' magnus opus riff of *The Alien Factor*, the directorial debut of Baltimore B-movie impresario Don Dohler. In the film, an extraterrestrial ship carrying three dangerous specimens crashlands on Earth, and only a mysterious stranger who calls himself Ben Zachary (Don Leifert) can save the day. In many ways *The Alien Factor* is the Platonic ideal of riffing fodder with its silly yet impressive monster effects and unsubtle yet earnest acting. The Titans' performance, filmed at Los Angeles' Largo at the Coronet and released in 2010, is a masterclass for study and a joy to revisit for its calibration of mockery of and grinning affection for a silly but guileless B-movie.

Hodgson begins the performance by introducing his castmates. With each introduction, Hodgson stresses their history as standup comedians in Minneapolis and collaborating on MST3K: "You don't fight like other comics: you write," Hodgson says, heightening the sense of unity while bringing the performers front and center. The Titans show they have not lost any heat on their fastballs since MST3K, delivering thirty-one jokes before the opening credits close, even riffing their own pre-movie countdown: "Five, what a stupid number," Conniff says; "Got to do your warm-ups," Weinstein adds reflexively.

One of the most striking aspects of Cinematic Titanic's live riffing is how each performer's distinct voice shines through in the performance. Hodgson specializes in conversational riffs, hilariously rambling jokes that span the time of multiple rapid-fire ones. "Oh yah, two light beers is my limit, you know?" Hodgson narrates in an exaggerated Scandinavian accent as a doomed bar patron to the bartender. "Good luck with the discount beer and everything and with your hair." Hodgson later trades his folksy Minnesotan accent for full-throated bombast, responding to a synthesizer sound effect with a boisterous rendition of Emerson, Lake & Palmer's "Karn Evil 9": "Welcome back my friends to the show that never ends! Come outside, *Alien Factor*'s about to start. Guaranteed to blow your head apart!" he sings to uproarious applause.

Beaulieu delivers tongue-in-cheek intertextual references ("Keep the beaches open," he says, riffing on *Jaws* as *The Alien Factor*'s mayor argues with the sheriff) and handles vocal impressions and in-character riffs with his gift for dynamic vocal delivery. Beaulieu elicits the biggest audience response of the evening when he punctuates a conversation between Deputy Pete and alien survivor Mary Jane with a perfectly hilarious burlesque riff: as Pete sits down after warmly conversing with Mary Jane, Beaulieu says with adolescent enthusiasm, "Oh man, that was a date. I was on a real live date"; as Pete curiously ends the scene by glancing downward toward his crotch, Beaulieu gulps, "uh oh." Somewhere in the atmosphere above Largo a decade-plus later, Conniff's infectious, bellowing laughter at Beaulieu's adept comic delivery may still be audible, illustrating how immediate feedback from audience and co-performers can elevate even an already clever joke to all-timer status.

Weinstein is the Titans' eagle-eyed go-to man for spotting textual flaws and tugging at the seams of the movie's production, often poking holes in and raising objections over the cast and crew's artistic choices. "What the hell emotion is he trying to play here? Hot?" Weinstein asks incredulously at assistant coroner Steven's (George Stover) close-shot emoting. "The Miller Light people just called to ask them to turn their sign off," Weinstein declares, highlighting the filmmaking cliché of product placement while riffing on an extended musical performance by Baltimore band Atlantis in the middle of the movie's bar scene. As Atlantis's performance stretches on, Weinstein exclaims, "Jesus, how much money did the director owe these guys?" Referring to the film's languorous pacing, Weinstein riffs with a metahumorous flourish, "You know the problem with our particular style of humor, this riffing thing, is that sometimes people are just walking through the goddamn woods." He later calls back to the ponderous scene, announcing, "Remember when I complained about watching people walk around in the woods? Well, that was before I knew walking around in the yard was an option."

Pehl shines at deadpan observational riffing that subverts the tone of the movie. During an early scene in which the sheriff and coroner recoil from the corpse of the film's first alien attack, Pehl comments, "That police car has a definite 'my brother's going to kill me if we don't have it back by six' quality to it," later adding, "Oh, I know the economy is bad, but is the state trooper driving a Beetle?" Later, after an alien is killed following a deadly attack on the mayor, Pehl jokes, "Well it's not the first time someone's passed out on the mayor's lawn without pants." Pehl also supplies 1970s-era pop culture references, embracing *The Alien Factor*'s funky "Me Decade" vibe by comparing the movie's incidental characters to members of the Bay City Rollers and Lynyrd Skynyrd.

Conniff excels with topical and political riffs, often circumventing clear signification for the joy of non sequiturs or exuberant outbursts. When coroner Ruth Sherman (Anne Frith) likens one alien's deadly life-sucking attack to the effects of progeria, saying "the internal organs deteriorate and fail," Conniff jokes, "like the ten o'clock [Jay] Leno show," humorously scoffing at a few scandalized murmurs from the audience. Later, when protagonist Ben describes two aliens as "basically non-thinking animal forms," Conniff answers, "which explains their fondness for Carlos Mencia." Beyond his riffing chops, Conniff also lends sheer joy to the performance thanks to his hearty laughter at his co-performers' best riffs, lending the proceedings an infectious energy. Conversely, he and the rest of the Titans also know when to lay out and let the film amuse the audience without assistance, as in one absurd moment when assistant coroner Steven, intent on burning an alien with gasoline while hunting it in the woods, throws the capped gas can at the alien and runs. In a non-live setting, such a moment would necessitate a riff to mark the ridiculous moment. Instead, the Titans expertly stand by and let the audience revel in the absurdity of the exchange, with Pehl giving the audience plenty of time to process it before adding, "throw the lighter at him."

Cinematic Titanic ended its run after a farewell tour in 2013. The performers went their separate ways with all but Weinstein transitioning quickly to other riffing projects.[41] Pehl became a regular contributor to RiffTrax, forming the riffing combo Bridget and Mary Jo with Jones-Nelson in 2015. The duo specializes in domestic hygiene shorts with titles such as *A Word to the Wives . . .*, *Naturally . . . a Girl*, and *Duties of a Secretary* while riffing such feature-length movies as *Gravity*, *Angels' Revenge* aka *Angels' Brigade*, and *Inspector Mom*.

Bridget and Mary Jo frequently riff on gender norms and roles, often employing a strategy of comedically exaggerating reductive attitudes toward women and femininity in ways that highlight the fact that said attitudes are both real and illogical. For instance, when riffing *The Maturing Woman*, a short highlighting social stigma surrounding women and aging, Jones-Nelson and Pehl comedically exaggerate negative anti-women stereotypes, ironically joking about having to go the bathroom frequently, not smiling enough, withholding sex, being subservient to a husband, being obsessed with cosmetics, and being poor drivers. When one of the characters laments struggling to choose between career and family, Jones-Nelson and Pehl suggest she take up a career as a recipe blogger before riffing on the inanities of endless blog photos and random musings.

When riffing *The Home of the Future: Year 1999 A.D.*, Jones-Nelson and Pehl recoil in horror when a young mother reveals her age to her child: "I didn't expect this movie to be so graphic," Jones-Nelson says, adding, "Back in those days 44 was like 244." In their updated riff on MST3K season six standout *Angels' Revenge*, the duo's approach of exaggerating, thereby exposing, a film's anti-women ideology is a masterclass. Jones-Nelson and Pehl frequently riff on the seven "Angels" with references to food avoidance ("It was only half a Twix. Eat!"), Spanx, driving a minivan poorly, Curves, Yelp, Skinnygirl cocktails, sun-damaged hair, and cheerleading camp, each riff overperforming the movie's grotesque conception of feminine empowerment. This dynamic of subverting the film by exaggerating its message can be summed up in two riffs: Pehl's wry observation, "Yeah right, a girl doing something all by herself," reminding the audience that women are regarded as less-than in their capacity for action, and Jones-Nelson's suggestion of "See, women kill bloodlessly because they know they'd have to clean it up," reminding the audience that women's action is defined by domesticity.

As a combo, Jones-Nelson and Pehl approach riffing with a distinctively interpersonal, conversational dynamic that stands out in contrast to the more rapid-fire riffing style of their fellow MST3K alumni. More so than any other riffers in the MST3K extended family, Jones-Nelson and Pehl project a sense that they are riffing for one another, often asking one another leading questions or riffing conversationally for extended periods. For example, when riffing *Sherlock Holmes and the Woman in Green*, Pehl responds to the title card by riffing, "The true story of an adult Girl Scout"—a recurring riffing technique of subverting the movie premise by purposefully misinterpreting its title card. Jones-Nelson piggybacks in a dramatic tone, "Her insatiable desire for Thin Mints will thrill . . . and shock! . . . you," to which Pehl replies, as if dropping the pretense of performing comedy, "Ooo, now you've got me thinking about Tagalongs." During "The Second Annual Bridget and Mary Jo Christmas Special!" Jones-Nelson and Pehl overtly ditch the task of riffing for conversation when guest Beez McKeever, MST3K's beloved prop diva, enters the audio feed. Though Bridget and Mary Jo's riffing is as cleverly scripted and rich in references and jokes as any troupe in the MST3K school, their warm interpersonal dynamics and conversational riffing style also lend their riffs a relaxed vibe reminiscent of the internet's most inviting livestream and let's play videos.

Beaulieu and Conniff revived their iconic partnership as the Mads, debuting their live "The Mads are Back" duo in 2015 and as co-hosts of the "Movie Sign with the Mads" podcast in 2016, where they discussed movies new and old until 2020. That is when everything changed: the planet shut down suddenly in March 2020 with the onset of the coronavirus pandemic, and the Mads' live touring agenda was suspended indefinitely. In July 2020, the Mads returned to live riffing in an unconquered space, the livestream, and kept the flame of live movie riffing alive during the indefinite global lockdown.

On July 21, 2020, the Mads beamed their live riff of Ed Wood classic *Glen or Glenda* to their sheltering-in-place audience, with a ten-dollar ticket buying access to the livestream and a download of the show later. The Mads began livestreaming one riff per month, mixing previously unriffed B-movies (*The Tingler*, *The Choppers*, *The Brain from Planet Arous*) with MST3K classics (*Santa Claus vs. The Devil*, *Manos: The Hands of Fate*, *I Accuse My Parents*) and their recurring "A Night of Shorts" shows. As a duo, Beaulieu and Conniff perform with all the chemistry honed from sharing stage and screen across four decades, with

Conniff adopting an excitable persona and Beaulieu using a comparatively conversational tone. Their dynamic is illustrated in their memorable riff of the kitschy 1968 short *Marijuana* starring Sonny Bono, with Conniff riffing on mask mandates and referencing orgies and the Manson family while Beaulieu mocks Bono's gold lamé pajamas and declares a scene in which young pot fiends rob a store to be "the worst episode of *CHiPs* ever." When *Marijuana* depicts a burning US map as Bono lectures on the potential dangers of nationwide marijuana addiction, Conniff sings the Bonanza theme, to which Beaulieu quips, "It is the Pot-terosa."

The Mads' riff is typically followed by a question-and-answer with the two comics along with moderator and producer Chris Gersbeck and special guests from the worlds of comedy, entertainment, and riffing. Pehl joined the Mads in the riffing livestream game in 2021, debuting *The Mary Jo Pehl Show* in which she and Gersbeck cover a variety of media on Twitch in a comparatively more unstructured and unscripted format, including After School Specials, vintage advertisements, Pehl's past media projects and old diaries, or Pehl accompanying her father on a guided tour of a local Menards.

The story of movie riffing's rebirth in the wake of MST3K's 1999 cancellation is one of technological adaptation, independence, and perseverance. After the decade began with a string of short-lived projects hamstrung by mass media's slow transition to the internet age, the successful launches of RiffTrax, Cinematic Titanic, the Mads are Back, and *The Mary Jo Pehl Show* saw MST3K's principal riffers rekindle their craft with new ventures that embraced emergent modes of distribution and a convergence of new (and old) avenues for engaging an audience that refused to disperse after MST3K's 1999 demise.

Through it all, it was undeniable that a large audience devoted to movie riffing existed well into the twenty-first century, one that was willing to support their favorite riffers whether it meant attending live shows, purchasing riffs à la carte, or tuning into livestreams. Fans refused to give up on the legacy of MST3K, and neither would the man who started it all. Following the end of Cinematic Titanic, Hodgson devised an opportunity to go public with his most famous invention in a brave new media landscape, one defined by fan participation and crowdfunding.

"JUST ANOTHER MUG
IN A YELLOW JUMPSUIT"

The Netflix Revival and the Gizmoplex

On June 28, 2016, the past, present, and future of *Mystery Science Theater 3000* converged at the birthplace of movie riffing for the *RiffTrax Live! MST3K Reunion Show*. MSTies who packed Minneapolis's State Theater or watched via livestream witnessed the most comprehensive reunion of MST3K onscreen talent to date: RiffTrax's Bill Corbett, Kevin Murphy, and Michael J. Nelson; Bridget Jones-Nelson and Mary Jo Pehl; Trace Beaulieu and Frank Conniff as the Mads (Beaulieu: "I forgot to tell you, Mike, I was going to be late for work for about thirty years"); and the creator of modern movie riffing, Joel Hodgson. The show featured live riffing of seven shorts culminating with the different troupes uniting for two joyous full-cast "riff-a-paloozas."

Anyone in the audience who tuned movie riffing out the day the Satellite of Love (SoL) was grounded in 1999 would have been mystified by the inclusion of a ninth riffer, one with no prior history aboard the SoL. The newcomer, introduced by Murphy as "new meat" and by Corbett as "the untested one," was actor, comedian, and podcaster Jonah Ray. Co-host of TV's *The Meltdown with Jonah and Kumail* and The Nerdist podcast, Ray was a familiar voice to fans tuned into the broader MST3K universe, having hosted and interviewed MST3K alumni on his shows and namechecking *Mystery Science Theater 3000: The Movie*'s riffing of *This Island Earth* on two comedy albums.

Ray's first public riffing trial under the MST3K flag commenced when he and Hodgson riffed *Americans at Work: Barbers & Beauticians*, a 1959 AFL-CIO-produced industrial short. Ray fit right in. He flashed strong intertextual chops;

"Let my sideburns grow!" Ray growls as Charlton Heston's Moses when the narrator discusses barbers in ancient Egypt, later evoking a Frank Nelson-esque "yeesss!" in response to a dapper, mustachioed barber. Identifying the short's agenda of framing 1950s barber shops as welcoming community spaces, Ray introduced a contradictory dose of Jim Crow–era realism by suggesting barbershops were xenophobic spaces in which patrons discussed "the coming race war." Responding to the short's suggestion that women's commitment to beautification is best rewarded by men's approving glances, Ray amplifies the short's problematic sexism with "So when you see a woman on the street, give her a shrill whistle and command her to smile," drawing the loudest audience applause of the short.

Funny and charming on stage as ever, Hodgson demonstrated impressive chemistry with Ray, the two feeding off one another with dueling Frankenstein's monster impressions in response to a square-headed beautician, jesting over Hodgson's hair or Ray flubbing a line, and infusing the performance with kinetic humor via an enthusiastic podium switch. Warm audience reception to the performance indicated that Ray passed his trial, and with Hodgson's affirmation—"Natural-born movie riffer right here"—Ray's MST3K debut went a long way toward demonstrating that he was indeed the right kind of people. "Can I thank all you guys for making *Mystery Science Theater 3000*?" Ray asked later in the performance. "It made me who I am." Many applauding in the audience, some of whom were not yet alive when new MST3K episodes were being produced, could identify with the sentiment. Ray had lived out MSTies' greatest collective fantasy: riffing alongside Hodgson with most of the principal cast there standing by to symbolically endorse him.

The RiffTrax-hosted MST3K reunion was neither riffing fantasy camp nor mere foray into nostalgia. It was known by June 2016 that Ray was the heir apparent to helm the SoL for the upcoming MST3K revival spearheaded by Hodgson, once again in charge of the franchise he invented after Shout! Factory acquired the rights to MST3K from Mallon and Best Brains, Inc. The excitement over MST3K's impending return had simmered since November 2015 when Hodgson announced a Kickstarter campaign to crowdfund the return of MST3K. The "Bring Back MYSTERY SCIENCE THEATER 3000" Kickstarter quickly rocketed past its initial two million dollar goal, ultimately raising an astonishing $5,764,229 from 48,270 backers, with the final six hundred thousand dollars needed to fund a full fourteen-episode season raised externally.[1] MST3K's phenomenal Kickstarter, along with creative involvement from celebrities such as Felicia Day, Joel McHale, and Patton Oswalt, captured the public imagination and drew mainstream media attention from outlets such as CNN, *Wired*,[2] NPR,[3] and UPI.[4] "Bring Back MYSTERY SCIENCE THEATER 3000" closed as the most profitable film- or TV-related Kickstarter campaign to date, eclipsing the $5,702,153 raised for 2014's hyped *Veronica Mars* movie.[5]

"I AM REOPENING MY FAMILY'S MOST LEGENDARY EXPERIMENT": RELAUNCHING MST3K

That MST3K's return was not only real but a pop culture phenomenon is a credit to Hodgson's ingenuity and a recognition of crowdfunding as an important sea change in the mass-mediated landscape, one ideally structured to liberate beloved cult texts like MST3K from the banalities of chasing the ghost of mass appeal. Using Kickstarter, the crowdfunding apparatus of choice for media and creative projects, artists seek start-up capital by securing modest monetary contributions from what they hope will be a sufficiently broad base of the right people who get the project, thus allowing fans to collectively fill the role of executive producer. In exchange for buying in, the artist offers backers tangible or intangible rewards, typically tiered based on level of contribution, in addition to the ultimate promise of producing the advertised work. For "Bring Back MYSTERY SCIENCE THEATER 3000," rewards included digital downloads; tangible goods such as t-shirts, coffee mugs, and physical media; and once-in-a-lifetime incentives such as appearing in an MST3K episode, having a personal inside joke appear in an episode, or actual Tom Servo or Crow T. Robot puppets used in an episode.[6]

Though independently funding a project while thumbing one's nose at old-media powerbrokers is an appealing fantasy for fans, successful Kickstarter campaigns are only the beginning. The crowdfunded total, even six million dollars, likely will function "as a tool as much for generating publicity and tangibly demonstrating an audience"[7] more than the actual budget to produce a show or product. Hodgson confirmed this to backers: "it helps us send a really clear message to all of those boardrooms of executives, to let them know that you're out there and waiting for more new MST3K."[8] Though there had been more lucrative Kickstarter campaigns than the one launched to raise money for MST3K, most were for discrete consumer products (tabletop games, video games) or one-off special productions. MST3K ventured into unconquered territory by crowd-funding capital to fund the open-ended existence of a media entity of its scope.[9]

Despite the reality that even six million dollars could not deliver MST3K to a utopia of pure autonomy, the role of fans in bringing MST3K back is undeniable. As communication scholar Annamarie Navar-Gill concluded in her study of the *Veronica Mars* Kickstarter, "The support of a fan audience boosts the artistic and authorial credibility of a creator, which has real implications for economic power and industry decision-making."[10] The enthusiasm surrounding the Kickstarter bestowed not only buzz but legitimacy for Hodgson to shop MST3K to distributors. Hodgson could boast a built-in audience ready to spend money to support the show. In an age characterized by media fragmentation and the decline of mass monoculture, a small yet passionate fanbase is often more attractive to content producers than a larger-but-dispassionate casual viewership. If fans were willing to fork over nearly six million dollars for the idea that MST3K would return, then they would surely pay to partake in the finished product.

In hindsight, MST3K was a poetically perfect vessel for crowdfunding success because it represents, as explored throughout this book, a culture and a sensibility as much as a media product. It was this dynamic from which Hodgson, along with his partners at his production company Alternaversal Productions, LLC (later renamed Gizmonic Arts), spun Kickstarter gold. To direct the "Bring Back MYSTERY SCIENCE THEATER 3000" campaign, Hodgson recruited Ivan Askwith, a guru on crowdfunding for cult media properties. As Askwith explained in 2018's *We Brought Back MST3K* documentary, fans perceive MST3K as not merely a television series but rather:

> as a cause that might stand for something, as kind of a sense of humor, as something that had brought certain kind of people together, meant something specific to people at a certain time in their lives and wasn't around on television or on the internet anymore except for old episodes, and what it would mean to bring that back, why somebody might actually care rather than just if they would care.[11]

This audience eager to buy into MST3K did not materialize en masse because there was a Kickstarter. Rather, fans bought in because the mechanisms of online crowdfunding made the collective action required to reinvigorate MST3K feasible to conceptualize.

Environmental activist Roger Hallam suggests the dynamic of "conditional commitment" used by crowdfunding websites enables participation because "potential participants in collective action can be reasonably confident, through the visibility of data on the pre-commitment, of what will happen: where, when and with whom."[12] When "Bring Back MYSTERY SCIENCE THEATER 3000" obliterated its initial two million dollar goal with the beloved and wholesome Hodgson leading the project, it gained credibility beyond the most hardcore fanbase. Fans could amplify their support through social and mediated networks without the cognitive dissonance of possibly chasing what could be a pipe dream. In contrast to 1999 when crestfallen MSTies could take out an ad in *Variety* imploring some corporate media broker to rescue MST3K with no certainty anything would come of it, the advent of web-based crowdfunding provided evidence that their support was tangibly contributing to their hearts' desire. Backer and Executive Producer Greg Tally articulates the allure of MST3K's perfect storm of goodwill and identification well, stating, "As a fan of the show, I was intrigued for the possibility of using this to leverage a tiny little business and support the arts through one of the best sci-fi shows ever. I couldn't help myself: I had to jump in."[13]

Like independent online distribution before it, the power of crowdfunding to circumvent material barriers to cultural expression has played a fundamental role in the twenty-first-century expansion of movie riffing. In 2013, RiffTrax launched its inaugural Kickstarter campaign to raise funds needed to secure rights to stage a live riff of the eminently mockable *Twilight*. Ultimately, 6,113 backers pledged $254,860 to the project. Crowdfunded movie riffing quickly reached its first stress test when, three months prior to the scheduled performance, RiffTrax announced it was unable to secure rights to *Twilight*, explaining via Kickstarter update: "[Summit/Lionsgate] just felt that the Twilight series is still very much a going concern for them, i.e. something that's still going to earn them millions and millions more dollars, and it didn't make sense to let a few guys crack jokes on top of it—at least not this summer."[14] Rebuffed but resilient, RiffTrax pivoted to fulfilling a longstanding fan request by instead riffing *Starship Troopers*. It was the first of several successful Kickstarter campaigns for RiffTrax, each playing an essential role in securing rights to publicly riff otherwise prohibitively expensive stinkburgers such as the 1998 American *Godzilla*, *Anaconda*, and *The Return of Swamp Thing*—not to mention facilitating RiffTrax's hosting of 2016's live MST3K reunion. "It was no six-and-a-half-million dollars," Murphy joked during the show, "but we truly can't do a show on this scale without you guys."

No doubt being rewarded for contributing with a shirt, poster, or souvenir enticed many backers to buy into the "Bring Back MYSTERY SCIENCE THEATER 3000" project, but research on crowdfunding suggests designated rewards are secondary to the sense of active participation in the creation of art and a feeling of connection with a beloved artist.[15] For MSTies unable to spend twenty-five thousand dollars to become an executive producer or spare eight thousand dollars for a genuine Crow or Servo puppet, frequent production updates from Hodgson and being immortalized in end credits as vital members of the *Mystery Science Theater 3000* Revival League both allowed fans behind the curtain of the show's production and let them take a bow before the world. When the documentary *We Brought Back MST3K* chronicled the creation of season eleven, there was no ambiguity as to the identity of the "we" in the title. On this rare occasion, being the entity named in the title of an MST3K production was safe from mockery.

"MEANWHILE, AT NETFLIX . . .": MST3K ENTERS THE STREAMING ERA

One month after Hodgson and Ray's live appearance with RiffTrax, streaming video behemoth Netflix announced via Twitter it was picking up MST3K's eleventh season.[16] The success of the Kickstarter campaign and the surrounding cultural buzz undoubtedly played a role in *MST3K: The Return* landing on the biggest platform possible. Securing digital distribution with the reigning and ascending titan of streaming media at a point when streaming was overtaking physical media as the United States' preferred home-entertainment medium was quite a coup. US citizens would increase spending on streaming services 22.6 percent in 2016,[17] Netflix leading the way with stalwarts *Orange is the New Black* and *House of Cards* joined by phenomenal newcomer *Stranger Things*. Netflix grew even bigger in 2017, eclipsing one hundred million subscribers[18] while going all in on producing original programming.

Releasing alongside significant competition from fellow debutants such as *Dear White People, Mindhunter, GLOW*, and *13 Reasons Why, MST3K: The Return* was a critical and audience darling right out of the gate. It was rated the top new Netflix series of 2017 by *Business Insider* based on critical and audience approval scores[19] and earned a 100 percent "fresh" rating on Rotten Tomatoes[20] based on positive reviews from critics at publications such as AV Club,[21] IndieWire,[22] *Slant Magazine*,[23] and Vox.[24] Eighteen years after being expelled by the great god Cable Television, MST3K once again capitalized on a changing media landscape while cable TV found itself clinging to relevancy with the streaming revolution underway.

Season eleven was initially conceived as interweaving the casts of the Comedy Central and Sci-Fi eras,[25] but Hodgson instead introduced the world to a new principal cast. Ray plays Jonah Heston, a cool and capable maverick intergalactic long-haul driver for Gizmonic Institute. Gallantly responding to a phony distress call, Heston pilots his ship to the dark side of the moon, where he is captured by chief antagonist Kinga Forrester (Day), daughter of Clayton and granddaughter of Pearl, and second banana Max (Oswalt), who longs to be known as TV's Son of TV's Frank.[26] Kinga, commander of the Moon 13 research station, has revived her family's evil movie-watching experiment, imprisoning Ray on the SoL where Cambot, Gypsy (Rebecca Hanson), Tom Servo (Baron Vaughn), and Crow (Hampton Yount) await. Two months after capture, easygoing Jonah has made the SoL his home, demonstrating Joel-esque talents for mechanical invention by rigging Gypsy's body to the ceiling (and giving her a Midwestern accent) and gifting Servo the power of in-theater flight. Despite being initially framed as something of a Mary Sue by his adoring overseers at Gizmonic (Erin Gray and Wil Wheaton in memorable cameos), Jonah is received with exasperated dismissal by Crow and Servo, who reject the new guy's earnest attempts at bonding outside the theater. "Joel is the father figure. Mike is the older brother," Ray explained. "I'm the irritating kid from next door that wants to hang out with Crow and Servo."[27]

Longtime MSTies will immediately recognize season eleven's efforts to capture the relaxed, soft sci-fi vibe of the Joel era with many of the show's original defining tropes returning after receding from view following Hodgson's departure. The invention exchange makes its triumphant return, as occasionally do fan letters. Like Joel, Jonah seems generally content with life on the SoL and seems minimally motivated to escape captivity, with IndieWire suggesting Ray's "complete lack of cynicism" and "good-hearted edge" are his defining characteristics as host.[28] Without sacrificing the show's classic do-it-yourself aesthetics, *MST3K: The Return* boasts impressive production values with intricate miniature models, Kinga's vibrant and richly rendered Moon 13 lair, and unprecedentedly active and ambulatory bots brought to articulate life by professional puppeteers.

The show's dramatic premise as an ongoing science experiment is again foregrounded with the nature of the experiment adapted for a new cultural epoch. The new stakes of the experiment provide fascinating insight into how media consumption has changed since the 1990s when MST3K could be understood as an extended allegory for being subject to and resisting the overwhelming seduction of mediated mass culture. Unlike her father who endeavored to subjugate the masses through the oppressive qualities of the perfect bad movie, Kinga's objective is malevolently adapted for the postmodern, fractured consumption habits of twenty-first-century audiences. Kinga's stated mission is simply to "blow up this brand and sell it to Disney for a billion dollars," chiding Max that the experiment (and thus the show itself) "isn't about ideas or making things—it's about sheer star power." Jonah's plight, the audience can surmise, stands in for our own always-plugged-in existence in which we are forever within a camera's gaze, our data is always being monetized, and influencers or YouTube personalities have replaced movie stars or pro athletes as today's most accessible avenues to relevance. Jonah is not being held captive as an experimental vessel to break like Joel or Mike; instead, Jonah and the bots' roles in the experiment are as cogs co-opted to revive a bankable product in a hypermediated hellscape in which hustling is synonymous with selling out and all culture and experience are commodified and exploited.

The experiment at the heart of *MST3K: The Return* also reflects the nature of twenty-first-century celebrity culture. Kinga's desire to torment and ultimately break Jonah stems from her assumption that if she can jellify his mind and spirit, he will become more compelling to a jaded audience attracted to human wreckage. "People don't watch TV for sane," Kinga lectures Max, lamenting Jonah's resilience to her bad movies. "They want crackpot housewives, drug-addled chefs, unstable bachelorettes." Kinga's defining evil traits, beyond general rudeness to Jonah and Max, are her Disney-esque lusts for reducing culture to capital and for hoarding and exploiting intellectual property, which extends to her repeatedly stealing Jonah and the bots' in-theater chatter for invention exchange fodder (Kinga: "Deal with it! Corporations do it all the time"). For Kinga Forrester, the perfectly perverted embodiment of post-capitalism's perpetual churning of culture into commodity, every thought, relationship, and ritual (even the rite of matrimony) is source material for potential monetization. "The only preferences of yours I care about," she tells Max, "are the ones I sell to Google for datamining." At first glance, Kinga's evil desires seem more benign and less ambitious than her father's. Yet, as its mega-successful Kickstarter demonstrated, MST3K represents a sensibility—a way of moving through and making sense of the world—to its fans as much as a TV show. What could be more poetically terrifying than a soulless, Disneyfied MST3K lumbering zombified through the motions of movie riffing, reborn eighteen years later as disposable content in some brand management company's portfolio?

When the nature of evil changes, the dialectical constitution of heroism changes with it. Within MST3K's dramatic universe, Joel and Mike are heroes because their respective resiliencies thwarted Dr. Forrester's discovery of a perfectly weaponized bad movie. By contrast, Jonah does not seem to be riffing defiantly to stave off domination from his evil nemesis like the classic sci-fi protagonists his surname namesake would play. He is not subverting Kinga's mission of co-optation and commodification by, for example, consciously tanking the show's marketability to Disney, etc. By 2017, conquering evil through singular will and determination is a relic as outdated and stale as the abrasive retrograde masculinity in one of season eleven's Doug McClure movies. Even trading captivity for freedom seems only a fleeting whim to Jonah during *MST3K: The Return.*

As the audience's avatar, Jonah is heroic not for his overt defiance but for his integrity and embrace of a riffer's constitution. Jonah Heston is a distinctly twenty-first-century fictional hero because he is uncorrupted and unbroken by the pressures of being constantly subjected to mediated culture. He willingly embraces his role as media consumer without sacrificing his agency and voice, resisting the threat of being subsumed and flattened by the threat of exploitation while finding fellowship and shared sensibility among his fellow riffers. Within the mythos of *MST3K: The Return,* selling out is the new world destruction; integrity is the new salvation.

For all its impressive multilayered characterization, would the new MST3K live up to the hype as entertainment? It would not be enough for MST3K to simply return; it would have to deliver the goods and stay true to the show's rich history while taking the premise in new directions. Anything less than reclaiming its throne as the funniest and smartest comedy on TV would be a letdown: no pressure from the 48,270 backers who chipped in $5.7 million to sit by digital proxy in the producer's chair.

The first new MST3K experiment in eighteen years is *Reptilicus*, a Danish-American *Kaiju* movie. "Nothing says 'international' like a picture of the U.S. Capitol building," Servo riffs in response to the American International Pictures logo, inaugurating a new era with his first riff in eighteen years. With that, Jonah and the bots settle into a comfortable rapid-fire riffing groove, lovingly pillorying *Reptilicus* by utilizing classic MST3K riffing techniques with references updated for the twenty-first century. There are intertextual references galore, with jokes alluding to *The Wicker Man, North by Northwest, Hamlet, The Elephant Man,* and *Gilligan's Island* that would have fit seamlessly into a Joel or Mike episode. Jonah and the bots observe the film's poor film stock, critique its use of stock footage to replicate military action against Reptilicus, and mock the film's incongruous tires squealing on a dirt road (Crow: "That Jeep's got its own Foley artist"). The riffers deploy levity to undermine the allegedly tense final showdown with Reptilicus: "Maybe a couple of souvenir t-shirts will make him think twice," Servo jokes as a soldier aims a bazooka at the rampaging Kaiju. In 2017, the riffing tools of yore cut through *Kaiju* cheese as sharply as ever.

Arguably the most enduring moment of *MST3K: The Return* comes outside the theater when Jonah and the bots serenade audiences with the original song "Every Country Has a Monster." Credited to songwriters Storm DiCostanzo and Paul Sabourin (aka Paul and Storm) and delivered impeccably by Ray, Vaughn, Yount, and Hanson, "Every Country Has a Monster" is the most lyrically adroit and vocally dexterous song in MST3K's rich musical history. An instant crowd-pleaser and watercooler moment within MST3K fandom, the two-and-a-half-minute song incorporates twenty-four fictional monsters (twenty-five if Kinga counts) from across film and folklore. "Every Country Has a Monster" established Ray and the actors behind the bots as dynamic and versatile performers, winning over musical theater lovers and *Kaiju* devotees in a single song.

Season eleven continues with the most bonkers movie of the season, *Cry Wilderness.* The comically inept Bigfoot fantasy—as Max warns, "Hope you like stock footage and incomplete Bigfoot costumes"—honors MST3K's historical role in reviving and preserving obscure, unspeakably bad films in the ignoble tradition of *Manos: The Hands of Fate, The Dead Talk Back, Werewolf,* and the Coleman Francis trilogy. Jonah and the bots feast on the film's amateurish Bigfoot effects ("Homo erectus [Zach] Galifianakis") and abundance of nature stock footage, including a recurring bit by which forest animals offer child protagonist Paul sensible homespun wisdom in mocking of Bigfoot's telepathic communications to Paul. The episode also establishes an important in-universe bridge to MST3K's past with cameos from Pearl, Bobo, and Brain Guy (Pehl, Murphy, and Corbett reprising their roles) while introducing Pearl's uncanny clone Synthia (Hanson), whom Pearl left as a surrogate to maintain a standoffish relationship with her love-deprived granddaughter. Star-studded season eleven also beheld the onscreen return of MST3K writer and supporting actor Paul Chaplin (playing an Observer hivemind manager) as well as celebrity cameos by Joel McHale, Neil Patrick Harris, Jerry Seinfeld, and Mark Hamill.

For the discerning connoisseur of movie riffing style and substance, there are salient and subtle differences between *MST3K: The Return* and the show's previous incarnations. The rate of riffs is consistently high, rivaling the highest riffs per minute in the show's history, and there are more multi-sentence riffs, giving season eleven's riffing a different cadence from the relatively more succinct riffing of previous seasons. The riffers' intertextual references have been both updated and broadened in scope. Joining late twentieth-century film, television, and pop culture references ("Ladies and gentlemen, the Bland-Tastic Four!"; "Peter Cushing: The Dr. Who that no one is tempted to cosplay") are more contemporary references to social media such as Twitter, Facebook, LinkedIn, and Tinder; MMORPGs and video game culture (Servo: "Wait, if we just hang back we'll get all the XP after Reptilicus dies"); youth-oriented cultural institutions such as Coachella and Bonnaroo; and distinctly twenty-first-century sociopolitical phenomena such as common core education, Alex Jones–esque false flag rhetoric, and the Bechdel Test.

There are still classic riffs on Midwestern culture, including Minnesota-centric references to New Ulm, Lake Minnetonka, the Mall of America, and the 2015 killing of Cecil the Lion by dentist Walter Palmer. With a more demographically diverse writing staff and the show no longer being produced in Minnesota, such references register as internal callbacks to MST3K's Midwestern legacy more than contemporary intertextual references recognizable to an international streaming audience. In service of bridging MST3K's past and present, *MST3K: The Return*'s riffing is liberally peppered with internal callbacks to legacy riffs—"It stinks!" "Watch out for snakes." "He tampered in God's domain"—along with deeper cuts for superfans: "This is where the fish lives." "We wanna hear 'California Lady.'" "Wonderful, wonderful Super Dragon."

The Netflix era of MST3K resumes and intensifies the show's historic sense of self-awareness. MST3K's experiment-within-a-show premise meant Joel, Mike, and the bots always acted as though they were aware they were being watched by both the Mads and an audience, but *MST3K: The Return* adds another layer. It is established that characters such as Jonah, Kinga, and Max are conscious of and literate in MST3K's vast internal vocabulary though, unlike the bots, they were not present for the show's first 197 experiments. This dynamic raises the interesting question of whether MST3K exists as an in-universe reality TV show or if recordings of experiments on Joel and Mike are available for archival viewing. This adds another layer to MST3K's self-referential universe-building; whereas Joel, Mike, and the bots once built in-world continuity through callback riffing to their own in-theater experiences,[29] Jonah and company tap into MST3K's previous callbacks as simultaneously intertextual riffs and self-aware nods to MST3K's metahistorical cultural impact.

Analytically inclined aficionados of movie riffing will find it interesting that Jonah and the bots often evoke pop culture references that would be lost to obscurity if not for their second life as part of the MST3K riffing lexicon, which is to say today's audiences will recognize them as MST3K references more than their pre-MST3K antecedents. In other words, some riffs during Netflix-era MST3K are more accurately riffs on cable-era MST3K riffs. Generally, most riffs referencing pop culture rely on the audience's immediate understanding of the antecedent being referenced. As an informative example, when riffing *The Land That Time Forgot*, Crow (apparently forgetting the theme song's imperative to "just relax") asks Jonah what he drinks while imprisoned on the SoL. "Well, have you ever seen the opening of *Waterworld*?" Jonah asks. "Ew," Crow responds, delivering the punchline, "you drink copies of *Waterworld*?" Here, the comedic impact of the joke requires the audience to (1) recognize *Waterworld* as the 1995 Kevin Costner movie, (2) to recall *Waterworld*'s infamous scene in which Costner's character drinks his own purified urine for survival, and (3) that *Waterworld* is an oft-mocked and stigmatized film—hence, Crow's ironic disgust of the film being less appetizing than consuming one's own urine. Without making each of those cognitive links, Crow's joke makes no sense.

By contrast, *Reptilicus* features references to advertising campaigns for *Rat Patrol* (in Color!), K-Tel's "Explosive Hits" music compilations, and Smucker's fruit jelly, all of which are far older and unknown or irrelevant to the average Netflix subscriber.[30] Yet fans fluent in MST3K will recognize that trio of moldy oldies as semi-recurring riffs from classic episodes, and new fans need only search for them on websites such as The Annotated MST (www.annotatedmst.com) to trace their origins. When riffing *Cry Wilderness*, for instance, Jonah references *Candid Camera* ("Little does Paul know we've got a real skunk waiting in the bushes. We think the joke will be on Paul"), a show that peaked in cultural relevance twenty years before Ray was born but would be familiar to veteran MSTies as a semi-recurring reference. When Crow says, "Diarrhea is like a storm raging inside you" as *Avalanche*'s titular antagonist rolls downhill, he is referencing an obscure Pepto-Bismol commercial but is more directly calling back to a half-dozen riffs on said commercial in past MST3K episodes. An online search for the phrase "diarrhea is like a storm raging inside you" returns multiple results for MST3K before Pepto-Bismol is pinged. In an age when seemingly every commercial, trailer, and memorable TV or film clip is uploaded to YouTube, learning the original significance of the reference is only a few clicks away, yet within MST3K fandom, the origins of the riff are more trivial than essential. With condolences to some pioneering 1990s ad wizard, "Diarrhea is like a storm raging inside you" has become MST3K's de facto intellectual property.

As when Joel inhabited the SoL, Jonah and the bots rarely attack the films they riff with venom, demonstrating general goodwill toward the hapless riffing fodder literally flushed their way via Kinga's proprietary liquid medium Kingachrome. This dynamic of riffing with a smirk instead of a sneer is deftly articulated in episode 1108, *The Loves of Hercules.* As Hercules drives a horse drawn cart through a misty field, Jonah earnestly says to the bots, "See that pink smoke? Nowadays all this would just be done in CGI, which I feel is cold and sterile." "Yeah," Crow responds enthusiastically, "you don't get the warmth of these shots of incompetent people trying their very hardest." This affection toward filmmakers trying their hardest is on display throughout the Netflix era of MST3K, from the selection of bright and colorful movies to the riffers' seemingly bottomless patience for the incompetent but redeemable films they riff. As head writer Elliot Kalan (co-host of the long-running bad movie podcast *The Flop House*) explains:

> We want to almost take a movie that is not good, to put it mildly, and . . . it's almost like alchemy. The riffing is the philosopher's stone that turns it into gold or something enjoyable, and you have to find the rights riffs and the right tone and the right style to . . . lead the movie through a transformation process until it become enjoyable to watch.[31]

This constructive, heuristic tone that has long permeated MST3K is amplified throughout *MST3K: The Return* and is a logical extension of the show's ethos for a new era in which entire subcultures have mushroomed online constituted around embracing and celebrating problematic media artifacts (movies, music, video games) through mockery. When fans fire up YouTube to watch The Nostalgia Critic go on a red-faced rant about *Batman & Robin* or The Angry Video Game Nerd faux-defecate on an Atari Jaguar CD console, they do so to celebrate bad movie or bad game culture, not to loath the target of their favorite online critic's performative wrath.

As with any cult media entity that resumes production after a period of discontinuance, fans passionately scrutinized the new MST3K, conducting micro analyses of episodes and comparing *MST3K: The Return* to previous MST3K eras in forums, comment sections, blog posts, and video essays. Some online commenters criticized the initial episodes of season eleven for their riffing being too rapid-fire and overly wordy. Some panned the show's new production model by which the riffers record their dialogue separately, rather than together on set, as creating a dynamic of disconnection between the characters in the theater. As with any passionate fanbase, particularly a fanbase once heatedly divided in allegiance to Mike over Joel or vice versa, such debates and comparisons can represent important (and mostly healthy) engagement with a beloved text, reconciling differences and organizing the new production in relation to the old. A survey of fan discourse online in comment sections and forums such as the Mystery Science Discourse 3000 forum on mst3k.com suggests that fans became increasingly comfortable with the show's updated style within a few episodes. Online fan reception became increasingly appreciative as season eleven progressed, suggesting that the fandom at large bought into the new MST3K in relatively quick order after initial anticipation faded out and the task of critical assessment set in.

On Thanksgiving 2018, a poetic date given the show's Thanksgiving 1988 birthday and longstanding association with Turkey Day, MST3K returned to Netflix for its twelfth season, dubbed "The Gauntlet." Season twelve consists of six episodes, tied with season seven for the shortest run in the show's history. Another six-episode season may have struck an ominous tone for MSTies who recall what transpired after the abbreviated seventh season, but the relative brevity of season twelve came with a twist: the season's entire eight-hour runtime is designed to be binge-watched with the concept of binge-watching incorporated diegetically into the show's in-universe experiment. "Forget binge-watching this show," Kinga gloats. "We're going to binge-make it!"

Hodgson explained in an interview with *The Nerdist* that season eleven's fourteen-episode run of eighty-plus minute episodes ran counter to viewing habits of Netflix viewers accustomed to powering through more compact, self-contained seasons.[32] Apparently, Netflix viewers were not bingeing their way through season eleven as they were other series such as *Stranger Things* or *House of Cards*. "We created this enchanted forest that people were wandering into, but they weren't wandering out of," Hodgson said, explaining,

> I just feel like we really satisfied *MST* fans, but they're used to lots and lots of *MST*s and they want really a lot. When you think of nice normal people who might go, "What's this weird show I've heard about?" Now, I feel like we made it in a shape that newcomers can get to it and people who like the show [;] it's the same format but it's more breezy I think.[33]

The implication that MST3K was not meeting Netflix's private audience-engagement expectations was foreboding, but it is fitting that MST3K, the show that conceptually foregrounded the comfort (or lack thereof) of extended screentime, would finally explore the binge-watching phenomenon through meta-storytelling.

The concept of binge-watching burst into the cultural lexicon in the early 2010s as streaming video services such as Netflix (mid-transition away from DVD service as its primary model), Amazon Prime Video, and Hulu approached maturity and began nudging DVD out as the home-viewing medium of choice. Defined in a *Television & New Media* study as "a consumption of more than one episode of the same serialized video content in a single sitting at one's own time and pace,"[34] binge-watching occupies an interesting liminal status within the United States' binge-and-purge relationship with mediation and indulgence. On one hand, the correlation of this practice to bingeing burdens it with negative stigma of lack of self-discipline and self-care, the viewer's equivalent of eating or drugging oneself toward an early grave. Outlets such as the *Wall Street Journal* reported of dazed TV viewers mindlessly "gobbling up" entire seasons of shows like *Breaking Bad* without regard for anything other than the idiot box and the body's base urges.[35] Binge-watching has been popularly associated with hedonism, laziness, social isolation, and disregard for hygiene, family, and society. "TV binges are replacing time once spent on more active parent-child experiences," professor and author Stephen Camarata lamented in *TIME*. "Bingeing indirectly sends the message, 'This screen is more important to me than spending time with you.'"[36]

Yet it was clear early on that despite social anxieties and reactionary hand-wringing, binge-watching was immediately popular among streaming audiences, and streaming services were keen on encouraging it. In 2013 Netflix crowed about survey results that indicated 61 percent of US streaming customers engaged in binge-watching and that 73 percent have positive feelings about doing so.[37] Research suggested that binge-watching was more strategic than mindless, with viewers setting aside extended blocks of leisure time to fully engage with particularly intriguing programs rather than rationing regular viewing periods, thereby exerting greater agency over their engagement with mediated programming. During 2020's society-altering coronavirus pandemic, binge-watching would assume a therapeutic form for some viewers pining for escape from the depression and anxieties resulting from extended social isolation.

Viewers with long memories (and stocked media shelves) may also note that the social phenomenon of binge-watching entire TV series was not new but rather an evolution of the DVD boxset boom of the prior decade, when fans eagerly purchased entire seasons of acclaimed series such as *The Sopranos*, *Lost*, and *The Wire* to own and consume on their own schedules. Along with the concept of binge-watching came the evaluative concept of binge-worthiness, the idea that shows of certain quality—often associated with cult status and complex narrative storytelling—deserved to be binged, which producers were thrilled to discover bestowed cultural capital on their most binge-worthy properties. Scholar Mareike Jenner suggests that the production of "bingeable texts" helps to legitimize new, good streaming programming, separating it from less-prestigious old, bad TV associated with traditional scheduling models. As Jenner writes, "if viewers stand to earn valued cultural capital, it is socially acceptable to binge, rather than watch several hours of scheduled television."[38]

MST3K fits sublimely into the ongoing conversation on binge-watching because its writers could play off both sides of the debate through layered storytelling. In terms of in-universe storytelling, "The Gauntlet" playfully taps into the negative stigma of binge-watching as eroding mental and bodily health. Within the show's universe, being forced to binge "The Gauntlet" inflicts Jonah and the bots with the intense physical and psychological punishment of being forced to endure eight nearly consecutive hours of bad movies, and outside the theater it shows. Crow, Servo, and Jonah (having just returned from season eleven's aborted cliffhanger in which he was to marry Kinga to boost ratings) express escalating despair and discomfort with each new movie, and for the first time during the Netflix era, the viewer is allowed to believe that Jonah could succumb to Kinga's experiment. Apart from Yongary's agonizing slow death in episode 1107, Jonah stays endlessly frosty throughout season eleven, never truly breaking down as Joel did versus *The Castle of Fu-Manchu* or Mike versus *Invasion of the Neptune Men*. Yet the idea of binge-watching six movies has Jonah and the bots on their heels immediately and keeps them reeling throughout season twelve's host segments.

On the other hand, MST3K as a Netflix-showcased media property benefits from positive associations with binge-watching. In several important facets, MST3K comfortably embodies the profile of an artistically superior binge-worthy series. An award-winning critical darling, MST3K boasts a passionate cult audience motivated to pour over its pleasures and micro details. Though it only fleetingly trades in traditional narrative storytelling (see chapter 3), the richness of its symbolically complex, vocabulary-building riffing rewards focused analysis and line-by-line engagement. Toward that end, MST3K's writers bestowed "The Gauntlet" with the most narrative coherence in the series since season eight, with an intriguing subplot unfolding by which Jonah and the bots slowly craft an escape plan between in-theater stints.

As it always has, movie riffing remains the centerpiece of season twelve. "The Gauntlet" begins with infamous *E.T.* knockoff *Mac and Me*, which Jonah and the bots mock for its ugly aliens (Jonah: "He's like a Teddy Ruxpin with the face torn off"), shameless derivative storytelling, and even more shameless product placement (Crow: "Mom, do we have any Reese's Pieces? I don't know, it just seems like they'd fit into this somehow"). *Atlantic Rim* follows, marking MST3K's first attempt at riffing a mockbuster (Crow: "*Atlantic Rim*? Could you be more Pacific?"). Jonah and the bots dispatch the dismal *Pacific Rim* rip-off for its unlikeable protagonist, uninteresting love triangle plotline, and terminal dearth of giant mech fight footage.

Third in line is *Lords of the Deep*, a Roger Corman–produced underwater sci-fi movie that borrows liberally from *Alien* and *2001: A Space Odyssey*. Jonah and the bots lambast the dimwitted mustachioed hero Jack, including Crow breaking out his deft Morgan Freeman impression ("Jack O'Brien crawled to freedom through five hundred yards of underwater air ducts so poorly directed I can't even imagine. Or maybe I just don't care enough to"). The episode also introduces its first new character of the season, effervescent movie monster conservationist Dr. Donna St. Phibes (Deanna Rooney) from the Habitat for B-Movie Monsters. Dr. St. Phibes pops in after *Lords of the Deep* to share the wonders of the film's adorable (but deadly) titular monster in the vein of Joan Embery or Jack Hanna's appearances on *The Tonight Show*. St. Phibes, who debuted in 2018's Mystery Science Theater 3000 30th Anniversary Tour, quickly became a fan favorite online, inspiring fan art and suggestions for a spinoff series to feature her.

The second half of "The Gauntlet" unfolds with *The Day that Time Ended*, *Killer Fish*, and the return of series icon Ator (*gesundheit*) in *Ator: The Fighting Eagle*. In addition to sharp riffing ("This'll make a great selfie for my Tinder photo," Servo riffs as Ator first wields the Sword of Torin. "Shooting down, chin up, duck face, boobs together"), episodes 1204 to 1206 feature some of MST3K's most exciting narrative storytelling and the return of the long-departed Dr. Erhardt (Weinstein, appearing in his first MST3K episodes since 1990). Erhardt arrives on Moon 13 to scatter the ashes of Dr. Forrester and TV's Frank as Kinga, with help from newly articulate Synthia,[39] attempts to recover a recording of season three favorite song "Idiot Control Now" to fulfill her father's last wish.

Upon completing the final film of "The Gauntlet," Jonah and the bots are to be forced back to Earth as captive performers in Kinga's live touring MST3K. Yet Jonah, Crow, and Servo, who between in-theater stints had been shuttled between the SoL and Moon 13 to drill storage holes for "The Gauntlet's" stored Kingachrome capsules, spring their trap, ensnaring Kinga and Max in a hidden theater in their storage facility where *Mr. B Natural* is showing. "Oh, no," Kinga realizes in horror, "Jonah's hoisted us by our own petard! We've become our own cautionary tale!" It is left ambiguous how long they are to be trapped or how long *Mr. B* will continue to play.

The most resonant emotional climax of season twelve—and ultimately, of the Netflix era of MST3K—comes when Kinga, just prior to being trapped by Jonah, delivers a truly chilling evil monologue down the lens to the at-home audience. In it, Kinga addresses viewers as "the lowlifes who just spent eight hours of this precious one-way trip we call life watching schlock" with her malevolent vision fully unfurled: "Every time you see a movie with a cheap set, I'll be there. Every gaping plot hole or monster costume with a zipper: I'll be there, too."

Midway through her monologue, Kinga transitions away from the narrative premise of her father's experiment—bad movies as being uniquely decapacitating—to a more chilling evocation of postmodern dread:

> Fact is, we've always been here. We're the ones who sucked all the art and replaced it with trash. We're the ones who fill your life with so much noise and visual clash, you can't tell the good from the crap anymore. Maybe the truth is out there, but we've mixed it up with so much other stuff; you're never gonna find it. You're alone in this whirlpool of meaningless images . . . your minds have been skillfully mismanaged since the beginning. You are not a person, you're just a data point, and with all the multitudes working to amuse and distract you, there's no one taking the time to look out for you.

Kinga's monologue, delivered with scary sneering malevolence by Day, taps deeply into contemporary anxieties over the diminishment of film and of art in general. More urgently for the viewer, Kinga appeals to the notion that engagement with art or film no longer offers authentic expression or insight. Kinga's taunting the at-home audience as being lost and disoriented in a "whirlpool of meaningless images" evokes Fredric Jameson's theories on postmodernism's "waning of affect"[40] and Jean Baudrillard's theories on simulation and hyperreality[41] which, broadly applied here, support Kinga's suggestion that our capacity to identify and connect to what's real and meaningful in life has been severed.

Unlike the contemporary media myth of *The Matrix* films that suggests we have been fooled by a false reality through our reliance on mediation, Kinga articulates a much more dreadful scenario truly out of Baudrillard: that we are not merely deceived but rather that our interpretive capacities have been permanently mutated with no way to disentangle reality from hyperreality. Even if we turn off partisan news, reality TV, social media disinformation, and the mass-marketing of unhealthy products or ideals, there is no going back because there is no "back" we could identify.

Fittingly, our final image of season twelve depicts Jonah and the bots departing for Earth over the end credits, leaving it ambiguous as to whether they have escaped their captors or if they will be forced to carry on with their overlords only temporarily detained. However, the audience can rest assured that their heroes remain resilient after enduring "The Gauntlet," with Jonah singing through his lingering pain on the doo-wop-flavored "Your Horrible Show (Your Show Stinks)." The ending reinforces *MST3K: The Return*'s distinct construction of heroism; though Kinga taunts, "there's no one taking the time to look out for" us, Jonah and the bots remain with us, helping us navigate and make sense of the mediated gauntlets we experience in our lives.

Just days before Thanksgiving 2019 and amid MST3K's third national live tour, The Great Cheesy Movie Circus Tour, MSTies received the all-too-familiar bad news: MST3K had been canceled again. Netflix would not be picking up a third season of the show, one of several popular series to be cut down by the streaming giant in a frenzy. "We don't know what the future holds for the show, it always seemed to figure out how to survive," Ray tweeted while breaking the news. "From Comedy Central to SyFy. Then kept alive by RIFFTRAX & Cinematic Titanic. whatever happens, I want everybody to know that getting a chance to be on this show was a dream come true."[42] Hodgson confirmed over Twitter that MST3K was done producing episodes for Netflix. Yet he assured his followers, "It's not the end of MST3K, [*sic*] It's just the end of the first chapter of bringing back MST3K."[43] Instead of sixteen years, MSTies would need wait only five months for the next chapter. It would prove to be MST3K's most ambitious and liberating move to date.

Mystery Science Theater 3000—The Return (Netflix), season 1, 2017. Shown: Jonah Ray.
NETFLIX / PHOTOFEST © NETFLIX

"F.Y.I., I LOVE HAVING MY OWN PANEL": RIFFING ON COMIC BOOKS WITH MST3K

While Netflix's cancellation of MST3K was certainly a blow to both creators and fans, neither group was ready to give up on the beloved series just yet. Prior to Netflix axing the show yet again, Hodgson had been playing around with the idea of piloting the SoL into previously uncharted territories, specifically comic books. Thus, in 2018, Hodgson partnered with Milwaukie, Oregon–based publisher Dark Horse Comics to launch the six-issue miniseries *Mystery Science Theater 3000: The Comic*. Co-written by Hodgson, Harold Buchholz, Matt McGinnis, Mary Robinson, Seth Robinson, and Sharyl Volpe and featuring art by Todd Nauck and Mike Manly, the comic spins out of the reboot series. In it, Kinga and Max use a device called the Bubbulat-R to drop Jonah and the bots—including new additions Growler and M. Waverly—into old public domain comics like *Horrific*, *Black Cat*, *Funny Animals*, and *Johnny Jason, Teen Reporter*. Jonah and pals replace characters from each story and comment on the overwrought action in self-aware fashion, all while Kinga and Max try to monetize the SoL crew's plight via sponsorship from Totino's Pizza Rolls.

Mystery Science Theater 3000: The Comic combines Nauck's expressive artwork with pages from the public domain comics, with the SoL crew added in over existing characters along with additional word balloons that signal when a character is riffing on the original dialogue. Meanwhile, Growler and M. Waverly pop in occasionally to inject additional humorous commentary on the proceedings. Running from September 2018 to May 2019, the limited series generated lots of laughs as Jonah and company made witty observations about the juvenile stories in which they found themselves. For instance, upon landing in the 1940s and assuming the role of sidekick to the scantily clad adventure heroine Black Cat, Jonah observes, "Even the darkness feels old." Elsewhere, speaking to the editor of the fictional *Green City Journal* while in the guise of plucky teen reporter Johnny Jason, Servo muses, "Isn't this the same cigar from the first issue?" Crow, meanwhile, dons the tattered robe of a Crypt Keeper–like figure who lurks in the pages of the short-lived 1950s horror anthology comic *Horrific*. At one point, Crow's hooded head looms ominously above an old castle, prompting the robot to excitedly declare "I'm huge!" in a callback to one of MST3K's most oft-repeated jokes. Throughout its six issues, *Mystery Science Theater 3000: The Comic* adroitly demonstrates that riffing can be adapted to almost any situation across a variety of media.

However, not everyone agreed that MST3K's transition to the printed page was entirely successful. Media blogger and MST3K fanatic Michael Cook of Thoroughly Modern Reviewer praised the series, writing "*Mystery Science Theater 3000* makes for a really funny, really enjoyable, and really good comic" thanks largely to the "clever, surprising, and enjoyable" way that the creative team "tweaked the *MST3K* formula to best work within the medium of comics."[44] Comics reviewer Stacy Baugher, on the other hand, writes that the comic "reads like an episode, but that reading is off from the series," mostly because some jokes "seem forced, and at times it reads like a contest to see who could deliver the most relevant, or irrelevant, joke the quickest."[45] Longtime MSTie Jason Segarra of the pop culture site AIPT describes *Mystery Science Theater 3000: The Comic* as "a fun experiment that proves the series' formula of quick-witted quips juxtaposed against mediocre films from yesteryear is best left in the theater."[46] According to Segarra, MST3K's humor feels "misplaced in this more visual format" mainly because "many of the crew's most successful jokes are not meant to be read, they're meant to be heard." He concludes by writing that though "a lot of the magic is lost in the translation from the screen to print," *Mystery Science Theater 3000: The Comic* is nevertheless "a fun and worthwhile read . . . that could maybe have used a more draconian editor."

Segarra's review represents probably the fairest assessment of *Mystery Science Theater 3000: The Comic* and perhaps best encapsulates the limited series' strengths and shortcomings. According to the critical consensus, MST3K's maiden voyage into comic books was a fun but not altogether successful experiment. Readers may disagree, of course, and at least one of your authors (that would be Christopher J. Olson[47]) would like to see the SoL crew tackle more public domain comics in the future with the help of Dark Horse. However, it should be obvious by now that MST3K's format is better suited to television—or a similar medium, at least—than to comic books. Thankfully, it would not be long before the series landed back on the small screen.

"AND WE'LL STREAM THEM IN THE GIZMOPLEX": A PROPRIETARY PLATFORM FOR RIFFING

Soon after their unceremonious departure from Netflix, Hodgson and his team hatched a plan to free MST3K from the shackles of traditional models of production, distribution, and exhibition. Instead, they would deliver new episodes directly to fans via a proprietary platform devoted solely to all things MST3K. As Gavin Jasper of the website Den of Geek put it, "Hodgson and friends are going the Bender route (minus the blackjack and hookers) of making their own streaming service of sorts specifically for MST3K."[48] This new platform would take the form of the Gizmoplex, which Hodgson envisioned as both a "premiere theater" and a "tourist attraction" that can be accessed "on a lot of your different devices and on smart TVs and stuff like that."[49] More importantly, perhaps, the Gizmoplex would allow fans to watch "with friends and chat,"[50] thus advancing the participatory fan culture that MST3K fostered from the very beginning. Starting with the show's first episode, MST3K's creators encouraged viewers to leave messages on KTMA's answering machine, to write letters that would be read on the show, and to "keep circulating the tapes," thereby sharing episodes with others. With the Gizmoplex, MSTies could engage with the show in real time thanks to advanced communication technologies like the internet and streaming video.

More than just encouraging participation, though, the Gizmoplex would grant fans a renewed sense of ownership over MST3K by once again making them executive producers of yet another iteration of the show. As with the Netflix revival, Hodgson and his collaborators turned to Kickstarter to fund their new venture. On April 6, 2021, Hodgson announced the new campaign titled "Let's Make More MST3K & Build the Gizmoplex!!" via an update to the previous "Bring Back MYSTERY SCIENCE THEATER 3000" Kickstarter campaign. To help promote the campaign, the MST3K team organized several livestream events, with the first taking place on April 26, 2021. Most consisted of members of the MST3K crew riffing on old episodes of the show, though one took the form of "The Jackbox Showdown!" which saw cast members compete against one another while playing humorous digital games like "Tee K.O." and "Talking Points." The whole thing culminated with "The Final Countdown, Part II," a livestream telethon featuring appearances from such guests as Dana Gould, Rhett Miller, and the Rock-afire Explosion, the animatronic band featured at ShowBiz Pizza Place restaurants from 1980 to 1992.

Fans were offered further enticement in the form of stickers, holiday cards, t-shirts, posters, Blu-ray box sets, new episode downloads, weekly production updates, acknowledgment of their support on social media, having their name featured in the end credits of an episode, and more. However, perhaps the most important reward was a months-long pass to the Gizmoplex streaming service, meaning that those who contributed gained access to brand new episodes of MST3K as soon as they premiered. Such incentives were hardly needed, though, as delighted fans rallied to support the new project; by May 8, 2021, more than thirty-six thousand MSTies had pledged a total of $6,519,019 to help build the Gizmoplex and resurrect their favorite show once more,[51] making it one of the most successful crowdfunding efforts in history. Thus, much like the muscle-bound protagonist of Zombie Nightmare, MST3K would once again rise from the grave of cancellation to continue its mission of mocking some of the worst movies ever made.

Production on MST3K season thirteen commenced almost immediately af-terward, with pre-production starting in June 2021. This phase consisted largely of clearing film rights, hiring writers, securing a production crew, determining the shooting schedule, and allocating the show's budget.[52] From there, things moved at a rapid clip as the crew started writing episodes in June 2021, while shooting kicked off in October of that year.[53] Episodes were shot piecemeal over the next few months, with production taking place mainly in Philadelphia, Pennsylvania, and Los Angeles, California. In this phase, actors performed against a green screen so that the new virtual sets could be added in later. Principal photography ran until January 2022, with post-production taking place throughout much of February. Following a whirlwind schedule, production of season thirteen officially wrapped near the end of February 2023, all while the MST3K crew simultaneously em-barked on the live MST3K Time Bubble Tour, which ran from October 30, 2021, to February 6, 2022. Throughout it all, Hodgson and his team kept fans in the loop throughout via their promised weekly production updates posted on Kickstarter, as well as sharing behind-the-scenes photos, taking backers on virtual set tours, and sending out blog posts detailing the entire process. In doing so, the creators kept the show's longstanding tradition of fan participation and dynamic media consumption alive and well in the digital age.

Preview versions of the new episodes debuted exclusively for Kickstarter backers starting in March 2022, with the completed episodes being made widely available in May 2022. The cast of the Netflix revival returned for season thirteen, but they were joined by some new faces and voices—well, new to anyone who had not attended any of the MST3K live shows, perhaps. Versatile performer Emily

Marsh, host of both the Great Cheesy Movie Circus and the Time Bubble live tours, made her Gizmoplex debut as hapless Gizmonic employee Emily Connor (originally Crenshaw), the latest unwilling subject of the Forresters' movie riffing experiment. With a name inspired by Linda Hamilton's character in *The Terminator*, Emily is portrayed as clever and resourceful, possessing deep knowledge of both popular culture and quantum mechanics, though a bit too trusting for her own good. She finds herself trapped aboard Kinga's latest nefarious invention the Simulator of Love, an exact replica of Jonah's satellite, after helping to install it. She is joined by duplicates of Servo (Conor McGiffin) and Crow (Kelsey Ann Brady, marking the first time the character was played by a woman), as well as GPC (Yvonne Freese), an updated version of Gypsy renamed to avoid cultural insensitivity toward people of Romani descent.

Longtime fans were excited to learn that Jonah and Emily would encounter some old friends as well; both Mary Jo Pehl and J. Elvis Weinstein returned to reprise their roles as Pearl Forrester and Dr. Laurence "Larry" Erhardt, respectively. Pearl joined Kinga in the newly constructed moon base Moon 1 to help her granddaughter torment the various SoL crews, largely because she wanted to forge a closer connection with Kinga before shuffling off this mortal coil. Kinga, however, dismissed her grandmother's affections, still bitter over the years of neglect. Dr. Erhardt, meanwhile, popped into the Gizmoplex to team with Pearl for a riff on *Cavalcade*, a short featuring vignettes about various unrelated topics including phone repair, amateur astronomy, and ostrich racing.

While fans greeted these homecomings warmly, diehard MSTies were overjoyed to welcome series creator Hodgson back aboard the SoL for the first time since his brief appearance in a special feature included in Rhino's DVD release of *The Giant Gila Monster*. Hodgson resumed his riffing duties after Kinga's new financier, the mysterious Dr. Kabahl (Baron Vaughn, playing a character inspired by the 1936 film *Things to Come*), ordered her to bring back one of the show's original hosts. With Dr. Erhardt's help, Kinga retrieved a version of the SoL from the year 3000 manned by Joel Robinson. However, because his bots were on a spacewalk at the time, Robinson is joined by the Crow and Servo from the Simulator of Love. Hodgson would also once again don the comically oversized hazmat suit of Ardy (a play on the acronym R&D, which stands for research and development), the put-upon lackey who "flushes" the liquified movie to the SoL crew, a role he originated during MST3K's Netflix years. Throughout season thirteen, riffing duties would be handled alternately by the three different crews, who came together for a holiday-themed riff in the season's final episode.

Though originally intended to consist of twelve episodes, the season thirteen Kickstarter proved so successful that Hodgson and his crew could afford to make a total of thirteen new installments, with the last one serving as a new holiday special and thus continuing a tradition started all the way back in season three. Across the new season, the different crews took turns speaking back to some of the goofiest cinematic atrocities ever made, from Mexican wrestling movies to superhero knockoffs, and from Italian sci-fi flicks to yet another adventure starring everyone's favorite flying turtle, Gamera. The films riffed in season thirteen harken back to many of movies featured in prior seasons of MST3K. Starting things off, Jonah and his robot pals faced down the horrors of *Santo in the Treasure of Dracula*, *Robot Wars*, *Gamera vs. Jiger*, *The Million Eyes of Sumuru*,[54] *The Mask*,[55] and *Munchie*, a film so inconceivably awful it gives both *Manos* and *Cry Wilderness* a run for their money. Over on the Simulator of Love, meanwhile, Emily and her crew try to survive against the overwhelming cheesiness of *Beyond Atlantis*, *Doctor Mordrid*, *The Batwoman*,[56] and *The Shape of Things to Come*. Joel and his bots stepped in to tackle *Demon Squad* and *The Bubble*. In the final episode of the season, all three crews teamed up to riff on the insipid fantasy film *The Christmas Dragon*. Along the way, the casts and crew of MST3K participated in livestream events, celebrated trash cinema via month-long themed programming, produced humorous ads for sponsors like BearManor Media and Onyx Path Publishing, and riffed on numerous shorts such as *The Wonder of Reproduction* and *Let's Keep Food Safe to Eat*.

Starting March 13, 2023, season thirteen of MST3K ventured outside of the Gizmoplex to land on both Tubi and Pluto TV, allowing more people to check out the new episodes. As with *Mystery Science Theater 3000: The Comic*, critical reception to season thirteen was decidedly mixed. Dan Wiencek of Pop Dose wrote that whereas the show's original incarnation "used to look comfortingly homemade, it now just looks cheap" due to shooting much of the new season in front of green screen,[57] necessitated by the ongoing COVID-19 pandemic. Wiencek continues, "Season 11 started with the lackluster *Reptilicus* before finding its groove with the far superior *Cry Wilderness,* and Season 13 unfortunately, in my view, repeats that dynamic." Conversely, Wiencek's colleague Tony Redman expressed more affection for the latest iteration of his favorite series, stating that real-world circumstances led "to some unfortunate (but creative) workarounds, but as long as the performing and riffing stay strong, everything else is gravy."[58] Other reviewers found a lot to love in the new season, such as Den of Geek's Eirik Gumeny, who wrote that while the latest version of MST3K "may be smaller and scrappier in every way," the riffs "are still rapid-fire."[59] Jim Vorel of *Paste Magazine* similarly observed that "once you get past technical issues with the livestream or the interruption of sponsored content in the broadcast, [episode 1301] shows a promising and comfortably familiar start for Season 13."[60] Overall, MST3K had managed to charm critics with its new season despite an updated aesthetic, primarily because the format remained intact.

Fans also appeared divided over the new episodes. Reddit user Spats_McGee started the "Unofficial season 13 review thread!" inviting other users to offer their thoughts on the most recent batch of episodes.[61] Some respondents had good things to say. For instance, RecallGibberish, who offered up the first response, felt that season thirteen "was worthy of the original series, in ways that I thought the two Netflix seasons fell a bit short, even if I liked them as well." User lunardaddy69 concurred with this assessment, writing "I was glad for every second of it, tbh. It's just fun to have it all back and I love how earnest and fun it all is." Other users, however, were less enamored of the show; GrandPriapus wrote rather disparagingly, "Maybe, just maybe, when the series wrapped on after season 10, it should have just stayed that way." Spats_McGee, the user who started the thread, also expressed a negative opinion, calling season thirteen "an unfunny slog" that lacked the "biting satirical edge that made the 90's episodes so funny." A user going by the handle of sandowd offered up perhaps the most measured assessment of the season, writing "Well, the sets were janky, the skits were hit-and-miss, and the riffs were good to great throughout. So, one of the better seasons, I'd say." Based on these comments, at least some fans were content to listen to the theme song and remember that MST3K is just a show, and they should really just relax.

"JOIN US, WON'T YOU?": THE PARTICIPATORY NATURE OF MST3K

While season thirteen may have proved somewhat divisive, it nevertheless indicates a bright future for MST3K, one that promises to amplify the show's relationship with its devoted fans and its willingness to embrace digital technologies such as the internet. From the start, the SoL crew invited viewers to become a part of the riffing experience, asking them to call in, write letters, send emails, and start comment threads. During the KTMA years, MST3K staved off an early cancellation thanks to the intervention of fans who inundated the small cable access station with missives of support in the form of letters and answering machine messages, some of which appeared on the show itself. This participatory spirit would continue during the show's basic cable days, as each episode ended with the SoL crew imploring viewers to write in to the "Mystery Science Theater 3000 Information Club," an official fan club that allowed viewers to connect with both the show's creator's and other MSTies.[62] The show also encouraged tape trading thanks to its repeated mantra of "keep circulating the tapes," urging fans to record episodes and share them with others, thus growing the fandom. This idea lives on in the form of Kickstarter campaigns and livestream events, all intended to spread the word about MST3K and keep it going for years to come. These days, rather than circulating the tapes, MSTies can keep circulating the URL.

At the same time, MST3K has long relied on advanced communication technologies to grow its audience. Starting with the answering machine messages that poured in throughout the KTMA era and continuing with dedicated UseNet groups and bulletin boards that sprang up during the World Wide Web's early days, MST3K has become synonymous with technologies that allow people to reach out and touch someone across vast distances. As mentioned, MST3K was one of the earliest series to embrace the connectivity offered by the internet, using it to develop a passionate fanbase willing to spread the word about the show via message boards, chat groups, and other digital avenues. Now, MST3K has embraced the power of crowdfunding, one of the most participatory platforms around, as Hodgson and his collaborators turn to Kickstarter to fund new episodes made outside of traditional production contexts. By eliminating the intermediary and launching their own streaming platforms, MST3K's creators can now deliver new episodes directly to MSTies, who in turn help to fund the production and thus gain an even greater sense of ownership of the beloved series. More than ever before, MST3K is truly for the fans.

Because of its focus on participation and digital media, the show has also fostered a vibrant and thriving community comprised of riffers from around the world and all walks of life. As mentioned, the spirit of movie riffing lives on in the form of podcasts such as *The Flop House*, *We Hate Movies*, *How Did This Get Made?* and more, which set out to mock such terrible films as *Fateful Findings*, *Nukie*, and *The Love Guru*. Digital gamers have also gotten in on the act with YouTubers like the Game Grumps and the Angry Video Game Nerd routinely tearing apart dreadful video games like *Link: The Faces of Evil* and *McKids*, a McDonald's tie-in game. In addition, movie riffing has gone global, making its way to places like Uganda and Germany courtesy of VJ Emmie and the comedy duo of Oliver Kalkofe and Peter Rütten. Emmie, who refers to himself as a "video joker," provides a running commentary on the films of self-taught Ugandan director Nabwana I.G.G., most famously *Who Killed Captain Alex?* and *Bad Black*. Produced in the Ugandan slum known as Wakaliga, these films are known for their low production values and high entertainment quotient. Throughout each film, VJ Emmie injects enthusiastic exclamations, including his repeated declaration of "Uganda!" during action sequences, and humorous observations, as when he dubs a performer with a slim physique as the "Ugandan Arnold Schwarzenegger." Your authors do not know whether VJ Emmie has ever seen MST3K, but his enthusiastic riffs are very much in the tradition of those featured on the show.

Kalkofe and Rütten, meanwhile, draw inspiration directly from MST3K to mock bad movies such as *Supershark* and *Mega Piranha* via their satirical show *SchleFaZ*, a German word that roughly translates to "the worst movies of all time." The show features a similar format, with Kalkofe and Rütten introducing the films and occasionally interrupting them to engage in humorous skits in between mocking them. Pop-ups reminiscent of those used in the VH1 series *Pop-Up Video* are used to provide background information on the film or to remind viewers of whatever drinking game the hosts are engaging in during the episode. The duo has proven themselves adept at making intertextual references while riffing on the films they watch. For instance, while watching the superhero fiasco *Superargo vs. Diabolicus*, an Italian/Spanish co-production, Kalkofe and Rütten compare the film to the *James Bond* franchise and turn its many allusions to that series into a drinking game. Similarly, they note that the fantasy flick *Orcs!* feels like an ultra-low-budget cousin to director Peter Jackson's luxurious *Lord of the Rings* trilogy. They also suffer through films previously mocked by the SoL crew, including *Laserblast*, *The Million Eyes of Sumuru*, *Santa Claus*, and *Wizards of the Lost Kingdom*. VJ Emmie and *SchleFaZ* both illustrate that MST3K's influence has spread far and wide since its inauspicious debut on a small Minnesota UHF channel in 1988.

Ultimately, MST3K's longevity results from its creators' willingness to embrace both its fans and new digital technologies, along with a tendency to experiment with new forms of production and distribution. By fostering an active fan community comprised of people willing to follow the show across different networks and platforms, Hodgson and his collaborators have ensured that the series will continue for years to come. They have also ensured that movie riffing will live on well into the future, as others use the SoL crew's tactics to respond to and poke fun at a variety of media from films to television to video games and more. In the end, so long as cheesy movies exist, people will continue to riff on them.

The saga of the Gizmoplex took a surprising turn in November 2023 when Hodgson and company's crowdfunding campaign to raise funds for season fourteen concluded without reaching its minimum four million dollar funding goal. The season fourteen crowdsourcing campaign was announced in October 2023 and was hosted entirely on MST3K.com. In stark contrast to its paradigm-shifting predecessors on Kickstarter, the campaign got off to a slow start, leaving the question of whether it would be successful ominously hanging over it for its duration. Despite Hodgson announcing a series of budget-minded compromises that dropped the funding minimum from $4.8 million to four million dollars, the campaign ended in heart-wrenching failure on Turkey Day weekend, topping out at $2,715,304 raised from 18,419 contributors,[63] less than half the totals of the two Kickstarter campaigns. The all-or-nothing dynamic of crowdfunding meant no money was collected, and the immediate future of MST3K was suspended in uncertainty.

As of this writing, a comprehensive postmortem of what went wrong with the 2023 crowdfunding campaign has yet to be conducted. A survey of online discourse points to several potential contributing factors. Some of the public was apparently under the misguided notion that the 2021 Kickstarter campaign to build the Gizmoplex was funding the show in perpetuity. Despite Hodgson swiftly addressing the misconception, a portion of previous backers apparently felt burned by being asked to contribute again and took to forums such as Reddit to voice their discontent. Some 2021 Kickstarter contributors expressed frustration about delays and unexpected additional shipping costs in receiving physical rewards, which Hodgson attributed to manufacturing and shipping delays caused by the coronavirus pandemic as well as issues with a contracted shipping partner.[64] Additionally, moving away from Kickstarter, the ubiquitous first name in crowdfunding, may have reduced visibility of the campaign. Some quality-related concerns over season thirteen's cost-cutting and reliance on greenscreen backgrounds lingered, prompting Hodgson to confirm Gizmonic Arts' commitment to returning to physical sets.[65] Given the essential role of goodwill in crowdfunding, it stands to reason that any lingering cognitive dissonance over contributing to past campaigns would dissuade many from contributing to future campaigns. Just as the immediate good vibes of the first two campaigns' early successes instigated a snowball effect, the 2023 campaign's slow start may have produced an inverse effect, perhaps dissuading potential contributors from signing on to what seemed like a futile effort despite a late rush of new backers in the final days.

Crucially, the 2023 Writers Guild of America strike (which lasted from May 2 to September 27) and Screen Actors Guild–American Federation of Television and Radio Artists strike (July 14 to November 9) severely limited Hodgson and Gizmonic Arts from involving MST3K's Screen Actors Guild actors, who while striking were prohibited from participating in or promoting the project. In contrast to past Kickstarter campaigns, which were amplified by the involvement of celebrities such as Day and Oswalt and garnered mainstream press coverage, the 2023 campaign never captured the public's imagination the same way. The strike also prevented returning cast members from negotiating or signing on for season fourteen, which meant Hodgson could only promise potential backers that the cast had been invited back. "Unfortunately, this represents literally millions of views we can't rely on to spread the word until the strike is over," Hodgson explained of the cast's absence from the crowdsourcing campaign. "Obviously this has been a big part of our efforts during the last two campaigns, and we can feel the effects."[66]

In a campaign-concluding message to backers, Hodgson suggested he and his collaborators would return with updates on the future of season fourteen in 2024:

One silver lining is that the continued support for this campaign, and the show, may have opened up some new conversations about potential partnerships and fundraising that could be key in getting the show another season. We'll spend some time now exploring those, and working to integrate all of the feedback and suggestions we've heard from you, and will follow up again next year, Lord willing and the creek don't rise, when we've had a chance to regroup and have more to share downstream.[67]

Rather than celebrating MST3K's thirty-fifth Turkey Day gearing up for up-coming episodes featuring highly riffable movies like *Battle Beyond the Stars* and *Plan 9 From Outer Space*, the production of which Hodgson suggested could begin as early as January 2024,[68] MSTies were left in the sadly familiar position of waiting indefinitely for new MST3K. Thus, the process of bringing back MST3K began anew.

CONCLUSION

"It's just a show, I should really just relax!"

Mystery Science Theater 3000 debuted in a stiflingly conservative 1980s television landscape. Like a nimble punk band blowing lumbering rock dinosaurs off the stage, its creativity and do-it-yourself aesthetic immediately stood out as fresh and fiercely independent amid a glut of family values sitcoms and hackneyed action and crime drama series. MST3K's memorable characters, Midwest-flavored humor, and mastery of pop culture references made it a favorite of viewers looking for something smarter than the average fare and earned praise from several influential television critics. The show was recognized for comedic excellence with a Peabody Award in 1993 and is frequently featured in retrospectives of the best television of its era. Though it never attracted a mass mainstream audience, MST3K captured the imagination of a dedicated cult fandom that spread the show's gospel by circulating its episodes and singing its praises. Many fans who grew up on MST3K would carry the show's unique riffing sensibilities and incisive sense of humor throughout their lives as writers, comedians, critics, or unclassified wiseacres.

Yet simply being popular and different from its contemporaries is not enough to capture the essence of how MST3K transcends entertainment to establish a profound cultural legacy that cannot be quantified in ratings, awards, or critical esteem. MST3K and its trademark ethic of movie riffing resonated as vital in a cultural epoch in which the public's relationship with media and fandom was shifting. Mass media of the late 1980s and 1990s became simultaneously more intrusive due to pervasive new technologies and less independent and trustworthy due to corporate encroachment and conglomeration—a trend that would only intensify after the turn of the twenty-first century. Meanwhile, the cultural lines between creation and consumption grew ever blurrier as did the dialectics of art and trash and authorship and spectatorship. MST3K appealed to audiences during a period in which critical media literacy became an increasingly essential life skill. Through comedy and storytelling that were at once fantastic and relatable, MST3K articulated an ethic of active, articulate, and intentional media consumption, its everyday heroes dramatizing the danger of passive spectatorship and modeling the transformative potential for deconstructing and refashioning the elements of media to articulate a response to the world.

MST3K did not invent talking back to the screen; rather, Joel Hodgson and MST3K's plucky cohort of comedians updated participatory audiencing practices with deep historical roots. MST3K's active audiencing ethic has roots in historically uproarious theatergoers such as the groundlings of Shakespeare's Globe Theatre[1] or the peanut galleries of the Vaudeville era.[2] MST3K's appropriation and refashioning of existing media for entertainment purposes can be seen in prior productions such as *Fractured Flickers* or *What's Up, Tiger Lily?* By expertly combining these elements to hone and codify a series of techniques for responding to contemporary media, MST3K presented viewers with a memorable and malleable heuristic vocabulary they could adapt to respond to media in their own lives. Both Generation X and Millennials grew up poking fun at movies, television shows, music videos, advertisements, comic books, and political debates (to name a handful of examples), and whether they were bona fide MSTies or they never stopped flipping channels long enough to find out what the show with the shadows at the bottom was all about, they likely utilized riffing techniques perfected on a little cow-town puppet show from the Twin Cities.

Riffing in front of the TV set was only a warmup for the internet era, a new age of convergent media production and consumption in which riffing on media improbably became even more of an essential practice. A new age of snark sprang forth from comment sections, livestreams, and homebrew commentary tracks. In a world in which seemingly everyone with a social media account is a practicing riffer, a cottage industry of riffing-adjacent media flourished on YouTube, Twitch, and TikTok (to name just a few) as appropriating and dissecting existing media became its own genre of popular entertainment. Unburdened by antiquated notions of authorship and with seemingly the entirety of recorded media at their disposal, a new generation of critics, streamers, and Let's Play entrepreneurs adapted the tone-contradicting, intertextual, callback-manufacturing, creatively articulated critiques perfected on the Satellite of Love to speak back to anything and everything. Some pioneers in web-based snark are openly indebted to MST3K's influence, such as Something Awful's late founder Rich "Lowtax" Kyanka,[3] the progenitor of the let's play genre Michael "Slowbeef" Sawyer,[4] and Game Grumps co-hosts Arin Hanson[5] and Dan Avidan.[6] Others may not have been consciously influenced by MST3K but trade so heavily in its characteristic tropes and riffing techniques that comparisons to MST3K are inescapable.

MST3K has become synonymous with the trope of recording humorously snarky media commentary for fun or profit, as is evident by the frequency with which the moniker "The MST3K of [fill-in-the-blank]" is bestowed upon content creators. Attempting to "MST" popular media is so widespread, an entire genre of riffing other peoples' riffing has emerged, including memorable projects such as Retsupurae (which riffed bad Let's Play videos), Bad Creepypasta (riffed bad internet scary stories), Fanfic Theater 3015 (riffed bad *My Little Pony: Friendship is Magic* fan fiction), and The Black Pawn Movement (riffed bad *Twilight* fan vlogs). If imitation is the sincerest form of flattery, the highest compliment to MST3K's legacy is that its style and tone of movie riffing has become one of the defining approaches to media production on the internet today.

Despite meaning so much to so many and anchoring the early lineups of two successful cable networks, MST3K was canceled by three different media corporations. It was mishandled by misguided network executives, abysmally marketed by its movie studio, and discarded by Netflix on its most sacred of holidays, Turkey Day. Its capacity for surviving and thriving by guiding its fanbase to exciting new media terrains is another essential and underappreciated element of MST3K's cultural legacy.

Hodgson deserves credit as a pioneer in the genre of spinning mediated gold from discarded materials. This is obvious in the fashioning of Crow, Servo, Gypsy, and Cambot from everyday objects, but this ethic of junk extends to MST3K's use of severely distressed movies for its riffing fodder—an artistic choice that participated in a wider cultural blurring between high and low art. This became both a feature and a bug, for the emergence of MST3K raised the tide of trash cinema. The show's business model eventually toppled when a combination of red tape and profiteering made MST3K untenable for bottom line–obsessed corporate cable.

Rather than fade away, the art of movie riffing needed only to pause for technological innovation and online distribution to be liberated from the constraints of old media. Beyond all the wonderful comedy produced under its flag, RiffTrax deserves to be celebrated not only for pioneering web-based commentary but also as a vanguard in the movement to decentralize the industries of media commentary and criticism. Prior to the innovation of standalone recorded commentary facilitated by internet-based distribution, a movement at which RiffTrax was at the fore, art and media criticism were primarily reserved for those with sufficient cultural capital to access sanctioned mass-media channels. Outsider criticism of the media and cultural varieties has long served an invaluable role but once could reach only limited audiences through media such as outsider publications, public access television, or college or pirate radio. With its downloadable MP3 commentaries for copyrighted Hollywood movies, Nelson and the RiffTrax crew contributed to a movement of outsider media criticism that flourished online on websites such as YouTube, Twitch, and Bandcamp. As cable and other old media became less essential to establishing an audience, MST3K's alumni grew movie riffing in new frontiers such as live performance and livestreaming. With each new stop, fans followed, but just as importantly, fans were actively participating in sustaining movie riffing.

The revival of MST3K in the streaming video age represents more than the latest in a succession of successful transplantations of movie riffing to a new medium. It represents a crowning achievement in fan participation in the production of media outside traditional studio and producers' channels. As its two paradigm-shifting Kickstarter campaigns demonstrated, MST3K is a potent vessel to thrive via crowdfunding because it has become both a lifestyle and an ethos, rather than just a consumer product. MST3K's latest revival, the founding of the Gizmoplex and the in-house production of season thirteen, represents another step: the crowdfunding of not merely a show but a potentially self-sustaining app on which, at long last, Hodgson and his allies have attained a direct line to funding and creating MST3K by the fans and for the fans.

As of this writing, the Gizmoplex has produced only one season of MST3K; there are no accurate means by which to predict how Hodgson and his collaborators at Gizmonic Arts will regroup after falling short of their 2023 crowdsourcing goals, or what this development will ultimately mean to MST3K's legacy. Perhaps one day the Gizmoplex era's episodes, characters, and innovations will warrant their own book. Perhaps the "new conversations and potential partnerships"[7] at which Hodgson hinted in his 2023-concluding missive to fans will take MST3K in a new direction altogether. Despite an uncertain future, the 2023 saga of the Gizmoplex brought the essential role of fan participation in sustaining MST3K into sharper focus than ever. The right people not only get *Mystery Science Theater 3000*; the right people are finally the ones responsible for guiding its destiny.

APPENDIX

The Little Gold Statue Best-of List: Essential Episodes

Since 1988, MST3K has produced 234 episodes across a total of fourteen seasons, including the KTMA era. What follows is our list of twenty essential episodes of MST3K. These are the episodes we would show to anyone unfamiliar with the series, as they all perfectly encapsulate the various elements that define MST3K, from the brilliantly funny riffs to the enjoyably cheesy movies to the delightfully absurd host segments.

Episode 212: *Godzilla vs. Megalon* (January 19, 1991)

After making major strides in riffing quality throughout season two, Joel and the bots hit transcendent levels with their greatest performance of the Comedy Channel era. Toho's stranglehold on the rights to its flagship monster makes this episode tricky to access these days, but thirty-plus years later it is absolutely worth MSTies' time to track down this lost classic. Highlights include riffing the climactic Godzilla/Jet Jaguar vs. Megalon/Gigan battle as if it were a pro wrestling tag team match, and the final segment in which Jet Jaguar's "Punch! Punch! Punch!" theme song gets uproarious English subtitles.

Episode 301: *Cave Dwellers* (June 1, 1991)

Joel and the bots watch the nonsensical 1983 Italian fantasy flick *Cave Dwellers* (aka *The Blade Master*), directed by Joe D'Amato and starring musclebound hunk Miles O'Keeffe. In between bouts of admiring O'Keeffe's melon-like pecs, the gang debut their new smoking jacket (a fancy robe that emits smoke), reenact scenes from the film, ponder the naming conventions of the fantasy genre, and teach viewers how to create sound effects using the art of Foley.

Episode 303: *Pod People* (June 15, 1991)

This time out, the Satellite of Love (SoL) crew riffs on director Juan Piquer Simón's *Pod People* (aka *Extra Terrestrial Visitors*), a 1983 Spanish/French co-production that borrows liberally from both *Alien* and *E.T. the Extra-Terrestrial*. During the host segments, the crew demonstrate an explosive new guitar chord, dabble in new age music, engage in some thoroughly confusing mayhem, and perform the original songs "Idiot Control Now" and "A Clown in the Sky."

Episode 321: *Santa Claus Conquers the Martians* (December 21, 1991)

MST3K's first holiday-themed episode, for countless MSTies it's not Christmas until they've rewatched Joel and the bots tear apart this cheery (though terrible) camp classic. Great riffing gets upstaged by Crow's Christmas carol "A Patrick Swayze Christmas" (a Michael J. Nelson original) and Servo's poem "A Child's Christmas in Space." *Santa Claus Conquers the Martians* was revisited by both Cinematic Titanic and RiffTrax, blessing fans with a wealth of options for celebrating the season.

Episode 421: *Monster A-Go Go* (January 9, 1993)

January 1993 holds claim as the greatest calendar month in MST3K history, and it begins with Joel and the bots struggling to make sense of a completely nonsensical, hot-glued-together "dung heap" of a monster movie (Joel: "four movies went into the making of this film") whose twist is there was no monster. Their pain is fans' pleasure. Also features classic short "Circus on Ice" and the Mads' most insidious invention exchange: Johnny Longtorso, the action figure who is himself sold separately. Best Brains followed *Monster A-Go Go* with classic episodes *The Day the Earth Froze* and *Bride of the Monster*, then closed their greatest month with . . .

Episode 424: *Manos: The Hands of Fate* (January 30, 1993)

What more can be said about the most iconic MST3K episode? In plucking El Paso fertilizer salesman Harold P. Warren's monumentally incompetent horror film out of obscurity, Best Brains produced their defining work. Joel and the bots need all their endurance and wit in facing an adversary like no other as they try to survive the grim tale of the Master (Tom Neyman) and gargantuan-kneed caretaker Torgo tormenting unfortunate visitors at Valley Lodge. The crew makes it just barely, and the world is better for it, as *Manos* ascends to bad movie royalty later revisited by both RiffTrax and the Mads.

Episode 506: *Eegah* (August 28, 1993)

An ideal gateway episode, *Eegah* is an instant primer to what Joel-era MST3K is all about. *Eegah* has it all: the best of gizmocrat Joel in an all-time invention exchange (the porkarina), great out-of-theater skits that encapsulate the dynamics of Joel's fatherly relationship with the bots—plus one of the most riffable movies in series history. Joel and the bots' dismantling of the silly yet icky story of a pre-historic caveman (Richard Kiel) in modern-day Burbank produces a full quota of callbacks, including the immortal "Watch out for snakes!"

Episode 512: *Mitchell* (October 23, 1993)

One of the most emotionally resonant episodes enters the pantheon for its historical significance as Joel departs from his creation, passing the hosting torch to head writer Michael J. Nelson. That alone would make *Mitchell* a must-see, but Joel and the bots complete takedown of Joe Don Baker's beefy, boozy titular cop-who-doesn't-play-by-the-rules is relentlessly funny and provides the template for spinning comedy gold from mocking ruggedly masculine anti-heroes.

Episode 519: *Outlaw* (December 11, 1993)

The episode that won MST3K its Peabody Award, the Mike era arrives in earnest with dynamite riffing of this most breasticaboobical of fantasy epics directed by John "Bud" Cardos. Riffs on buffalo shots and Jack Palance impressions flow like wine during the movie, but Mike and the bots save their best work for the mid-movie song "Tubular Boobular Joy" and a credits-length riff on USA Network's lascivious late-night original movies ("Jeff Conaway is a college professor whose secret life catches up with him in *Death Spank*").

Episode 619: *Red Zone Cuba* (December 17, 1994)

There may be no more fascinating auteur in MST3K history than Coleman Francis, whose profoundly bleak, morally dubious, crudely assembled trilogy haunts Mike and the bots throughout season six. Francis, whom Kevin Murphy likens to "Curly Howard possessed by demons from Hell," not only directs but stars in *Red Zone Cuba*. Perhaps not an episode for MST3K newbies, it is essential for those fans who believe that the more the movie hurts, the better the episode. *Red Zone Cuba*'s unremitting bleakness breaks just long enough for the short "Speech: Platform Posture and Appearance," which introduces the giggle-inducing "knee test" to the MST3K lexicon. To complete the Coleman Francis experience, check out episodes 609: *The Skydivers* and 621: *The Beast of Yucca Flats*.

Episode 704: *The Incredible Melting Man* (February 24, 1996)

Season seven is perpetually underrated due to its association with MST3K's painful first cancellation, but *The Incredible Melting Man* is the brightest of its underappreciated treasures. Written as a horror parody but tragically filmed as straight horror, Mike and the bots have a blast with the most tonally confused film in the series' history, as well as effects maestro Rick Baker's ever-gooey monster. The episode is also memorable for its cathartic host segments, in which the writers vent their frustrations on the studio meddlers who hampered *Mystery Science Theater 3000: The Movie* via a series of skits in which screenwriter Crow has his opus "Earth vs. Soup" greenlit by Clay and Pearl (Mary Jo's finest performance in the role pre–Sci-Fi era) before having his dreams dashed one cut corner at a time.

Episode 810: *The Giant Spider Invasion* (May 31, 1997)

Sometimes all MST3K's writers need is one theme to produce a classic. Mike and the bots pile on the state of Wisconsin with every drunk cheesehead stereotype in the book for the duration of Bill Rebane's *Jaws*-but-Wisconsin Dairyland sci-fi spectacular, and the joke never gets old. Highlights include a giant spider fashioned from a Volkswagen Bug consuming lecherous villain Dan Kester (voice-acting legend Robert Easton) via its butt and Mike and the bots riffing mercilessly on the Skipper Alan Hale's jovial performance as the ineffective sheriff. Whether the Packers win the Super Bowl, they always will come out on top in MSTies' hearts thanks to this classic, revisited by RiffTrax in 2019.

Episode 816: *Prince of Space* (August 16, 1997)

Mike and the bots struggle to maintain their sanity when faced with the inane Japanese kid's movie *Prince of Space*, which features a ridiculously overpowered superhero saving the Earth from an armada of birdlike aliens. In this episode, the SoL crew find themselves trapped inside a wormhole that warps reality. This leads to one of the series' best bits, as Mike and the bots move at different temporal speeds and have a hilarious conversation in which they each respond to things that have not yet been said. Elsewhere, Mike turns into a robot that resembles a ventriloquist's dummy, the satellite is replaced by a pastoral wooded glen, and the villainous Krankor (the antagonist of *Prince of Space*, here played by Bill Corbett) makes an appearance that leaves the crew feeling uncomfortable.

Episode 820: *Space Mutiny* (November 7, 1997)

A fan favorite from the Sci-Fi era, *Space Mutiny* is a masterclass on developing a handful of riffing themes and hammering them home until they are all the audience remembers about the movie. Between giving beefy action hero Dave Ryder forty ridiculous nicknames (Stump Beefknob! Smash Lampjaw!), tracking the movie's many railing kills, and poking fun at Captain Santa Claus (Cameron Mitchell) and his grandma-daughter (Cisse Cameron), this episode is a prime example of Mike and the bots aggressively mocking a terrible movie with no quarter—with unforgettably hilarious results.

Episode 822: *Overdrawn at the Memory Bank* (December 6, 1997)

In this episode, the SoL crew plumb the Canadian-flavored depths of mid-1980s public broadcasting only to come face to face with *Overdrawn at the Memory Bank*, a sci-fi clunker starring Raul Julia (1940–1994, R.I.P.) and based on the short story of the same name by legendary sci-fi author John Varley. Set in a futuristic dystopia that resembles a mall, the film follows corporate lackey Aram Fingal (Julia) as he becomes trapped inside a computer program. In this standout episode from the Sci-Fi era, Mike and the bots participate in Pearl's bogus pledge drive, acquire a pet monkey via the internet ("Get your monkeys instantly with Instant Monkeys Online!"), and send Servo's consciousness into the microscopic realm of the ship's nanites.

Episode 904: *Werewolf* (April 18, 1998)

In this Z-grade horror film from director Tony Zarindast, an archeologist unearths the remains of a werewolf in the Arizona desert and the project's director uses the skeleton to transform a romantic rival into a strangely accented lycanthrope. While this episode features some potentially questionable humor as the crew poke fun at the accents of the ethnically ambiguous leads it also boasts some of the series' funniest jokes, as when Crow observes "Well so far, the 'star power' consists of Charlie Sheen's uncle" in response to Joe Estevez's credit. *Werewolf* also inspired some hilarious host segments, with Mike and the bots speculating about which celebrity relatives they would like to cast in their own werewolf movies, a list that includes Spike Knotts and Chip Hitler. The episode also spawned the original song "Where, Oh Werewolf," a toe-tapping ditty inspired by the girl groups of the 1950s and 1960s. Most disturbingly, perhaps, Mike cuts his hand on Crow's head and starts turning into a Werecrow.

Episode 910: *The Final Sacrifice* (July 25, 1998)

From the wilderness of Canadian student film, an icon is born in hard-drinking, pickup-driving, hockey-hair rocking action star and meme legend Zap Rowsdower. Brain Guy introduces *The Final Sacrifice* (also released as *Quest for the Lost City*) by declaring it "The worst thing to ever come out of Canada," but MSTies could not have fallen harder for Rowsdower and company's battle against the Ziox cult. Tragically, MSTies loved *The Final Sacrifice* a bit too much, as director Tjardus Greidanus reclaimed copyright of the film in the wake of its post-MST3K popularity, making it difficult to access. Tracking down a DVD of MST3K Volume XVII is expensive but infinitely worth it for a heartwarming interview with the man behind the Canadian tuxedo, Bruce J. Mitchell (1945–2018, R.I.P.).

Episode 1201: *Mac and Me* (November 22, 2018)

A high point of the Netflix era, this episode sees Jonah and the bots riff their way through cinematic punchline *Mac and Me*, made infamous by comedian Paul Rudd who showed a clip from the film every time he appeared on Conan O'Brien's various talk shows. *Mac and Me*, one of several blatant rip-offs of *E.T. the Extra-Terrestrial* (a list that includes *Pod People*), sees a wheelchair-bound boy befriending a hideous alien on the run from NASA. Ostensibly a feature-length commercial for Coca-Cola and McDonald's restaurants, the film inspired some of the funniest riffs in the history of the series, as when Crow references *Mad Max: Fury Road* by screaming "Witness me!" over a shot of a remote-controlled racecar. The episode introduces the intelligence-boosting drug Algernon (which grants defective clone Synthia the power of speech), sees Crow throw Servo a McDonald's-themed birthday party, and ends with the SoL crew facing down the horrors of the mockbuster *Atlantic Rim*.

Episode 1303: *Beyond Atlantis* (May 8, 2022)

After hosting the two MST3K live tours, Emily Connor (played by Emily Marsh) makes her Gizmoplex debut by riffing on this cheap US/Philippine co-production alongside the bots aboard the Simulator of Love. The film, directed by exploitation legend Eddie Romero, follows a band of intrepid adventurers who invade a native island to find a rumored treasure, only to encounter a village full of bug-eyed merpeople and their beautiful blonde princess Syrene (Leigh Christian). During breaks from savaging the movie (which the crew alternately refers to as "Weekend at Bernie's 3: Havana Nights" and "Mike Brady's lost weekend"), Emily and pals invent a toothpaste for plants, participate in a game show inspired by the film, and perform the original rap song "Mother Crabber."

Episode 1304: *Munchie* (May 21, 2022)

Easily the apotheosis of season thirteen, this episode subjects Jonah and the bots to the 1992 family film *Munchie*, an in-name-only sequel to the 1987 *Gremlins* knockoff *Munchies*. In the film, directed by Jim Wynorski (*Chopping Mall*, *Deathstalker II*), a bullied kid's life turns around when he meets a magical imp voiced by comedian Dom Deluise. At one point, the movie proves so punishing that the SoL crew simply screams in existential horror. Of course, the crew manage to drop some hilarious riffs throughout, as when they refer to the film as "Apt Pupil 2" or invoke Stephen King's story "The Body" by joking "I was 12 going on 13 the first time I saw a dead Munchie." The episode also features the debut of Kinga's new zombie-powered treadmill known as the Deadmill, Jonah and the bots discovering the recording of Deluise's highly improvisational and abusive voice-over sessions, Growler and M. Waverly landing jobs as Kinga's new henchmen, and Dr. Donna St. Phibes giving a presentation on Munchie's ancestry.

NOTES

INTRODUCTION

1. Synthia later spawned her own clone, Mega-Synthia, bane of Emily Connor, the host of Mystery Science Theater 3000 Live - The Great Cheesy Movie Circus Tour.

2. Longtime writer and cast member Kevin Murphy, who voiced and operated Tom Servo and later donned a *Planet of the Apes*–style get-up to play Professor Bobo, frequently described the show as such. See Katharine Coldiron, "No Longer a Cowtown Puppet Show," published November 28, 2018, https://bookandfilmglobe.com/television/tv -review-mystery-science-theater-3000/.

3. For more on MST3K's influences see Paul Anthony Ita, "The Patron Saint of Smart Alecks: An Interview with Joel Hodgson," published March 25, 2019, https://www .masslive.com/details-are-sketchy/2010/04/interview_with_joel_hodgson.html.

4. Mack Rawden, "Insane Clown Posse Has a Strangely Awesome MST3K Style Show," published March 13, 2014, https://www.cinemablend.com/television/Insane-Clown -Posse-Has-Strangely-Awesome-MST3K-Style-Show-62780.html.

5. For more on the phenomenon of participatory culture, see Henry Jenkins, *Textual Poachers: Television Fans and Participatory Culture* (Routledge, 1992); Henry Jenkins, *Convergence Culture: Where Old and New Media Collide Fans* (New York University Press, 2006); and Henry Jenkins, *Bloggers, and Gamers: Media Consumers in a Digital Age* (New York University Press, 2006).

6. According to Jeffrey T. Nealon, contemporary society has entered an era of post-postmodernism, during which the postmodern capitalist economic sphere has come to saturate nearly every facet of everyday cultural life. Therefore, citizens must develop new skills that allow them to better understand the relations between economic production and cultural production. For more, see Jeffrey T. Nealon, *Post-Postmodernism, or The Cultural Logic of Just-in-Time Capitalism* (Stanford University Press, 2012).

CHAPTER ONE

1. PACKERS! WOOOOO!

2. Marc Maron, "811: Joel Hodgson/Jonah Ray," May 15, 2017, in *WTF with Marc Maron*, produced by Brendan McDonald, podcast, MP3 audio, 1:47:50, https:// www.poorstuart.com/podcast-episode/WTF-with-Marc-Maron/Episode-811-Joel -Hodgson-Jonah-Ray/179424/.

3. Brian Raftery, "Mystery Science Theater 3000: The Definitive Oral History of a TV Masterpiece," published April 22, 2014, https://www.wired.com/2014/04/mst3k -oral-history/.

4. Witney Siebold, "The Mystery Science Theater 3000 Robots Are Quintessential Gen-Xers," published March 8, 2022, https://www.slashfilm.com/791431/the-mystery-sci ence-theater-3000-robots-are-quintessential-gen-xers/?utm_campaign=clip.

5. Zeke Jarvis, *Make 'em Laugh! American Humorists of the 20th and 21st Centuries* (Santa Barbara: ABC-CLIO, 2015), 140.

6. Jeff Strickler, "Local Comedian Gets Last Laugh in Competition," published October 1, 1982, https://web.archive.org/web/20090123024106/http://mst3k.booyaka.com /articles/mst-joel/8_1_82.html.

7. Raftery, "Oral History of MST3K."

8. Brian Boone, "The Untold Truth of Mystery Science Theater 3000," published May 8, 2017, https://www.looper.com/48365/untold-truth-mystery-science-theater-3000/.

9. Colin Covert, "Seinfeld and Hodgson," published May 5, 1986, https://web.ar chive.org/web/20090123024040/http://mst3k.booyaka.com/articles/mst-joel/5_5_86.html.

10. For more, see Margaret Rouse, "Ultra High Frequency (UHF)," last modified July 14, 2015, https://www.techopedia.com/definition/9811/ultra-high-frequency-uhf.

11. Raftery, "Oral History of MST3K."

12. Eirik Gumeny, "20 Things You Didn't Know About Mystery Science Theater 3000," published April 13, 2017, https://screenrant.com/mst3k-mystery-science -theatre-3000-trivia/.

13. CBR Staff, "Mystery Science Theater: 15 Things Only Hardcore MST3K Fans Know," published October 6, 2018, https://www.cbr.com/mst3k-mysteries/.

14. See Jon Ellis, "Broadcast History: The Innovative UHF Era That Created MST3K," published June 4, 2022, https://www.northpine.com/blog/2022/06/04/the -innovative-uhf-era-that-created-mst3k-ktma-kitn-kxli/.

15. Trace Beaulieu et al., *The Mystery Science Theater 3000 Amazing Colossal Episode Guide* (New York: Bantam Books, 1996), xxxi.

16. No, not the actor who played Cosmo Brown in the classic movie musical *Singin' in the Rain*, but someone else entirely.

17. Raftery, "Oral History of MST3K."

18. Beaulieu et al., xxxii.

19. *This is MST3K*, directed by Bill Price, written by Glen Eichler, featuring Penn Jillette, Neil Patrick Harris, and Joel Hodgson, aired November 14, 1992, on Comedy Central.

20. David Cassel, "A Farewell Tour with His Puppet Robot Pals for MST3K Creator Joel Hodgson," published February 9, 2020, https://thenewstack.io/a-farewell -tour-with-his-puppet-robot-pals-for-mst3k-creator-joel-hodgson/.

21. Beaulieu et al., xxxi.

22. Ibid., xxxii.

23. Ibid., 2.

24. Ibid., xxxii.

25. *This is MST3K*.

26. Dick Hebdige, *Subculture, the Meaning of Style* (New York: Methuen & Co. Ltd, 1979), 90.

27. Peter Webb and John Lynch, "'Utopian Punk': The Concept of the Utopian in the Creative Practice of Björk," *Utopian Studies* 21, no. 2 (2010): 313–30.

28. Graham St. John, "Protestival: Global Days of Action and Carnivalized Politics in the Present," *Social Movement Studies* 7, no. 2 (2008): 167–90.

29. Teal Triggs, *Fanzines: The DIY Revolution* (San Francisco: Chronicle Books, 2010), 9.

30. Martin Esslin, "The Theatre of the Absurd," *The Tulane Drama Review* 4, no. 4 (1960): 4.

31. In episode 321, the crew riff on the campy kids' flick *Santa Claus Conquers the Martians*, which co-stars a ten-year-old Pia Zadora as the Martian child Girmar. At one point, after benevolent Martian daddy Kimar (Leonard Hicks) orders his despondent children to bed, Crow affects a high-pitched little girl voice and jokes "Will you buy me a Golden Globe then?" Here, Crow refers to a scandal in which hotel magnate Meshulam Riklis allegedly influenced members of the Hollywood Foreign Press Association to nominate Zadora, whom he was courting at the time, for the "best new star of the year in a motion picture" award for her performance in the 1982 film *Butterfly*. For more, see Dariel Figueroa, "The Story of How a Wall Street Tycoon and a Broadway Actress Nearly Ended the Golden Globes in 1982," published January 11, 2015, https://uproxx.com/movies/story-behind-golden-globes-1982-scandal/.

32. For instance, while watching *Monster A-Go Go* in episode 421, Servo humorously refers to the eponymous monster as "Billy Pilgrim," evoking the protagonist of Vonnegut's most celebrated novel, *Slaughterhouse-Five*, originally published in 1969.

33. Founded in Minneapolis, Minnesota, in the early 1980s, Trip Shakespeare released five albums between 1986 and 1992: *Applehead Man, Are You Shakespearienced?, Across the Universe, Lulu,* and *Volt*. Members Dan Wilson and John Munson would go on to found 1990s alt-rock group Semisonic.

34. According to one estimate, MST3K's original budget was around $250 per episode, with Hodgson receiving fifty dollars for creating, starring, writing, and building all the props. The rest of the crew split the remaining two hundred dollars among themselves, though Beaulieu claims that he and fellow puppeteer Josh Weinstein received only twenty-five dollars per episode. For more on the show's budget, see Gumeny, "20 Things You Didn't Know About MST3K," and Raftery, "Oral History of MST3K."

35. Jacob Shelton, "Vampira, The First Horror Host: Her Short, Frustrating Story," accessed August 23, 2022, https://groovyhistory.com/vampira-horror-host-elvira-true-story/8.

36. For more see "Horror Mistresses Battle in Court," published February 27, 1989, https://www.upi.com/Archives/1989/02/27/Horror-mistresses-battle-in-court/1180604558800/; and Cassandra Peterson, *Yours Cruelly, Elvira: Memoirs of the Mistress of the Dark* (New York: Hachette, 2021), 171–83.

37. Created and portrayed by announcer/actor/disc jockey Ernie Anderson. The character hosted the derivatively titled *Shock Theater*, which ran from January 13, 1963, to December 16, 1966, on WJW-TV in Cleveland, Ohio.

38. Radio and TV personality Jerry G. Bishop portrayed the original incarnation of the character from 1970 to 1973, hosting a self-titled show that originally aired on WFLD in Chicago, Illinois. In 1979, actor/broadcaster Rich Koz revived the character for the series *Son of Svengoolie*, which ran on WLFD from 1979 to 1986. However, much like a zombie in one of the movies presented by Svengoolie, the series rose from the grave in 1994 as simply *Svengoolie*, this time airing on Chicago's WCIU, which continues to produce new episodes well into the twenty-first century. The show also airs on the MeTV network. At the time of this writing, Koz continues to inhabit the character.

39. The erudite redneck, played by comedian, writer, actor, and film critic John Irving Bloom, originally debuted as the host of *Joe Bob's Drive-in Theater*, which aired on the Movie Channel from 1986 to 1996. The character then made the jump to Ted Turner's TNT network, where he hosted the show *MonsterVision* from 1996 to 2000. In 2018, Bloom teamed with the newly launched Shudder streaming service to revive the character, this time as the host of *The Last Drive-In with Joe Bob Briggs*.

40. The superheroic Commander USA, played by disc-jockey-turned-actor Jim Hendricks, served as the host of *Commander USA's Groovie Movies* on the USA Network from 1985 to 1989.

41. Played by newscaster and radio personality Steve Brenzel, Ned the Dead hosted *Ned the Dead's Chiller Theater* (not to be confused with Zacherley's *Chiller Theater*), which originally aired on Green Bay's WLUK Channel 11 from 1983 to 1989. Six years later, the show was revived on Channel 26, where it ran from 1995 to 2005. In 2009, *Ned the Dead's Chiller Theater* clawed its way out of the grave for one last run, this time airing on WBAY's RTV 2.3 subchannel until 2010.

42. Kristen Hunt, "How Local TV Made 'Bad' Movies a Thing," *JSTOR Daily*, November 21, 2019, https://daily.jstor.org/how-local-tv-made-bad-movies-a-thing/.

43. Guy Barefoot, *Trash Cinema: The Lure of the Low* (New York: Wallflower Press, 2017).

44. Hunt, "Local TV."

45. Kendra Meinert, "Joel Hodgson Riffs on 'MST3K' and Its Green Bay Roots," published August 2, 2017, https://www.greenbaypressgazette.com/story/entertainment/television/2017/08/02/joel-hodgson-riffs-mst-3-k-and-its-green-bay-roots/529221001/.

46. For more, see Henry Jenkins, *Textual Poachers: Television Fans & Participatory Culture* (New York: Routledge, 1992).

47. See Jef Burnham and Joshua Paul Ewalt, "*Mystery Science Theater 3000* and the Restricted Universe of Popular Culture Production," in *Reading Mystery Science Theater 3000: Critical Approaches*, edited by Shelley S. Rees (Lanham: The Scarecrow Press, 2013), 33.

48. John King, "Mystery Science Theater 3000, Media Consciousness, and the Postmodern Allegory of the Captive Audience," *Journal of Film and Video* 59, no. 4 (2007): 39.

49. Alan Siegel, "'Freaks and Geeks': The Last Great High School TV Show?" published October 20, 2010, https://www.theatlantic.com/entertainment/archive/2010/10/freaks-and-geeks-the-last-great-high-school-tv-show/64563/.

50. Steven Johnson, *Interface Culture: How New Technology Transforms the Way we Create and Communicate* (San Francisco: Harper, 1997), 29.

51. ILoveMST3KPromos, "MST3K KTMA Commercials," YouTube, December 2, 2011, video, 2:06, https://www.youtube.com/watch?v=bCoKX6P53B8.

52. Beaulieu et al., 97.

53. Joe Dante and Josh Olson, "13: Jonah Ray," October 8, 2018, in *The Movies That Made Us*, produced by Trailers from Hell, podcast, MP3 audio, 1:06:05, https://trailersfromhell.com/podcast/jonah-ray/.

54. *Stingray* (1964–1965) and *Captain Scarlet and the Mysterons* (1967–1968), respectively.

55. Later riffed by MST3K alumni Michael J. Nelson, Kevin Murphy, and Bill Corbett under the Rifftrax banner. The film was also recycled for the ninth episode of

season thirteen of MST3K (originally streamed via the Gizmoplex streaming service on September 2, 2022), this time heckled by Jonah Ray Rodriguez and his crew.

56. It is the opinion of the authors that *Phase IV* contradicts Dante's assertion that the MST3K showrunners only picked on bad films, as it is in fact an excellent science fiction thriller about hyperintelligent ants terrorizing a group of researchers in a remote desert laboratory.

57. Beaulieu et al., xxxii (emphasis in original).

58. Tom Shales, "'MST3K' Means Fine Television," *Washington Post*, November 27, 1991, https://www.washingtonpost.com/archive/lifestyle/1991/11/27/mst3k-means-fine -television/582a1a46-a971-4aed-9982-526243f0f0b6/.

59. Though, as author John McMurria argues, such expression was often bound by social hierarchies that revolve around class, gender, and race inequalities. For more, see John McMurria, *Republic on the Wire: Cable Television, Pluralism, and the Politics of New Technologies, 1948–1984* (New Brunswick: Rutgers University Press, 2017), 111–36.

60. *This is MST3K.*

61. ILoveMST3KPromos, "MST3K KTMA Commercials."

62. Beaulieu et al., xxxiii.

CHAPTER TWO

1. Claire Schmidt and Laurel Schmidt, "'Do You Even Live Here?': Regionalism, Humor, and Tradition in *Mystery Science Theater 3000*," in *Reading Mystery Science Theater 3000: Critical Approaches*, edited by Shelley S. Rees (Lanham: The Scarecrow Press, 2013), 77–91.

2. Brian Raftery, "Mystery Science Theater 3000: The Definitive Oral History of a TV Masterpiece," *Wired*, April 22, 2014, https://www.wired.com/2014/04/mst3k-oral-history/.

3. Trace Beaulieu et al., *The Mystery Science Theater 3000 Amazing Colossal Episode Guide* (New York: Bantam Books, 1996), 147–49.

4. Raftery, "Oral History of MST3K."

5. See *This is MST3K*, directed by Bill Price, written by Glen Eichler, featuring Penn Jillette, Neil Patrick Harris, and Joel Hodgson, aired November 14, 1992, on Comedy Central.

6. Ibid.

7. Raftery, "Oral History of MST3K."

8. Bridget Jones and Michael J. Nelson would marry while working on the show, and she would eventually adopt the professional name of Bridget Jones-Nelson.

9. This character, played by Pehl, parodies Jan Compton (Virginia Leith), the tragic heroine of *The Brain That Wouldn't Die*. In the film, Jan, a nurse engaged to dashing transplant specialist Dr. Bill Cortner (Jason Evers), is decapitated in an automobile accident. Bill retrieves her head from the wreckage, wraps it in gauze and surgical tape, and places it in a pan filled with his experimental "life-giving serum." Jan spends the rest of the movie as a living disembodied head stuck in a pan, though she eventually gains the power to telepathically control the hideous mutant creature that Bill keeps locked in a dark room, so she has that going for her.

10. In episode 524, Mike and the bots riff the musical short *Design for Dreaming*. In this ten-minute advert, an unnamed woman dreams that a mysterious masked man

whisks her away to the future, which for some reason resembles the 1956 General Motors Motorama auto and appliance show. Jones appears as this woman, now called Nuveena, during one of the episode's host segments.

11. With this character, Nelson spoofs respected reporter, commentator, war correspondent, and anchorman Jack Perkins, who appeared on *NBC Nightly News* and *The Today Show* before hosting the long-running A&E series *Biography*.

12. In this episode, Joel and the bots riff on the sensationalistic 1956 teen flick *The Beatniks*, in which thirty-four-year-old teenager Eddy Crane (Tony Travis), a petty thief with a talent for singing, finds his efforts to attain fame threatened when his hoodlum pals accidentally murder a plus-sized barkeep. The trio also savage a brief segment from the long-running soap opera *General Hospital*, in which put-upon nurse Jessie Brewer (Emily McLaughlin) hosts an awkward engagement party comprised of her husband, Phil (Roy Thinnes), his mistress, Cynthia (Carolyn Craig), and Cynthia's fiancé, Dr. Ken Martin (Jack Betts aka Hunt Powers).

13. This episode sees Mike, Servo, and Crow riff on *Laserblast*, a cheesy, low-budget sci-fi thriller about a disgruntled teenager who stumbles on a powerful alien weapon that turns him into a cadaverous, green-skinned killer who embarks on a murderous rampage.

14. Creator of the cult smash indie comic book *Scud: The Disposable Assassin*, which debuted in 1994.

15. An Emmy-winning writer/performer/producer known for his work on shows like *Veronica's Closet* and *Gilmore Girls*.

16. Whiting is a writer/performer who appeared in the 1986 horror spoof *Blood Hook*, directed by Jim Mallon.

17. Raftery, "Oral History of MST3K."
18. Ibid.
19. Ibid.
20. Ibid.
21. No, not the Art Bell who hosted the radio show *Coast to Coast AM* from 1988 to 2007, a different one.
22. Raftery, "Oral History of MST3K."
23. Ibid.
24. Ibid.
25. Ibid.
26. Ibid.
27. See Beaulieu et al., 153–54.
28. Raftery, "Oral History of MST3K."
29. Ibid.
30. Ibid.
31. Darragh McManus, "My Generation's Irony: So Bad It's Not Good?" *The Guardian*, March 11, 2010, https://www.theguardian.com/commentisfree/2010/mar/11/generation-x-sarcasm-seriously.
32. Paul Brownfield, "Don't Like the Movie? Let's Talk About It," *New York Times* (New York, NY), June 3, 2012.
33. *This is MST3K*.
34. Paul Kix, "Midwestern Nice: A Tribute to a Sincere and Suffocating Way of Life," *Thrillist*, October 21, 2015, https://www.thrillist.com/lifestyle/nation/my-life-living-midwestern-nice.

35. "Midwest Nice," *Urban Dictionary,* accessed June 30, 2023, https://www.urban dictionary.com/define.php?term=Midwest+Nice.

36. Charlie McCarthy is a character created by famed ventriloquist Edgar Bergen (1903–1978), who imbued a dummy attired in a top hat, tuxedo, and monocle with the personality of a wisecracking, mischievous little boy.

37. Howdy Doody, eponymous star of *The Howdy Doody Show,* is a marionette made to look like a redheaded, freckle-faced boy dressed in cowboy garb. The chatty, fun-loving puppet attained massive popularity throughout the 1950s and remains well-loved to this day.

38. Gumby is an oddly shaped green humanoid character created and modeled by pioneering stop-motion clay animator Art Clokey. The character headlined the long-running *Gumby* media franchise, which debuted in 1953 and spans multiple TV series, a feature-length film, toys, books, and a variety of other media.

39. Pokey, Gumby's sidekick, is a sarcastic orange pony with a black mane and tail.

40. Kukla, a hand puppet that resembles a cranky clown, was one of the title characters on the Chicago-based live-action children's series *Kukla, Fran, and Ollie.* The character was performed by puppeteer Burr Tillstrom.

41. The roguish one-toothed dragon puppet Ollie (aka Oliver J. Dragon) was another titular star of *Kukla, Fran, and Ollie.* Like Kukla, Ollie was performed by Burr Tillstrom.

42. Beaulieu et al., 24.

43. Basehart (1914–1984) was American actor known for his portrayal of Admiral Harriman Nelson in the television science-fiction drama *Voyage to the Bottom of the Sea.*

44. *This is MST3K.*

45. Frederic Ogden Nash (1902–1971) was an American poet known for his light verse and unconventional rhyming schemes.

46. Raftery, "Oral History of MST3K."

47. Ibid.

48. Ibid.

49. Ibid.

50. Ibid.

51. Beaulieu et al., 87.

52. Michael J. Nelson, *Mike Nelson's Movie Megacheese* (New York: Dey Street Books, 2000), 231.

53. Ibid., 240.

54. It should be noted here that Christopher J. Olson considers *Hobgoblins*—along with other Rick Sloane joints like *Blood Theatre, The Visitants,* and *Vice Academy Part 2*—to be quite fun all things considered. However, he believes that *Werewolf* is every bit as bad as its reputation suggests.

55. Beaulieu et al., 99.

56. Raftery, "Oral History of MST3K."

57. Ibid.

58. Ibid.

59. Beaulieu et al., 87.

60. Raftery, "Oral History of MST3K."

61. Ibid.

62. Ibid.

63. Ibid.

64. Ibid.

65. Beaulieu et al., 105.

66. Ibid.

67. Ibid.

68. John Kelly, "Sweet 'Mystery' of Life," *Washington Post* (Washington, DC), April 19, 1996.

69. Peter Stack, "FILM REVIEW – 'Barb' Armed with Blanks/'Baywatch' Star Shows No Mercy," published August 23, 1996, https://www.sfgate.com/movies/article/FILM-REVIEW-Barb-Armed-With-Blanks-2969464.php.

70. "MST3K: The Movie," accessed August 27, 2023, https://mst3kinfo.com/mstfaq/movie.html.

71. Raftery, "Oral History of MST3K."

72. *This is MST3K.*

73. Raftery, "Oral History of MST3K."

74. Ibid.

75. *This is MST3K.*

76. Ibid.

77. Ibid.

78. Your humble authors, however, think both these cats are keen, especially Corman, whose shadow still looms large over modern Hollywood due to mentoring numerous acclaimed filmmakers and performers, including Joe Dante, James Cameron, Jack Nicholson, and Peter Fonda.

79. Raftery, "Oral History of MST3K."

CHAPTER THREE

1. According to Corbett, his lack of puppeteering skills resulted from being "given this job on the show on the Friday before the Monday we started production." For more, see "Episode 801- Revenge of the Creature," accessed August 28, 2023, http://www.mst3kinfo.com/aceg/8/801/ep801.html.

2. Ibid.

3. Brian Raftery, "Mystery Science Theater 3000: The Definitive Oral History of a TV Masterpiece," published April 22, 2014, https://www.wired.com/2014/04/mst3k-oral-history/.

4. An American film and television actor best known for starring alongside John Wayne in the films *Fort Apache*, *Sands of Iwo Jima*, and *She Wore a Yellow Ribbon*, John Agar would later star in such schlock classics as *The Mole People*, *Invisible Invaders*, and *Zontar: The Thing from Venus*.

5. The Observers are likely inspired by the Talosians, a race of highly advanced aliens appearing in the unaired pilot of the original *Star Trek* series, "The Cage."

6. Raftery, "Oral History of MST3K."

7. Barry Brummett, "Double Binds in Publishing Rhetorical Studies," *Communication Studies* 59, no. 4 (2003): 366.

8. Kenneth Burke, *The Philosophy of Literary Form: Studies in Symbolic Action* (Baton Rouge: Louisiana State University Press, 1941), 304.

9. James Poniewozik, "All-TIME 100 TV Shows," published September 6, 2007, https://time.com/collection-post/3103672/mystery-science-theater-3000/.

10. Will Sloan, "'You Can't Just Be the Voice of Generic Sarcasm': The Art of Movie Riffing," published August 16, 2012, https://www.npr.org/2012/08/16/158922001 /you-cant-just-be-the-voice-of-generic-sarcasm-the-art-of-movie-riffing.

11. Ibid.

12. "Project: Riff," accessed September 14, 2023, http://www.magicmarkerweb.com /mst3kreview/projriff.htm#project.

13. "Problematic," accessed September 14, 2023, https://dictionary.cambridge.org /us/dictionary/english/problematic.

14. "Problematic," accessed August 28, 2023, https://www.merriam-webster.com /dictionary/problematic.

15. Elizabeth Ellsworth, *Teaching Positions: Difference, Pedagogy, and the Power of Address* (New York: Teachers College Press, 1997), 23.

16. Played by venerable character actor Jonathan Harris, the cowardly and greedy Dr. Zachary Smith is a stowaway who successfully sabotages the maiden voyage of the spaceship *Jupiter 2* in the original incarnation of the campy sci-fi series *Lost in Space* that ran from 1965 to 1968.

17. Kenneth Burke argues that the framing of heroes and villains influences our acceptance of those values. See Kenneth Burke, *Attitudes Toward History*, volume 1 (Berkeley: University of California Press, 1937).

18. Kevin Murphy, *A Year at the Movies* (New York: Harper Collins, 2002), 271.

19. Robert Holtzclaw, "*Mystery Science Theater 3000*," in *The Essential Cult TV Reader*, edited by David Lavery (Lexington: University of Kentucky Press), 181–88.

20. Conversely, imagine the existential horrors of being stuck watching *Invasion of the Neptune Men* or *Carnival Magic* and only being able to address what is on screen at that moment, perhaps due to the evil handiwork of Intertextual-y the Intertextuality Sprite after some oaf got fed up following one too many *Family Guy* cutaway gags and wished to never see one again.

21. Backmasking refers to a recording technique in which a message is recorded backward onto a track meant to be played forward. The technique gained widespread recognition during the infamous "Satanic Panic" of the 1980s, as parents throughout the United States became convinced that heavy metal albums contained such hidden messages. For more, see Jake Rossen, "A Brief History of Satanic Panic," published May 14, 2021, https://www.mentalfloss.com/article/642372/satanic-panic-history-1980s.

22. WOOOOOO!

23. "Between the Riffs," *Cinematic Titanic Live: Danger on Tiki Island*, performed by Trace Beaulieu, Frank Conniff, Joel Hodgson, Mary Jo Pehl, and J. Elvis Weinstein, Cinematic Titan, LLC, 2010, DVD.

24. Servo's murderer's row of celebrity riffs: Robby Benson, Jack Burns, Andrea Martin, Dennis Hopper, Jody? (Tom gets tongue-tied), Garry Shandling, Paul Reiser, Peter Cook, Junior Samples, Elayne Boosler, Adam Sandler, Barry Sobel, Garth Brooks, Bruce Mahler, Les Paul, Patrick Swayze as Gandhi, Sheryl Lee Ralph, Robert Carradine, Bruno Kirby, Griffin Dunne, Mike Nichols, Ron Reagan, Demi Moore, Gabriel Byrne, Gallagher, Robert Loggia, Janis Joplin, Jonathan Schwartz, Lyle Waggoner, Tom Dreesen, Steve Rubell, Alan Alda, Michael Ironside, k.d. lang, Kate Clinton, Lee Van Cleef, Marlee Matlin, David Birney, Linda Hunt, Leslie West, Sandy Duncan, Craig T. Nelson, David Letterman, Tony Danza, Anthony Quinn, Edie Brickell, Tony Bill, Roland Gift, Jerzy Kosiński, Rene Auberjonois, John Hurt, Cicely Tyson, and Michael Pare. Crosschecking credit to MST3KInfo.com's Ward E. See "List: Celebrity Crowd at the Rally," accessed September 18, 2023, https://www.mst3kinfo.com/ward_e/List501a.html.

25. Trace Beaulieu et al., *The Mystery Science Theater 3000 Amazing Colossal Episode Guide* (New York: Bantam Books, 1996), 17.

26. Kenneth Burke uses the metaphor of verbal atom cracking in his exploration of perspective by incongruity as a form of comic critique. See Burke, *Attitudes Toward History*, 308.

27. It should be noted here that Christopher J. Olson enjoys a good pun. In fact, you could say he has a pun-chant for clever wordplay.

28. *Castle of Fu-Manchu* from the Joel era comes closest to breaking the SoL crew during the Comedy Central years.

29. Neil Nehring, "Jigsaw Youth versus Generation X and Postmodernism," in *GenXegesis: Essays on "Alternative" Youth (Sub)Culture*, edited John M. Ulrich and Andrea L. Harris (Madison: University of Wisconsin Press), 70.

30. Addressing a live audience in New York, Murphy deemed the film a "gift from God." See "Daddy-O's Drive-in Dirt: 904 - WEREWOLF (1996; 1995; R; 99m)," accessed September 14, 2023, https://www.mst3kinfo.com/daddyo/di_904.html.

31. Though episode 1013, "Diabolik," concludes the story and was the final episode produced before cancellation, episode 1003, "Merlin's Shop of Mystical Wonders," was delayed until September 1999, one month after "Diabolik" debuted. "Merlin's Shop of Mystical Wonders" was technically the final new episode of MST3K until season eleven in April 2017.

32. Beaulieu et al., 81.

CHAPTER FOUR

1. "The Yahoo Movies Interview: Gillian Flynn on 'Gone Girl,' 'Game of Thrones,' and Great Cheesy Movies," published October 2, 2014, https://www.yahoo.com/entertainment/gillian-flynn-gone-girl-interview-yahoo-98910212677.html.

2. Gillian Flynn, "MST3k Cancelled," last modified April 16, 1999, https://ew.com/article/1999/04/16/mst3k-cancelled/.

3. "Fan-Contributed Daily Variety Ad," accessed September 16, 2023, https://en.wikipedia.org/wiki/Mystery_Science_Theater_3000#cite_note-39.

4. John Dempsey, "Schulman Ankles Sci-Fi VP Post," published July 27, 1998, https://variety.com/1998/biz/news/schulman-ankles-sci-fi-vp-post-1117478846/.

5. Richard Corliss, "Cinema: Robocritics Take Flight," published April 22, 1996, https://content.time.com/time/subscriber/article/0,33009,984436,00.html.

6. Jim McConville, "Cult Status Doesn't Cut It on Cable Anymore," *Electronic Media* 18, no. 11 (1999): 4.

7. Flynn, "MST3k Cancelled."

8. "TimmyBigHands," accessed September 16, 2023, https://web.archive.org/web/20010203004200/http://www.timmybighands.com/default.asp.

9. After starting as an intern at Best Brains in 1992, Brantseg eventually worked his way up to the show's art director. In season eight, he also took over the duties of puppeteering and voicing the character of Gypsy after producer Jim Mallon stepped down from the role.

10. Chaplin, a writer and comedian from Chicago, Illinois, joined MST3K's writing staff in season three. In addition to his writing duties, Chaplin also portrayed several recurring characters, including an Observer, Ned the Nanite, Pitch the Demon, and Ortega

(inspired by Don Russell's villainous henchman character in *The Incredibly Strange Creatures Who Stopped Living and Became Mixed-Up Zombies!!?*).

11. "Reviews: Guys Who Are About Five-Eight, Five-Nine," accessed September 16, 2023, https://web.archive.org/web/20010208143636/http://www.timmybighands.com /reviews/fivefootguys.asp.

12. In 2023, the RiffTrax crew would revive the offbeat concept of the writing hand-off with the digital novel *Nick Nolte, P.I.*, created as a stretch goal for RiffTrax's 2023 Kickstarter to fund their riff of director Hal Needham's cult BMX epic, *Rad*. See "RiffTrax is Writing a Nick Nolte Novel: New Stretch Goal!" published March 2, 2023, https:// www.kickstarter.com/projects/rifftrax/rifftrax-live-2023-rad-the-classic-1986-bmx-movie /posts/3746911.

13. "The Tort: A Serial Novel by Timothy B. Hands – Chapter IV: Finger," accessed September 16, 2023, https://web.archive.org/web/20010211154728/http://www.timmy bighands.com/serial/tort4.asp.

14. Paul Czarnowski, "Michael J. Nelson," accessed September 16, 2023, https:// web.archive.org/web/20030122222815/http://www.crcradio.net/i13/mikenelson.html.

15. In addition to *Movie Megacheese*, Nelson published the essay collection *Mike Nelson's Mind Over Matters* (2002), the satirical Minnesota-spoofing novel *Mike Nelson's Death Rat!* (2003), and the trilogy *Love Sick: A Smoldering Look at Love, Lust, and Marriage* (2005), *Happy Kitty Bunny Pony: A Saccharine Mouthful of Super Cute* (2005), and *Fluffy Humpy Poopy Puppy: A Ruff Dog-Eared Look at Man's Best Friend* (2006), all riffs on illustrated children's books.

16. Michael J. Nelson, *Mike Nelson's Movie Megacheese* (New York: Harper Entertainment, 2000), 42.

17. Ibid., 79.

18. Ibid., 76.

19. Ibid., 124.

20. Shadowrama refers to the use of Lumakey or Chromakey to create the silhouette used on MST3K. Here, three characters are superimposed over a movie and made to look as though they are watching it and providing a running commentary. The theater seats consist of a black-painted foam core board placed behind the host's seat while recessed stages support the performers operating the Crow and Tom puppets. The host wears black clothing while the robot puppets are painted black, with the screen being a white Lumakey screen that helps to create the appearance of silhouettes.

21. Kevin Murphy, *A Year at the Movies* (New York: Harper Collins, 2002), 14–15.

22. Ibid., 138.

23. Per literary theory, the term paratext refers to any material that surrounds a published main text supplied by the authors, editors, printers, and publishers. In the case of films released on DVD, paratexts include special features such as making-of documentaries, interviews with casts and crews, and commentary tracks.

24. The fiasco of volume ten being yanked due to the unauthorized presence of *Godzilla vs. Megalon* (1973) had one silver lining: it begat a bonus feature on volume 10.2 in which Joel Hodgson, Trace Beaulieu, and Frank Conniff appeared for the first time as a trio on MST3K since Hodgson's 1993 departure. In it, Beaulieu and Conniff explain how to replace the contraband *Godzilla vs. Megalon* DVDs with the replacement DVDs of *The Giant Gila Monster*.

25. Eric Bangeman, "DVD Players Finally Outnumber VCRs," published December 22, 2006, https://arstechnica.com/gadgets/2006/12/8484/.

26. "Movies to Go," published July 7, 2005, https://www.economist.com/business/2005/07/07/movies-to-go.

27. Frank Conniff (@FrankConniff), "When I worked on @MST3K, we were very conscious about not doing misogynistic or homophobic jokes. We were proudly woke before it was called being woke. We still are. People were laughing then and they're still laughing now, dipshit," Twitter, May 30, 2022, https://twitter.com/FrankConniff/status/1531477088854745089.

28. See Robert Hariman, "Political Parody and Public Culture," *Quarterly Journal of Speech* 94, no. 3 (2008): 247–72.

29. See Jamie Warner, "Political Culture Jamming: The Dissident Humor of *The Daily Show with Jon Stewart*," *Popular Communication* 5, no. 1 (2007): 17–36.

30. Mikhail Bakhtin, *The Dialogic Imagination: Four Essays by M. M. Bakhtin*, edited by Michael Holquist, translated by Caryl Emerson and Michael Holquist (Austin: University of Texas Press, 1981), 23.

31. See Matthew Hindman, *The Myth of Digital Democracy* (Princeton, NJ: Princeton University Press, 2009).

32. Matt Hills, "From the Box in the Corner to the Box Set on the Shelf: 'TVII'" and the Cultural/Textual Valorizations of DVD," *New Review of Film and Television Studies* 5, no. 1 (2007): 52.

33. Ibid., 53.

34. Though *The Matrix* is a notable exception as its tenth-anniversary Blu-ray release includes two commentary tracks, one recorded by philosophers praising the film and the other by film critics who dislike the influential blockbuster. This latter track features Todd McCarthy, John Powers, and David Thomson discussing what they consider the film's many failings.

35. Nell Minow, "Interview: Mike Nelson of MST3000 and Rifftrax," published June 2, 2009, https://moviemom.com/interview-mike-nelson-of-mst30/.

36. Megan Condis, "Converging Fan Cultures and the Labors of Fandom," in *In the Peanut Gallery with Mystery Science Theater 3000: Essays on Film, Fandom, Technology, and the Culture of Riffing*, edited by Robert G. Weiner and Shelley E. Barba (Jefferson: McFarland, 2011), 82.

37. Christopher Bahn, "Cinematic Titanic," published October 14, 2011, https://www.avclub.com/cinematic-titanic-1798227923.

38. "conventions," accessed September 16, 2023, https://www.mst3kinfo.com/mstfaq/concon.html.

39. Richard Corliss, "1950s Sci-Fi Movies: *Plan 9 from Outer Space*," published December 11, 2008, https://entertainment.time.com/2008/12/12/top-ten1950s-sci-fi-movies/slide/plan-9-from-outer-space-1956/.

40. Bahn, "Cinematic Titanic."

41. Weinstein later confirmed that his disappearance from public movie riffing was in part because he was likely dealing with cancer for much of the group's run but did not learn of it until the end of Cinematic Titanic's final tour. Weinstein made his triumphant return to MST3K in 2018, reprising his role as Dr. Ehrhardt for the first time since 1990. See J. Elvis Weinstein, "J. Elvis Weinstein—The Cancer Chunk (stand-up)," March 15, 2018, video, https://www.youtube.com/watch?v=6c_qmseW05Q.

CHAPTER FIVE

1. Emmanuella Grinberg of CNN reported the externally raised figure at $425,000. See Emanuella Grinberg, "'Mystery Science Theater 3000' Revival Sets New Kickstarter Record," last modified December 14, 2015, https://www.cnn.com/2015/12/12/entertain ment/mystery-science-theater-kickstarter-feat/index.html.

2. Kevin McFarland, "MST3K Revival Hits Kickstarter, Back-Sassers Rejoice," published November 18, 2015, https://www.wired.com/2015/11/mst3k-kickstarter/.

3. Bill Chappell, "'Mystery Science Theater 3000' Creator Raises $500K Toward New Season," published November 10, 2015, https://www.npr.org/sections/thetwo-way /2015/11/10/455518678/-mystery-science-theater-3000-creator-raises-500k-toward-new -season.

4. Marilyn Malara, "'Mystery Science Theater 3000' Revival Breaks Kickstarter Record," published December 12, 2015, https://www.upi.com/Entertainment_News /2015/12/12/Mystery-Science-Theater-3000-revival-breaks-Kickstarter-record/986144 9927479/.

5. For more, see "The Veronica Mars Movie Project," accessed August 28, 2023, https://www.kickstarter.com/projects/559914737/the-veronica-mars-movie-project.

6. For more, see "Bring Back MYSTERY SCIENCE THEATER 3000," accessed August 28, 2023, https://www.kickstarter.com/projects/mst3k/bringbackmst3k.

7. Annamarie Navar-Gill, "Fandom as Symbolic Patronage: Expanding Understanding of Fan Relationships with Industry Through the Veronica Mars Kickstarter Campaign," *Popular Communication* 16, no. 3 (2018): 215.

8. Joel Hodgson, "A Quick One. Longer Update coming in the Not-Too-Distant Future . . ." published December 14, 2015, https://www.kickstarter.com/projects/mst3k /bringbackmst3k/posts/1443969.

9. The only possible rival to this distinction would be the 2014 *Reading Rainbow* Kickstarter that ultimately became mired in rights issues.

10. Navar-Gill, 222.

11. *We Brought Back* MST3K, directed by Daniel Griffith (Chickamauga, GA: Ballyhoo Motion Pictures, 2018), DVD.

12. Roger Hallam, "How the Internet Can Overcome the Collective Action Problem: Conditional Commitment Designs on Pledgebank, Kickstarter, and The Point/Groupon Websites," *Information, Communication & Society* 19, no. 3 (2016): 364.

13. *We Brought Back* MST3K.

14. "RiffTrax Wants to Riff TWILIGHT Live in Theaters Nationwide!" accessed August 28, 2023, https://www.kickstarter.com/projects/rifftrax/rifftrax-wants-to-riff -twilight-live-in-theaters-n/posts/488630s.

15. Navar-Gill, 214.

16. @Netflix, "In the not-too-distant future. @MST3K," Twitter, July 23, 2016, https://twitter.com/netflix/status/757055576903778304?s=20.

17. Claire Atkinson, "Video Streaming Services Saw Giant Leap in 2016," published January 6, 2017, https://nypost.com/2017/01/06/video-streaming-services-saw-giant-leap -in-2016/.

18. Mark Sweeney, "Netflix Tops 100m Subscribers as it Draws Worldwide Audience," published July 18, 2017, https://www.theguardian.com/media/2017/jul/18/netflix-tops -100m-subscribers-international-customers-sign-up.

19. John Lynch, "All 26 Notable Netflix Original Shows That Debuted in 2017, Ranked from Worst to Best," published December 1, 2017, https://www.businessinsider .com/best-new-netflix-original-shows-released-in-2017-ranked-2017-11.

20. "Mystery Science Theater 3000: The Return (2017)," accessed August 28, 2023, https://www.rottentomatoes.com/tv/mystery_science_theater_3000_the_return/s01.

21. Erik Adams, "We're Watching the New Season of *Mystery Science Theater 3000*," published July 14, 2017, https://www.avclub.com/we-re-watching-the-new-season -of-mystery-science-theate-1798288578.

22. Liz Shannon Miller, "'Mystery Science Theater 3000: The Return' Review: Faces Change, but the Anarchic Spirit Remains the Same," published April 14, 2017, https:// www.indiewire.com/2017/04/mst3k-review-netflix-jonah-ray-joel-hodgson-season-11 -1201805884/.

23. Scout Tafoya, "Review: *Mystery Science Theater 3000: The Return: Season One*," published April 21, 2017, https://www.slantmagazine.com/tv/mystery-science-theater -3000-the-return-season-one/.

24. Emily St. James, "Mystery Science Theater 3000 is the Same as Always in Its New Season. That's a Good Thing," published April 14, 2017, https://www.vox.com /culture/2017/4/14/15212400/mystery-science-theater-3000-new-season-netflix-good.

25. *We Brought Back* MST3K.

26. In episode 1204, Dr. Laurence Erhardt (J. Elvis Weinstein) confirms that Max is the Son of TV's Frank; previously, the nature of Max's connection to Frank was left ambiguous as possibly only aspirational.

27. *We Brought Back* MST3K.

28. Miller, "Faces Change."

29. The writers previously played with this dynamic in episode 613 (*The Sinister Urge*) when Mike riffed that a car with a distinctive smiling grill resembled Jet Jaguar (star of season two's *Godzilla vs. Megalon*), to which Crow asked, "How would you know?"

30. Katie Canales, "Meet the Average Netflix User, a Millennial Woman Without a College Degree Living in the American Suburbs Earning Less Than $50,000 a Year," published September 18, 2021, https://www.businessinsider.com/typical-netflix-user-sub scriber-demographic-millennial-age-political-views-income-2021-9.

31. *We Brought Back* MST3K.

32. Kyle Anderson, "How MYSTERY SCIENCE THEATER 3000's New Season Plays on Binge-Watching," published November 12, 2018, https://nerdist.com/article /mst3k-gauntlet-joel-hodgson-jonah-ray-hampton-yount/.

33. Ibid.

34. Jani Merikivi et al., "Binge-watching Serialized Video Content: A Transdisciplinary Review," *Television and New Media* 21, no. 7 (2020): 702.

35. John Jurgensen, "Binge Viewing: TV's Lost Weekends," published July 13, 2012, https://www.wsj.com/articles/SB10001424052702303740704577521300806686174.

36. Stephen Camarata, "Binge Watching Is a Loss for Families," published September 16, 2015, https://time.com/collection-post/4029794/stephen-camarata-how-much-binge -watching-is-too-much/.

37. "Netflix Declares Binge Watching is the New Normal," published December 13, 2013, https://www.prnewswire.com/news-releases/netflix-declares-binge-watching-is-the -new-normal-235713431.html

38. Mareike Jenner, "Binge-watching: Video-on-demand, Quality TV and Mainstreaming Fandom," *International Journal of Cultural Studies* 20, no. 3 (2017): 305.

39. Synthia's newfound talents for speech and thought are thanks to episode 1201's invention exchange, Kinga's dangerous experimental smart drug Algernon.

40. Fredric Jameson, "Postmodernism, or the Cultural Logic of Late Capitalism," in *Postmodernism: A Reader*, edited by Thomas Docherty (New York: Routledge, 1993), 62–92.

41. See Jean Baudrillard, *Simulacra and Simulation*, translated by S. Faria Glaser (Ann Arbor: University of Michigan Press, 1994).

42. See Marianne Garvey, "Netflix Cancels Its 'Mystery Science Theater 3000' Revival," published November 27, 2019, https://www.cnn.com/2019/11/27/entertainment /netflix-mystery-science-theater-3000/index.html.

43. Joel Hodgson (@JoelGHodgson). "If you didn't see the backer update, I announced today that #MST3K is not doing a third season for Netflix. It's not the end of MST3K, It's just the end of the first chapter of bringing back MST3K." Twitter, November 26, 2019. https://twitter.com/JoelGHodgson/status/1199482835150749704.

44. Michael Cook, "REVIEW: "Mystery Science Theater 3000: The Comic #1," published September 12, 2018, https://thoroughlymodernreviewer.com/2018/09/12 /review-mystery-science-theater-3000-the-comic-1/.

45. Stacy Baugher, "Mystery Science Theater 3000: The Comic #1 Review," published September 12, 2018, https://majorspoilers.com/2018/09/12/mystery-science -theater-3000-the-comic-1-review/.

46. Jason Segarra, "'Mystery Science Theater 3000: The Comic' Faces Some Stumbles in a New Medium," published September 11, 2019, https://aiptcomics.com/2019/09/11 /mystery-science-theater-3000-the-comic-review-tpb/.

47. Your other author, Matt Foy, was never much of a comic book guy but will gladly check it out upon coming across a copy of the trade.

48. Gavin Jasper, "MST3K: Joel Hodgson Reveals the Secrets of the Gizmoplex, Teases 'the Next Manos,'" published May 1, 2021, https://www.denofgeek.com/tv/mst3k -joel-hodgson-reveals-the-secrets-of-the-gizmoplex-teases-the-next-manos/.

49. Ibid.

50. Ibid.

51. Joel Hodgson, "Let's Make More MST3K & Build the Gizmoplex!" accessed September 19, 2023, https://www.kickstarter.com/projects/mst3k/makemoremst3k.

52. Joel Hodgson, "What We've Been Doing for the Last Three Weeks. Plus: Reward Updates & Sneak Peeks!" published June 2, 2021, https://www.kickstarter.com/projects /mst3k/makemoremst3k/posts/3207798.

53. Ivan Askwith, "MST3K Weekly Update: Oct 4-8, 2021," published October 8, 2021, https://www.kickstarter.com/projects/mst3k/makemoremst3k/posts/3324535.

54. Also riffed by the good folks over at Rifftrax.

55. No, not the adaptation of the Dark Horse Comic book starring Jim Carrey in his breakout role, but rather a three-dimensional horror film from 1961 about a psychiatrist who falls under the spell of a mysterious mask. Also, it should be noted here that this film represents MST3K's first Halloween special, continuing the theme of holiday episodes. The film was also presented in 3D, marking the first time the SoL crew riffed on such a film. Kickstarter backers could enjoy the effect thanks to the MST3K-themed three-dimensional glasses sent out as a reward.

56. No relation to the excruciating 1966 "comedy" *The Wild World of Batwoman*, riffed by the SoL crew in episode 515.

57. Dan Wiencek and Tony Redman, "TV Review: 'Mystery Science Theater 3000,' Season 13," published April 30, 2022, https://popdose.com/tv-review-mystery-science-theater-3000-season-13/.

58. Ibid.

59. Eirik Gumeny, "MST3K Season 13 is Embracing the Chaos," published September 27, 2022, https://www.denofgeek.com/tv/mst3k-season-13-is-embracing-the-chaos/.

60. Jim Vorel, "*MST3K: Santo in the Treasure of Dracula* (Ep. 1301)," published March 9, 2022, https://www.pastemagazine.com/comedy/mst3k/mst3k-season-13-review-santo-in-the-treasure-of-dracula-gizmoplex-issues.

61. Spats_McGee, "Unofficial season 13 review thread!" accessed September 20, 2023, https://www.reddit.com/r/MST3K/comments/zq3cks/unofficial_season_13_review_thread/.

62. Christopher J. Olson still has his membership club certificate and welcome letter along with several issues of the *Satellite News* newsletter he received in response to a fan letter he sent to the show back in the early 1990s.

63. "Let's Make MST3K Season 14!" accessed November 26, 2023, https://showmaker.mst3k.com/makeseason14?ref=ab_7OMTrB7ka3b7OMTrB7ka3b.

64. Ibid.

65. Ibid.

66. Ibid.

67. Ibid.

68. Erik Adams, "Mystery Science Theater 3000 Creator on the Show's Latest Crowdfunding Campaign and Its Future," published November 23, 2023, https://www.ign.com/articles/mystery-science-theater-3000-joel-hodgson-season-14.

CONCLUSION

1. See Amanda Mabillard, "Shakespeare's Audience: The Groundlings," published August 20, 2000, http://www.shakespeare-online.com/essays/shakespeareaudience.html.

2. See Melissa Belanta, "Voting for Pleasure, or a View from a Victorian Theatre Gallery," *M/C Journal* 11, no. 1 (2008).

3. Rich "Lowtax" Kyanka, "Interview: Mike Nelson," published November 15, 2006, https://www.somethingawful.com/feature-articles/interview-mike-nelson/.

4. The true creator of the Let's Play genre is a disputed distinction, but Slowbeef is often credited with the honor. See Patrick Klepek, "Who Invented Let's Play Videos?" published May 6, 2015, https://kotaku.com/who-invented-lets-play-videos-1702390484.

5. "Arin Hanson," accessed September 29, 2023, https://www.gamegrumps.com/about/Arin-Hanson.

6. "Dan Avidan," accessed September 29, 2023, https://www.gamegrumps.com/about/Dan-Avidan.

7. "Let's Make MST3K Season 14!" accessed November 26, 2023, https://showmaker.mst3k.com/makeseason14?ref=ab_7OMTrB7ka3b7OMTrB7ka3b.

BIBLIOGRAPHY

Adams, Erik. "We're Watching the New Season of Mystery Science Theater 3000." Published July 14, 2017. https://www.avclub.com/we-re-watching-the-new-season-of-mystery-science-theate-1798288578.

Amaya, Erik. "Joel Hodgson On That Special Mystery Science Theater 3000 Season 12 Cameo." *ComicCon.com*. Published November 23, 2018. https://www.comicon.com/2018/11/23/joel-hodgson-on-that-special-mystery-science-theater-3000-season-12-cameo/.

Anderson, Kyle. "How MYSTERY SCIENCE THEATER 3000's New Season Plays on Binge-Watching." Published November 12, 2018. https://nerdist.com/article/mst3k-gauntlet-joel-hodgson-jonah-ray-hampton-yount/.

"Arin Hanson." Accessed September 29, 2023. https://www.gamegrumps.com/about/Arin-Hanson.

Askwith, Ivan. "MST3K Weekly Update: Oct 4-8, 2021." Published October 8, 2021. https://www.kickstarter.com/projects/mst3k/makemoremst3k/posts/3324535.

Atkinson, Claire. "Video Streaming Services Saw Giant Leap in 2016." Published January 6, 2017. https://nypost.com/2017/01/06/video-streaming-services-saw-giant-leap-in-2016/.

Bahn, Christopher. "Cinematic Titanic." Published October 14, 2011. https://www.avclub.com/cinematic-titanic-1798227923.

Bakhtin, Mikhail. *The Dialogic Imagination: Four Essays by M. M. Bakhtin*, edited by Michael Holquist, translated by Caryl Emerson and Michael Holquist. Austin: University of Texas Press, 1981.

Band, Charles, and Adam Felber, *Confessions of a Puppetmaster: A Hollywood Memoir of Ghouls, Guts, and Gonzo Filmmaking*. New York: William Morrow, 2021.

Bangeman, Eric. "DVD Players Finally Outnumber VCRs." Published December 22, 2006. https://arstechnica.com/gadgets/2006/12/8484/.

Barefoot, Guy. *Trash Cinema: The Lure of the Low*. New York: Wallflower Press, 2017.

Baudrillard, Jean. *Simulacra and Simulation*, translated by S. Faria Glaser. Ann Arbor: University of Michigan Press, 1994.

Baugher, Stacy. "Mystery Science Theater 3000: The Comic #1 Review." Published September 12, 2018. https://majorspoilers.com/2018/09/12/mystery-science-theater-3000-the-comic-1-review/.

Bellanta, Melissa. "Voting for Pleasure, or a View from a Victorian Theatre Gallery." *M/C Journal* 11, no. 1 (2008).

Beaulieu, Trace, et al. *The Mystery Science Theater 3000 Amazing Colossal Episode Guide*. New York: Bantam Books, 1996.

"Between the Riffs." *Cinematic Titanic Live: Danger on Tiki Island*, featuring Trace Beaulieu, Frank Conniff, Joel Hodgson, Mary Jo Pehl, and J. Elvis Weinstein. Cinematic Titan, LLC, 2010. DVD.

Boone, Brian. "The Untold Truth of Mystery Science Theater 3000." Published May 8, 2017. https://www.looper.com/48365/untold-truth-mystery-science-theater-3000/.

"Bring Back MYSTERY SCIENCE THEATER 3000." Accessed August 28, 2023. https://www.kickstarter.com/projects/mst3k/bringbackmst3k.

Brownfield, Paul. "Don't Like the Movie? Let's Talk About It." *New York Times*, June 3, 2012. https://www.nytimes.com/2012/06/03/movies/joel-hodgson-on-mystery-sci ence-theater-and-riffs.html.

Brummett, Barry. "Double Binds in Publishing Rhetorical Studies." *Communication Studies* 59, no. 4 (2003): 364–69.

Burke, Kenneth. *The Philosophy of Literary Form: Studies in Symbolic Action*. Baton Rouge: Louisiana State University Press, 1941.

Burke, Kenneth. *Attitudes Toward History*, volume 1. Berkeley: University of California Press, 1937.

Burnham, Jef, and Joshua Paul Ewalt. "*Mystery Science Theater 3000* and the Restricted Universe of Popular Culture Production." In *Reading Mystery Science Theater 3000: Critical Approaches*, edited by Shelley S. Rees, 31–44. Lanham, MD: The Scarecrow Press, 2013.

Camarata, Stephen. "Binge Watching Is a Loss for Families." Published September 16, 2015. https://time.com/collection-post/4029794/stephen-camarata-how-much-binge -watching-is-too-much/.

Canales, Katie. "Meet the Average Netflix User, a Millennial Woman Without a College Degree Living in the American Suburbs Earning Less Than $50,000 a Year." Published September 18, 2021. https://www.businessinsider.com/typical-netflix-user-subscriber -demographic-millennial-age-political-views-income-2021-9.

"Cancellation and its Aftermath." Accessed August 28, 2023. https://www.mst3kinfo.com /mstfaq/cancel.html.

Cassel, David. "A Farewell Tour with His Puppet Robot Pals for MST3K Creator Joel Hodgson." Published February 9, 2020. https://thenewstack.io/a-farewell -tour-with-his-puppet-robot-pals-for-mst3k-creator-joel-hodgson/.

CBR Staff. "Mystery Science Theater: 15 Things Only Hardcore MST3K Fans Know." Published October 6, 2018, https://www.cbr.com/mst3k-mysteries/.

Chappell, Bill. "'Mystery Science Theater 3000' Creator Raises $500K Toward New Season." Published November 10, 2015. https://www.npr.org/sections/thetwo-way /2015/11/10/455518678/-mystery-science-theater-3000-creator-raises-500k-toward -new-season.

Coldiron, Katharine. "No Longer a Cowtown Puppet Show." Published November 28, 2018. https://bookandfilmglobe.com/television/tv-review-mystery-science-theater-3000/.

Condis, Megan. "Converging fan cultures and the labors of fandom." In *In the Peanut Gallery with Mystery Science Theater 3000: Essays on Film, Fandom, Technology, and the Culture of Riffing*, edited by Robert G. Weiner and Shelley E. Barba, 76–87. Jefferson, NC: McFarland & Company, Inc., 2011.

Conniff, Frank (@FrankConniff). "When I worked on @MST3K, we were very conscious about not doing misogynistic or homophobic jokes. We were proudly woke before it was called being woke. We still are. People were laughing then and they're still laughing now, dipshit." Twitter, May 30, 2022. https://twitter.com/FrankConniff/status/1531477088854745089.

"conventions." Accessed September 16, 2023. https://www.mst3kinfo.com/mstfaq/concon.html.

Cook, Michael. "REVIEW: "Mystery Science Theater 3000: The Comic #1." Published September 12, 2018. https://thoroughlymodernreviewer.com/2018/09/12/review-mystery-science-theater-3000-the-comic-1/.

Corliss, Richard. "1950s Sci-Fi Movies: *Plan 9 from Outer Space.*" Published December 11, 2008. https://entertainment.time.com/2008/12/12/top-ten1950s-sci-fi-movies/slide/plan-9-from-outer-space-1956/.

Corliss, Richard. "Cinema: Robocritics Take Flight." Published April 22, 1996. https://content.time.com/time/subscriber/article/0,33009,984436,00.html.

Covert, Colin. "Seinfeld and Hodgson." *Minneapolis Star and Tribune*, May 5, 1986. https://web.archive.org/web/20090123024040/http://mst3k.booyaka.com/articles/mst-joel/5_5_86.html.

Czarnowski, Paul. "Michael J. Nelson." Accessed September 16, 2023. https://web.archive.org/web/20030122222815/http://www.crcradio.net/i13/mikenelson.html.

"Daddy-O's Drive-in Dirt: 904 - WEREWOLF (1996; 1995; R; 99m)." Accessed September 14, 2023. https://www.mst3kinfo.com/daddyo/di_904.html.

"Dan Avidan." Accessed September 29, 2023. https://www.gamegrumps.com/about/Dan-Avidan.

Dante, Joe, and Josh Olson. "13: Jonah Ray." Produced by Trailers from Hell. *The Movies That Made Us*. October 8, 2018. Podcast, MP3 audio, 1:06:05. https://trailersfromhell.com/podcast/jonah-ray/.

Dempsey, John. "Schulman Ankles Sci-Fi VP Post." Published July 27, 1998. https://variety.com/1998/biz/news/schulman-ankles-sci-fi-vp-post-1117478846/.

Eichler, Glen. *This is MST3K*, directed by Bill Price, featuring Penn Jillette, Neil Patrick Harris, and Joel Hodgson. Aired November 14, 1992, Comedy Central. https://www.youtube.com/watch?v=rtTLlhz-EAA.

Ellis, Jon. "Broadcast History: The Innovative UHF Era That Created MST3K." Published June 4, 2022. https://www.northpine.com/blog/2022/06/04/the-innovative-uhf-era-that-created-mst3k-ktma-kitn-kxli/.

Ellsworth, Elizabeth. *Teaching Positions: Difference, Pedagogy, and the Power of Address.* New York: Teachers College Press, 1997.

"Episode 801—Revenge of the Creature." Accessed August 28, 2023. http://www.mst3kinfo.com/aceg/8/801/ep801.html.

Esslin, Martin. "The Theatre of the Absurd." *The Tulane Drama Review* 4, no. 4 (1960): 3–15.

"Fan-Contributed Daily Variety Ad." Accessed September 16, 2023. https://en.wikipedia.org/wiki/Mystery_Science_Theater_3000#cite_note-39.

Figueroa, Dariel. "The Story of How a Wall Street Tycoon and a Broadway Actress Nearly Ended the Golden Globes in 1982." Published January 11, 2015. https://uproxx.com/movies/story-behind-golden-globes-1982-scandal/.

Flynn, Gillian. "MST3k Cancelled." Last modified April 16, 1999. https://ew.com/article/1999/04/16/mst3k-cancelled/.

Garvey, Marianne. "Netflix Cancels Its 'Mystery Science Theater 3000' Revival." Published November 27, 2019. https://www.cnn.com/2019/11/27/entertainment/net flix-mystery-science-theater-3000/index.html.

Griffith, Daniel, dir. *We Brought Back* MST3K. Chickamauga, GA: Ballyhoo Motion Pictures, 2018). DVD.

Grinberg, Emmanuella. "'Mystery Science Theater 3000' Revival Sets New Kickstarter Record." Last modified December 14, 2015. https://www.cnn.com/2015/12/12/enter tainment/mystery-science-theater-kickstarter-feat/index.html.

Gumeny, Eirik. "MST3K Season 13 is Embracing the Chaos." Published September 27, 2022. https://www.denofgeek.com/tv/mst3k-season-13-is-embracing-the-chaos/.

Gumeny, Eirik. "20 Things You Didn't Know About Mystery Science Theater 3000." Published April 13, 2017. https://screenrant.com/mst3k-mystery-science-theatre -3000-trivia/.

Hallam, Roger. "How the Internet Can Overcome the Collective Action Problem: Conditional Commitment Designs on Pledgebank, Kickstarter, and The Point/ Groupon Websites." *Information, Communication & Society* 19, no. 3 (2016): 362–79.

Hamill, Dennis. "ONE SCARY GUY 'Shock Theater's' Zacherley Still Gives Us the Chills." Published October 28, 2000. https://www.nydailynews.com/scary-guy-shock -theater-zacherley-chills-article-1.894905.

Hariman, Robert. "Political Parody and Public Culture." *Quarterly Journal of Speech* 94, no. 3 (2008): 247–72.

Hayward, Chris, et al., writer. *Fractured Flickers*. Season 1, episode 1, "Rose Marie." Aired August 1, 1963 in syndication. Jay Ward Productions.

Hebdige, Dick. *Subculture, the Meaning of Style*. New York: Methuen & Co. Ltd, 1979.

Hills, Matt. "From the Box in the Corner to the Box Set on the Shelf: 'TVIII' and the Cultural/Textual Valorizations of DVD." *New Review of Film and Television Studies* 5, no. 1 (2007): 41–60.

Hindman, Matthew. *The Myth of Digital Democracy*. Princeton, NJ: Princeton University Press, 2009.

Hodgson, Joel. "Let's Make More MST3K & Build the Gizmoplex!" Accessed September 19, 2023. https://www.kickstarter.com/projects/mst3k/makemoremst3k.

Hodgson, Joel. "What We've Been Doing for the Last Three Weeks. Plus: Reward Updates & Sneak Peeks!" Published June 2, 2021. https://www.kickstarter.com/projects /mst3k/makemoremst3k/posts/3207798.

Hodgson, Joel (@JoelGHodgson). "If you didn't see the backer update, I announced today that #MST3K is not doing a third season for Netflix. It's not the end of MST3K, It's just the end of the first chapter of bringing back MST3K." Twitter, November 26, 2019. https://twitter.com/JoelGHodgson/status/1199482835150749704.

Hodgson, Joel. "A Quick One. Longer Update coming in the Not-Too-Distant Future . . ." Published December 14, 2015. https://www.kickstarter.com/projects/mst3k/bringback mst3k/posts/1443969.

Holtzclaw, Robert. "*Mystery Science Theater 3000*." In *The Essential Cult TV Reader*, edited by David Lavery, 181–88. Lexington, KY: University of Kentucky Press, 2010.

"Horror Mistresses Battle in Court." UPI, February 27, 1989. https://www.upi.com /Archives/1989/02/27/Horror-mistresses-battle-in-court/1180604558800/.

Hunt, Kristen. "How Local TV Made 'Bad' Movies a Thing." *JSTOR Daily*, November 21, 2019. https://daily.jstor.org/how-local-tv-made-bad-movies-a-thing/.

ILoveMST3KPromos. "MST3K KTMA Commercials." YouTube. December 2, 2011. Video, 2:06. https://www.youtube.com/watch?v=bCoKX6P53B8.

Ita, Paul Anthony. "The Patron Saint of Smart Alecks: An Interview with Joel Hodgson." Published March 25, 2019. https://www.masslive.com/details-are-sketchy/2010/04 /interview_with_joel_hodgson.html.

Itzkoff, Dave. "The Show That Turned the Mockery into the Message." Published November 9, 2008. https://www.nytimes.com/2008/11/09/arts/television/09dave.html.

Jameson, Frederic. "Postmodernism, or the Cultural Logic of Late Capitalism." In *Postmodernism: A Reader*, edited by Thomas Docherty, 62–92. New York: Routledge, 1993.

Jarvis, Zeke. *Make 'em Laugh! American Humorists of the 20th and 21st Centuries*. Santa Barbara, CA: ABC-CLIO, 2015.

Jasper, Gavin. "MST3K: Joel Hodgson Reveals the Secrets of the Gizmoplex, Teases 'the Next Manos.'" Published May 1, 2021. https://www.denofgeek.com/tv/mst3k-joel -hodgson-reveals-the-secrets-of-the-gizmoplex-teases-the-next-manos/.

Jenkins, Henry. *Bloggers, and Gamers: Media Consumers in a Digital Age*. New York: New York University Press, 2006.

Jenkins, Henry. *Convergence Culture: Where Old and New Media Collide Fans*. New York: New York University Press, 2006.

Jenkins, Henry. *Textual Poachers: Television Fans & Participatory Culture*. New York: Routledge, 1992.

Jenner, Mareike. "Binge-watching: Video-on-demand, Quality TV and Mainstreaming Fandom." *International Journal of Cultural Studies* 20, no. 3 (2017): 304–20.

Johnson, Steven. *Interface Culture: How New Technology Transforms the Way we Create and Communicate*. San Francisco: Harper, 1997.

Jurgensen, John. "Binge Viewing: TV's Lost Weekends." Published July 13, 2012. https:// www.wsj.com/articles/SB10001424052702303740704577521300806686174.

Kelly, John. "Sweet 'Mystery' of Life," *Washington Post*, April 19, 1996. https://www .washingtonpost.com/wp-srv/style/longterm/review96/mysterysciencetheaterkelly .htm.

King, John. "Mystery Science Theater 3000, Media Consciousness, and the Postmodern Allegory of the Captive Audience." *Journal of Film and Video* 59, no. 4 (2007): 37–53.

Kix, Paul. "Midwestern Nice: A Tribute to a Sincere and Suffocating Way of Life." Published October 21, 2015. https://www.thrillist.com/lifestyle/nation/my-life -living-midwestern-nice.

Klepek, Patrick. "Who Invented Let's Play Videos?" Published May 6, 2015. https:// kotaku.com/who-invented-lets-play-videos-1702390484.

Kyanka, Rich "Lowtax." "Interview: Mike Nelson." Published November 15, 2006. https:// www.somethingawful.com/feature-articles/interview-mike-nelson/.

"List: Celebrity Crowd at the Rally." Accessed September 18, 2023. https://www.mst 3kinfo.com/ward_e/List501a.html.

Lynch, John. "All 26 Notable Netflix Original Shows That Debuted in 2017, Ranked from Worst to Best." Published December 1, 2017. https://www.businessinsider.com /best-new-netflix-original-shows-released-in-2017-ranked-2017-11.

Malara, Marilyn. "'Mystery Science Theater 3000' Revival Breaks Kickstarter Record." Published December 12, 2015. https://www.upi.com/Entertainment_News/2015/12 /12/Mystery-Science-Theater-3000-revival-breaks-Kickstarter-record/986144992 7479/.

Maron, Marc. "811: Joel Hodgson/Jonah Ray." Produced by Brendan McDonald. *WTF with Marc Maron*. May 15, 2017. Podcast, MP3 audio, 1:47:50. https://www.poorstuart.com/podcast-episode/WTF-with-Marc-Maron/Episode-811-Joel-Hodgson-Jonah-Ray/179424/.

McConville, Jim. "Cult Status Doesn't Cut It on Cable Anymore." *Electronic Media* 18, no. 11 (1999): 4.

McFarland, Kevin. "MST3K Revival Hits Kickstarter, Back-Sassers Rejoice." Published November 18, 2015. https://www.wired.com/2015/11/mst3k-kickstarter/.

McManus, Darragh. "My Generation's Irony: So Bad It's Not Good?" Published March 11, 2010. https://www.theguardian.com/commentisfree/2010/mar/11/generation-x-sarcasm-seriously.

McMurria, John. *Republic on the Wire: Cable Television, Pluralism, and the Politics of New Technologies, 1948-1984*. New Brunswick, NJ: Rutgers University Press, 2017.

Meinert, Kendra. "Joel Hodgson Riffs on 'MST3K' and Its Green Bay Roots." *Green Bay Press Gazette*, August 2, 2017. https://www.greenbaypressgazette.com/story/entertainment/television/2017/08/02/joel-hodgson-riffs-mst-3-k-and-its-green-bay-roots/529221001/.

Merikivi, Jani, et. al. "Binge-watching Serialized Video Content: A Transdisciplinary Review." *Television and New Media* 21, no. 7 (2020): 697–711.

"Midwest Nice." Accessed June 30, 2023. https://www.urbandictionary.com/define.php?term=Midwest+Nice.

Miller, Joshua M. "Our Q&A with Joel Hodgson, Creator of 'Mystery Science Theater 3000.'" *Milwaukee Magazine*, July 13, 2017. https://www.milwaukeemag.com/qa-joel-hodgson-creator-mystery-science-theater-3000/.

Miller, Liz Shannon. "'Mystery Science Theater 3000: The Return' Review: Faces Change, but the Anarchic Spirit Remains the Same." Published April 14, 2017, https://www.indiewire.com/2017/04/mst3k-review-netflix-jonah-ray-joel-hodgson-season-11-1201805884/.

Minow, Nell. "Interview: Mike Nelson of MST3000 and Rifftrax." Published June 2, 2009. https://moviemom.com/interview-mike-nelson-of-mst30/.

"Movies to Go." Published July 7, 2005. https://www.economist.com/business/2005/07/07/movies-to-go.

"MST3K: The Movie." Accessed August 27, 2023. https://mst3kinfo.com/mstfaq/movie.html.

Murphy, Kevin. *A Year at the Movies*. New York: Harper Collins, 2002.

"Mystery Science Theater 3000: The Return (2017)." Accessed August 28, 2023. https://www.rottentomatoes.com/tv/mystery_science_theater_3000_the_return/s01.

Navar-Gill, Annamarie. "Fandom as Symbolic Patronage: Expanding Understanding of Fan Relationships with Industry Through the Veronica Mars Kickstarter Campaign." *Popular Communication* 16, no. 3 (2018): 211–24.

Nealon, Jeffrey T. *Post-Postmodernism or, The Cultural Logic of Just-in-Time Capitalism*. Redwood City, CA: Stanford University Press, 2012.

Nehring, Neil. "Jigsaw Youth versus Generation X and Postmodernism." In *GenXegesis: Essays on 'Alternative' Youth (Sub)Culture*, edited by John M. Ulrich and Andrea L. Harris, 59–78. Madison: University of Wisconsin Press, 2003.

Nelson, Michael J. *Mike Nelson's Movie Megacheese*. New York: Harper Entertainment, 2000.

@Netflix. "In the not-too-distant future. @MST3K." Twitter, July 23, 2016. https://twitter
.com/netflix/status/757055576903778304?s=20.

"Netflix Declares Binge Watching is the New Normal." Published December 13, 2013.
https://www.prnewswire.com/news-releases/netflix-declares-binge-watching-is-the
-new-normal-235713431.html

O'Neal, Sean. "We Got it All on UHF: An Oral History of 'Weird Al' Yankovic's Cult
Classic." Published March 23, 2015. https://www.avclub.com/we-got-it-all-on-uhf-an
-oral-history-of-weird-al-yan-1798278657.

Ott, Brian, and Cameron Walter. "Intertextuality: Interpretive Practice and Textual
Strategy." *Critical Studies in Media Communication* 17, no. 4 (2000): 429–46.

Peterson, Cassandra. *Yours Cruelly, Elvira: Memoirs of the Mistress of the Dark*. New
York: Hachette, 2021.

Poniewozik, James. "All-TIME 100 TV Shows." Published September 6, 2007. https://
time.com/collection-post/3103672/mystery-science-theater-3000/.

"Problematic." Accessed September 14, 2023. https://dictionary.cambridge.org/us
/dictionary/english/problematic.

"Problematic." Accessed August 28, 2023. https://www.merriam-webster.com/dictionary
/problematic.

"Project: Riff." Accessed September 14, 2023. http://www.magicmarkerweb.com/mst
3kreview/projriff.htm#project.

Raftery, Brian. "Mystery Science Theater 3000: The Definitive Oral History of a TV
Masterpiece." Published April 22, 2014. https://www.wired.com/2014/04/mst3k
-oral-history/.

Rawden, Mack. "Insane Clown Posse Has a Strangely Awesome MST3K Style Show."
Published March 13, 2014. https://www.cinemablend.com/television/Insane-Clown
-Posse-Has-Strangely-Awesome-MST3K-Style-Show-62780.html.

"Reviews: Guys Who Are About Five-Eight, Five-Nine." Accessed September 16, 2023.
https://web.archive.org/web/20010208143636/http://www.timmybighands.com
/reviews/fivefootguys.asp.

"RiffTrax is Writing a Nick Nolte Novel: New Stretch Goal!" Published March 2, 2023.
https://www.kickstarter.com/projects/rifftrax/rifftrax-live-2023-rad-the-classic-1986
-bmx-movie/posts/3746911.

"RiffTrax Wants to Riff TWILIGHT Live in Theaters Nationwide!" Accessed August 28,
2023. https://www.kickstarter.com/projects/rifftrax/rifftrax-wants-to-riff-twilight-live
-in-theaters-n/posts/488630s.

Rossen, Jake. "A Brief History of Satanic Panic." Published May 14, 2021. https://www
.mentalfloss.com/article/642372/satanic-panic-history-1980s.

Rouse, Margaret. "Ultra High Frequency (UHF)." Last modified July 14, 2015. https://
www.techopedia.com/definition/9811/ultra-high-frequency-uhf.

Sajdak, Stephen. "Joel Hodgson: The WHM Interview." YouTube. January 19, 2012.
Video, 37:56. https://www.youtube.com/watch?v=YRtV55iTPq0.

Schmidt, Claire, and Laurel Schmidt. "'Do You Even Live Here?': Regionalism, Humor,
and Tradition in *Mystery Science Theater 3000*." In *Reading Mystery Science Theater
3000: Critical Approaches*, edited by Shelley S. Rees, 77–92. Lanham, MD: The
Scarecrow Press, 2013.

Segarra, Jason. "'Mystery Science Theater 3000: The Comic' Faces Some Stumbles in
a New Medium." Published September 11, 2019. https://aiptcomics.com/2019/09/11
/mystery-science-theater-3000-the-comic-review-tpb/.

"Shakespeare's Audience." Accessed August 28, 2023. http://www.shakespeare-online.com/essays/shakespeareaudience.html.

Shales, Tom. "'MST3K' Means Fine Television." *The Washington Post*, November 27, 1991. https://www.washingtonpost.com/archive/lifestyle/1991/11/27/mst3k-means-fine-television/582a1a46-a971-4aed-9982-526243f0f0b6/.

Shelton, Jacob. "Vampira, The First Horror Host: Her Short, Frustrating Story." Accessed August 23, 2022. https://groovyhistory.com/vampira-horror-host-elvira-true-story/8.

Sherlock, Ben. "Pulp Fiction: 10 Best Movie References, Ranked." Published January 22, 2020. https://screenrant.com/pulp-fiction-quentin-tarantino-best-movie-references-ranked/.

Siebold, Witney. "The Mystery Science Theater 3000 Robots Are Quintessential Gen-Xers." Published March 8, 2022. https://www.slashfilm.com/791431/the-mystery-science-theater-3000-robots-are-quintessential-gen-xers/?utm_campaign=clip.

Siegel, Alan. "'Freaks and Geeks': The Last Great High School TV Show?" *The Atlantic*, October 20, 2010. https://www.theatlantic.com/entertainment/archive/2010/10/freaks-and-geeks-the-last-great-high-school-tv-show/64563/.

Sloan, Will. "'You Can't Just Be the Voice of Generic Sarcasm': The Art of Movie Riffing." Published August 16, 2012. https://www.npr.org/2012/08/16/158922001/you-cant-just-be-the-voice-of-generic-sarcasm-the-art-of-movie-riffing.

Spats_McGee. "Unofficial Season 13 Review Thread!" Accessed September 20, 2023. https://www.reddit.com/r/MST3K/comments/zq3cks/unofficial_season_13_review_thread/.

St. James, Emily. "Mystery Science Theater 3000 is the Same as Always in Its New Season. That's a Good Thing." Published April 14, 2017. https://www.vox.com/culture/2017/4/14/15212400/mystery-science-theater-3000-new-season-netflix-good.

St. John, Graham. "Protestival: Global Days of Action and Carnivalized Politics in the Present." *Social Movement Studies* 7, no. 2 (2008): 167–90.

Stack, Peter. "FILM REVIEW – 'Barb' Armed with Blanks / 'Baywatch' Star Shows No Mercy." Published August 23, 1996. https://www.sfgate.com/movies/article/FILM-REVIEW-Barb-Armed-With-Blanks-2969464.php.

"The Steel Cage Chat!" Accessed August 28, 2023. https://www.mst3kinfo.com/chats/cagechat.html.

Strickler, Jeff. "Local Comedian Gets Last Laugh in Competition." *Minneapolis Tribune*, October 1, 1982. https://web.archive.org/web/20090123024106/http://mst3k.booyaka.com/articles/mst-joel/8_1_82.html.

"Subtleties, Obscurities, Odds and Ends." Accessed February 11, 2023. https://mst3kinfo.com/mstfaq/subtle.html.

Sweeney, Mark. "Netflix Tops 100m Subscribers as it Draws Worldwide Audience." Published July 18, 2017. https://www.theguardian.com/media/2017/jul/18/netflix-tops-100m-subscribers-international-customers-sign-up.

Tafoya, Scout. "Review: Mystery Science Theater 3000: The Return: Season One." Published April 21, 2017. https://www.slantmagazine.com/tv/mystery-science-theater-3000-the-return-season-one/.

"TimmyBigHands." Accessed September 16, 2023. https://web.archive.org/web/20010203004200/http://www.timmybighands.com/default.asp.

"The Tort: A Serial Novel by Timothy B. Hands—Chapter IV: Finger." Accessed September 16, 2023. https://web.archive.org/web/20010211154728/http://www.timmybighands.com/serial/tort4.asp.

Triggs, Teal. *Fanzines: The DIY Revolution.* San Francisco: Chronicle Books, 2010.

"The Veronica Mars Movie Project." Accessed August 28, 2023. https://www.kickstarter
.com/projects/559914737/the-veronica-mars-movie-project.

Vorel, Jim. "*MST3K: Santo in the Treasure of Dracula* (Ep. 1301)." Published March
9, 2022. https://www.pastemagazine.com/comedy/mst3k/mst3k-season-13-review
-santo-in-the-treasure-of-dracula-gizmoplex-issues.

Warner, Jamie. "Political Culture Jamming: The Dissident Humor of *The Daily Show with
Jon Stewart.*" *Popular Communication* 5, no. 1 (2007): 17–36.

Webb, Peter, and John Lynch. "'Utopian Punk': The Concept of the Utopian in the Creative
Practice of Björk." *Utopian Studies* 21, no. 2 (2010): 313–30.

Weinstein, J. Elvis. "J. Elvis Weinstein - The Cancer Chunk (stand-up)." March 15, 2018.
Video. https://www.youtube.com/watch?v=6c_qmseW05Q.

Wiencek, Dan, and Tony Redman. "TV Review: 'Mystery Science Theater
3000,' Season 13." Published April 30, 2022. https://popdose.com/tv-review
-mystery-science-theater-3000-season-13/.

INDEX

ABOUT THE AUTHORS

Matt Foy (PhD, speech communication, Southern Illinois University) is an associate professor of communication at Upper Iowa University. He studies popular culture at the intersections of rhetorical, cultural, and performance studies.

Christopher J. Olson is assistant professor of English and digital media at Dickinson State University. An avid MSTie, his books include *The Greatest Cult Television Shows of All Time* (Rowman & Littlefield, 2020), *100 Greatest Cult Films* (Rowman & Littlefield, 2018), and *Possessed Women, Haunted States: Cultural Tensions in Exorcism Cinema* (Lexington, 2016).